Interdisciplinary Teaching Through Outdoor Education

Camille J. Bunting

Human Kinetics

Library of Congress Cataloging-in-Publication Data

Bunting, Camille J.
  Interdisciplinary teaching through outdoor education / Camille J. Bunting.
    p. cm.
  Includes bibliographical references.
  ISBN 0-7360-5502-9 (soft cover)
  1. Outdoor education. 2. Interdisciplinary approach in education. I. Title.
  LC1038.B86 2006
  371.3'8—dc22

                        2005011855

ISBN-10: 0-7360-5502-9
ISBN-13: 978-0-7360-5502-4

Acquisitions Editor: Gayle Kassing, PhD; **Developmental Editor:** Ragen E. Sanner, Jennifer Sekosky; **Assistant Editor:** Carmel Sielicki; **Copyeditor:** Alisha Jeddeloh; **Proofreader:** Andrew Smith; **Permission Manager:** Dalene Reeder; **Graphic Designer:** Fred Starbird; **Graphic Artist:** Dawn Sills; **Photo Manager:** Sarah A. Ritz; **Cover Designer:** Keith Blomberg; **Photographer (cover):** Jim Whitmer (bottom left), Camille J. Bunting (top and bottom right); **Photographer (interior):** Camille J. Bunting, unless otherwise noted.; **Art Manager:** Kelly Hendren; **Illustrator:** Keri J. Evans; **Printer:** Versa Press

Printed in the United States of America   10 9 8 7 6 5 4 3 2

Human Kinetics
Web site: www.HumanKinetics.com

United States: Human Kinetics
P.O. Box 5076
Champaign, IL 61825-5076
800-747-4457
e-mail: humank@hkusa.com

Canada: Human Kinetics
475 Devonshire Road Unit 100
Windsor, ON N8Y 2L5
800-465-7301 (in Canada only)
e-mail: info@hkcanada.com

Europe: Human Kinetics
107 Bradford Road
Stanningley
Leeds LS28 6AT, United Kingdom
+44 (0) 113 255 5665
e-mail: hk@hkeurope.com

Australia: Human Kinetics
57A Price Avenue
Lower Mitcham, South Australia 5062
08 8372 0999
e-mail: info@hkaustralia.com

New Zealand: Human Kinetics
Division of Sports Distributors NZ Ltd.
P.O. Box 300 226 Albany
North Shore City
Auckland
0064 9 448 1207
e-mail: info@humankinetics.co.nz

I want to dedicate this book to all current and future teachers who will introduce their students to the joys and responsibilities of our natural world, and to the people listed below who have been influential in my life.

Alene and Warren Bunting—My parents, who first took me to the Comal River at age 2.

Ruth Jeanette Bunting—An aunt and my 2nd-grade teacher.

Ouieda Carrol—My junior high school guidance counselor.

Mary Lee Bartlett—One of my high school teachers who hired me as a summer camp counselor.

Mary Tindle—One of my college professors who gave me responsibilities and encouragement.

Wadell Hill—The principal of the junior high school where I was allowed to start an outdoor education class in the mid-1970s.

Mickey Little—My graduate school professor and mentor who introduced me to many people and provided opportunities for professional growth.

Irma Lewis—An inspirational colleague and friend of outdoor education in Texas.

Gayle Kassing—The acquisitions editor for this book, whose excellent work and positive support helped me through the publishing process.

Contents

Preface

During the last century, outdoor education has gone from short treks into the outdoors for learning about the natural environment to a much more expansive and multidisciplinary concept. The more current concept of outdoor education includes skills for camping and outdoor recreation, environmental conservation education, adventure education, and a diverse assortment of educational experiences.

This book is for teachers who would like to include outdoor education in their teaching of students from 5th to 10th grade (ages 10-15). It has three goals.

- Goal 1: To provide a basic introduction to
  - what outdoor education is,
  - how it has developed,
  - the social psychology theories that provide a basis for its methodology and its success, and
  - some pertinent research findings.
- Goal 2: To provide several topical units designed specifically for teaching outdoor adventure activities to adolescent students.
- Goal 3: To serve as an integrated resource that highlights character qualities and reinforces academic curriculum standards in a way that enhances students' ability to make interdisciplinary connections.

The goal of reinforcing knowledge and skills from a variety of curriculum areas comes with the understanding that using information in a context other than the isolated subject area in which it was presented provides an authentic context for that information or skill. One of the results of brain research over the past 15 to 20 years is that we are now aware of the importance of perceiving and understanding patterns and context in order for learning to occur. Outdoor education provides naturally occurring opportunities for perceiving and understanding interrelationships and connections.

Character development is highlighted in the lessons because of the interrelatedness of the ecosystem and human character qualities in outdoor recreational activities. The natural environment and successful experiences of outdoor recreational activities help to develop character. The opportunity to learn the importance of character through directly experiencing activities is a unique way to learn positive character qualities, whereas lecturing on character does less to inspire.

The outdoor education content of this book includes a few activities that depend upon the natural environment. Because most of these activities are not usually taught in a school setting, are unique to most adolescent students, and seem a lot like play, they are natural motivators. Since many teachers get frustrated with their students' lack of motivation, outdoor education might open the way to a new learning environment for both students and teachers.

There are many books on specific topics and activities encompassed by outdoor education, but very few are written to help teachers organize and deliver interdisciplinary lessons using adventure activities. For example, there are multiple books on orienteering, backpacking, or rock climbing, but teachers still have to spend large amounts of time sifting through an overload of information in an effort to select what is appropriate for students and then plan sequential lessons. This book is designed to present enough background information on the various activities so that novices to a particular activity can teach that unit at an appropriate level. Planning time is in short supply for teachers, and the hope is that this book will offer enough help that teachers will give outdoor education a try.

My hope is that this book will facilitate the inclusion of these outdoor activities in more school curricula and that teachers who use it will discover or recover "the secret of the making of the best person. It is to grow in the open air and to eat and sleep with the earth" (Walt Whitman).

How to Use This Book

The purpose of this book is to provide information that will facilitate the teaching of outdoor adventure activities while reinforcing various curriculum standards and highlighting positive character qualities. With that in mind, a reader can turn to any activity chapter and begin using the lessons. Each activity unit and lesson plan can be modified to better fit a particular situation or group of students. In fact, teachers are encouraged to adapt the lessons to fit their teaching style and repertoire. Some teachers may only use a few of the activity units or lesson plans and then decide to create others on their own.

To use the activity lessons, it is not necessary to read the material found in part I. However, part I offers greater understanding about outdoor education as both a content area and a teaching method. Some outdoor education professionals would argue that while there is great value in what you teach, how you teach is just as important. Part I provides guidance for how to teach experientially.

Part I is comprised of two chapters. Chapter 1 provides foundational information on what outdoor education is and discusses pedagogical specifics that can be applied to outdoor education, such as methods of learning and teaching outdoor education as well as classroom strategy, planning, and implementation. Chapter 1 also includes guidelines for interdisciplinary and character-development applications. Chapter 2 offers a brief overview of outdoor education's historical evolution and a justification for offering outdoor education in schools. The justification is supported by relevant social psychology theories as well as educational and brain-based research.

Symbols representing five psychosocial theories presented in chapter 2 are used to indicate a particular point in the lesson plans where a theory is especially applicable. The theories included are Maslow's hierarchy of needs and the theories of optimal arousal, flow, self-efficacy, and attribution. As you read through the lesson plans in this book, look for the theory symbols.

- Maslow's hierarchy of needs $\triangle$
- Theory of optimal arousal $\sqcap$
- Flow theory (theory of competence-effectance) $\sqcup$
- Theory of self-efficacy ☺
- Attribution theory ↄ

Part II consists of the specific activity chapters, chapters 3 through 11. Each of these chapters begins with information about the activity that teachers will need for conducting the unit. The activity information is followed by a multiday unit plan, and then a few of the lessons are developed in detail. The activities and information in the lesson plans have been cross-referenced with national standards from various curriculum areas for kindergarten through 12th grade. These standards were selected because they are more general in nature, and it would be too cumbersome to attempt detailed lesson plans using specific grade level standards. The activity units and lesson plans are designed to provide assistance to teachers in organizing content and teaching outdoor adventure activities while reinforcing concepts from a variety of subject areas as well as highlighting the value of positive character qualities that are especially significant to that particular activity.

Chapters 3 through 9 of part II are organized as follows:

- Activity background information
- Unit plan
  - Unit objectives
  - Character focus
  - Curriculum areas
  - Assessment activity
- Lesson plans
  - Lesson objectives—What you should accomplish by utilizing this lesson.

- Character focus—The potential character qualities that the lesson plan allows you to highlight.
- Curriculum standards—The potential interdisciplinary standards that the lesson plan allows you to reinforce.
- Materials—What you need to gather before you can use the lesson.
- Preparation—The steps you need to take before you use the lesson.
- Lesson sequence—A simple, step-by-step list for you to follow through the lesson. The lesson sequence may include individual activity breakdown with questions and character affirmations for that activity.
- Discussion and review—Suggested questions and comments to help your students link the concepts to the activities.
- Teaching tips—Helpful hints to get you through the lesson.
- Safety tips—Tips for keeping your students safe.
- Possible character affirmations—Suggestions for reinforcing the character qualities that you have witnessed throughout the lesson.
- References—Additional resources such as reproducibles or stories appear at the end of that day's lesson.

In part II, chapters 10 and 11 cover rock climbing and canoeing and kayaking. These are subjects that many teachers may want to discuss with their students but do not have the resources for actually providing hands-on experience. Sample lessons for these activities have not been included due to the specific safety issues that are involved, the specialized resources necessary for these activities, and to discourage teachers from attempting these activities without specific skill and safety training.

Part III presents ideas on starting an outdoor education program, including getting support, training, and information for planning and implementing field trips. Field trips are not a necessity in an outdoor education program. However, this section will provide organizational information and follow-up considerations should this be an option for your program. Some teachers may have no use for this information, but others may find this to be the most valuable part of the book.

Part I

Introduction to Outdoor Education and Its Role in Schools

Defining and Teaching Outdoor Education

At first glance, the term *outdoor education* may seem to define itself. However, if you asked 10 different people to define outdoor education, you would probably get 10 different definitions. Is outdoor education a curriculum content area, a group of activities, or a method of teaching? The answer typically depends on one's experience.

How teachers understand outdoor education influences the type of program they conceive. This chapter discusses a definition of outdoor education that encompasses its multiple dimensions. Since the focus of this book is the teaching method of outdoor education, it is necessary to know what sets it apart from other teaching methods, so this chapter focuses on the experiential method in an outdoor education context. The teaching method presented in this book involves specific brain-friendly teaching practices, such as helping students make interdisciplinary and character connections with the outdoor educa-

tion content as well as with real-life situations. In addition, the chapter covers the advantages the outdoor education method affords students, lesson content, curricular standards that teachers should present and test, and how to organize a class so that teaching can take place outdoors. The chapter concludes with a discussion of four fundamental components of outdoor education: structured experiences, environmental involvement, reflection and discussion, and linkages for transfer.

Outdoor Education Defined

Outdoor education is multifaceted and cannot be easily defined in one concise sentence. Yet a single-sentence definition has been offered by one of the pioneers of outdoor education in the United States, Julian Smith. Smith was influential in making outdoor education part of school physical education programs in the 1940s, and he offered the following definition: "Outdoor education is education in and for the outdoors." Several years later Phyllis Ford, who followed in Julian Smith's footsteps at the University of Michigan and at Michigan State University, added *about* to that definition: outdoor education includes education *about* the relationships within the natural environment and between the environment and human societies.

In addition to *in, for,* and *about,* a fourth useful addition is *through.* Education *through* activities in the natural environment means that through participation in such activities other subject areas become interesting and more easily understood. Although the single-sentence definition, "Outdoor education is education in, for, about, and through the outdoors," is concise, it remains limited in what it is actually able to communicate. Since outdoor education is multidimensional, it is worth focusing on some of those dimensions.

Outdoor education is actually comprised of three dimensions—extension, content, and teaching method. One dimension of outdoor education is the process of extending structured learning activities beyond the classroom into the community, natural environment, and other locations of topics being studied. The students

Children need to learn about the natural environment and how they affect it.

© Ronald & Diane Salmon

go out of the classroom to delve more deeply into any topic in any curriculum. For example, if a class is studying about Native Americans, learning activities could be extended beyond the classroom by

- having students interview Native Americans or people associated in some way with Native Americans,
- guiding the class through the building of various Native American living structures and the tools used, or
- taking a field trip to a museum or Native American village.

Another dimension of outdoor education is the content, or what is being taught. The content can include information about the natural environment and its relationships, specific skills to be used in the outdoors, or our relationship with the environment and how our activities as individuals and as a society affect it.

The final dimension of outdoor education is teaching method. Outdoor education is a method that uses activities as a means for developing skills and understanding concepts in a variety of subjects. This method typically uses activities to highlight connections and initiate reflective discussions and journaling. Outdoor education as a teaching method links the cognitive, affective, and psychomotor domains of learning. Curriculum areas that at first glance seem unrelated can be better understood as a result of intentionally experiencing some of their connections. For example, the experience of rock climbing can be used to teach the concepts of structure and strength in three different curriculum areas. Climbers rely on the structure and strength of the rock formations, a geology and geography curriculum area. It is an activity that depends on the structure and strength of the belay equipment, which can address math and physics concepts. There is also necessary trust in the knowledge, skill, and responsibility, or structure and strength, of the belayer. Just as the structure and strength of the climber's belay system can be assessed by knowing the breaking strength of the equipment along with the belayer's skill, level of care, and understanding, the geologic structure and strength of different types of rocks and rock formations and the importance of structure and strength in human relationships can be learned and assessed. The internal relationships among these three connections show that they have much in common. However, if a teacher doesn't highlight the connections, the activity of rock climbing is limited to the psychomotor domain rather than including the cognitive (rock structure) and affective (human relationships) domains.

Teaching Outdoor Education

The act of teaching is both a science and an art. Specific knowledge must be conveyed, and how that knowledge is conveyed is the art of teaching. A few technical considerations are presented, but most of the teaching considerations are in the realm of art.

Methods

Outdoor recreational activities are excellent educational tools for incorporating experiential teaching methods and interdisciplinary lesson design because they engage the student's whole self:

- The physical self is moving and active.
- The mental self is thinking and questioning.
- The emotional self is feeling and engaging the physical and mental processes.

This is what takes place during the experiential learning process.

Experiential Learning

The Association for Experiential Education (AEE) defines experiential education as, "The process through which the learner constructs knowledge, skill, and values through direct experience." This is a more specific definition than the often-used "learning by doing" definition, and it communicates the message of the experiential learning cycle. AEE's 2005 definition is, "Experiential education is a philosophy and methodology in which educators purposefully engage with learners in direct experience and focused reflection in order to increase knowledge, develop skills, and

clarify values" (see www.aee2.org/customer/pages.php?pageid=47).

The experiential learning cycle, illustrated in figure 1.1, is a four-step process that begins with an experience. An experience engages the students through direct participation in an activity. It usually, though not always, involves a psychomotor component. The second step of the experience is reflecting on or discussing the experience by answering questions such as, "What did we just do and what things did I observe, think, or feel during the experience?" The third step, generalization, takes reflection and discussion to another level and considers what meaning there may have been and how the meaning might relate to areas of life separate from the immediate experience. In this step learners transfer the meaning from the present experience to situations in daily life that might have similarities with the present activity. Finally, the fourth step is applying the generalized learning to a situation that was discussed in terms of transferability. That application becomes another experience in itself.

Looking at this cycle, you get the idea that the majority of experiential teaching occurs after an activity has happened, during a period of reflection and discussion. Guided reflection, discussion, and generalization are important. Yet in a school setting, when you are using outdoor adventure activities as a means to teach specific objectives, the most critical part of the teaching process happens before (in planning) and during the activity. Simply knowing and following the experiential learning cycle

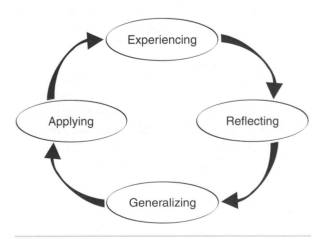

Figure 1.1 Experiential learning cycle.

is not enough for teaching interdisciplinary standards. You cannot be content with letting the experience speak for itself if you want to address specific curriculum objectives. You must structure the experiences in a manner that will focus on the desired objectives.

Experiential Teaching

Experiential teaching requires a somewhat different model that includes more detail for teachers. Experiential teaching looks easy to outsiders watching the students doing an activity, and often the teacher seems to be doing nothing but watching. However, these outside observers were not part of the planning process and are not aware of the lesson's objectives. In addition, if they are not close enough to hear the teacher's comments and questions during the activity, they can't discern the embedded objectives. The examples given in the six stages of the experiential teaching cycle (see figure 1.2) illustrate the particular importance of the following stages 1, 2, and 3: thinking creatively, planning for embedded curriculum, and implementing the plan with the objectives in mind.

• **Stage 1—Knowledge.** This stage usually begins with the teacher's intention to teach experientially using interdisciplinary highlights and with an idea and basic information, such as knowing your class, time frame, facilities, equipment, and what objectives or standards you want to address. Then comes the creative thinking.

For example, a lesson about the use of a map and compass lends itself quite easily to interdisciplinary teaching. You could relate the skills to history, geography, geology, math, or science. Consider what the students study in those subject areas and choose one or two subjects that are appropriate for each grade level. It is possible that you decide to reinforce concepts from each of these subjects. Making compasses using a small glass of water and magnetizing a needle that floats on the water in the glass could teach the science of magnetism. Touch on geology and geography by drawing a chalk map of the North American continent on a concrete or blacktop surface and using a large metal object to illustrate how the magnetic north pole affects the compass needle. Teaching students to use a compass to walk in a perfect square,

isosceles triangle, hexagon, or octagon could reinforce math skills. A Lewis and Clark trail could be reconstructed for an interactive history lesson.

• **Stage 2—Planning.** Planning involves structuring activities in ways that enhance the opportunity to use each activity to illustrate a concept or skill. It also involves identifying standards from other areas that you can connect to the activity in order to reinforce it. For example, look around the school grounds to find areas that are most appropriate for the activities you would like to do. Don't yield to the temptation of doing all activities in the same area just because you always use that area. Visual aids are also important. We often think that because our students are being active it is not necessary to have visual aids; however, they can be very effective in making connections between curriculum areas, so be sure to plan and prepare them in advance.

• **Stage 3—Implementation.** For the teacher, the implementation phase means actively engaging in the students' experiences, making observations and comments during the activity and asking leading, challenging questions that are pertinent to the planned objectives. In other words, the teacher does not just present the instructions and then leave the students to do the activity. Admittedly, there are times when the "introduce and back off" approach is appropriate, but it should not be the norm. Teachers have a choice of presentation styles, including the didactic or expository style and the experiential style. The didactic style focuses on the teacher, who is the "teller" or "explainer" of information and sets the pace and order of information delivery or activities. The experiential style, on the other hand, is focused on the desired learning, with elements of choice for the students, more time for small group activities, some degree of uncertainty regarding outcomes, and the understanding that learning is a process. A combination of these two styles is often a good choice.

For example, you could begin the first map and compass lesson by putting the students in groups of three and asking the groups to decide which direction is north and to point in that direction. Give each group a map of town and

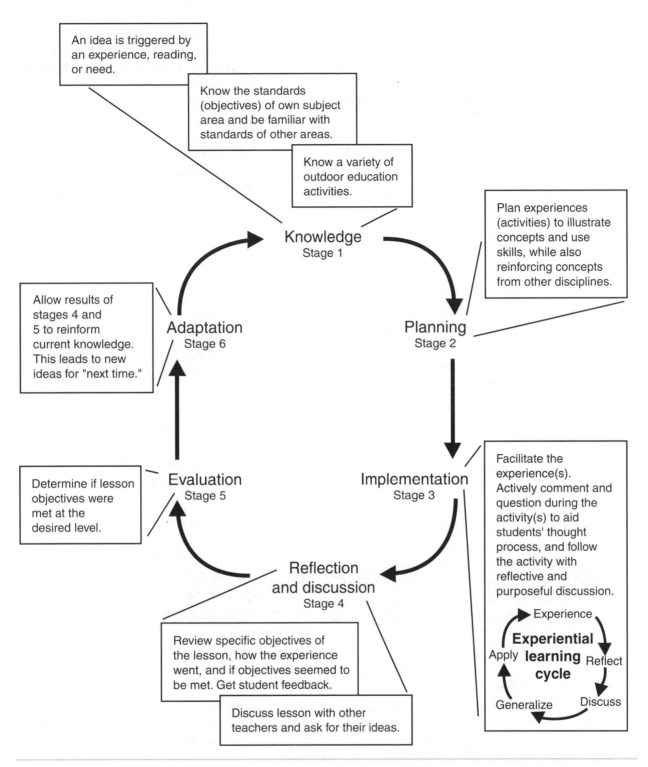

An idea is triggered by an experience, reading, or need.

Know the standards (objectives) of own subject area and be familiar with standards of other areas.

Know a variety of outdoor education activities.

Plan experiences (activities) to illustrate concepts and use skills, while also reinforcing concepts from other disciplines.

Allow results of stages 4 and 5 to reinform current knowledge. This leads to new ideas for "next time."

Determine if lesson objectives were met at the desired level.

Knowledge
Stage 1

Adaptation
Stage 6

Planning
Stage 2

Evaluation
Stage 5

Implementation
Stage 3

Reflection and discussion
Stage 4

Facilitate the experience(s). Actively comment and question during the activity(s) to aid students' thought process, and follow the activity with reflective and purposeful discussion.

Experience

Experiential learning cycle

Apply

Reflect

Generalize

Discuss

Review specific objectives of the lesson, how the experience went, and if objectives seemed to be met. Get student feedback.

Discuss lesson with other teachers and ask for their ideas.

Figure 1.2 Experiential teaching cycle.

ask them to "orient" the map. Then give each group a compass and ask them if the north arrow on their map is pointing in the same direction as the red end of the compass needle. Students are generally fascinated by maps, and after all

these questions, they will be hooked! You have given no lecture, but have gotten the students engaged and interested so that now you can begin giving some information that will be received with interest.

The art of being an experiential outdoor educator requires teachers to think of themselves as facilitators. The term *facilitator* encourages an attitude of assistance, encouragement, and coaching, whereas the term *teacher* is too often associated with an attitude of just providing the facts. Simmons and Cannon (1991, p. 7-11) have described 10 principles of being an effective facilitator:

1. Know why you are doing what you are doing.

2. Put the focus on the participants (students), not the facilitator. The facilitator plans and structures the activities and environment to be instructional.

3. Encourage students to explore and discover meaning and understanding from the activities. Do not succumb to the temptation to be the star of "show and tell." Experiential learning is much more powerful than being told how to do something.

4. Design situations that will encourage students to want to learn or figure out something. The more real-life context you can use, the better.

5. Look for and be flexible enough to use teachable moments. Such moments occur when something engages a student's interest, or when a student asks a question that has other students saying, "Yeah, what about that?" These moments may or may not be on topics that are part of the teacher's lesson plan, but the students are interested and want to learn. This does not mean there is never a need for a schedule, but don't be a slave to it.

6. Use sequenced progressions that move from simple to complex. Plan each activity as a building block for the next.

7. Anticipate how to use students' failures as well as their successes to maximize learning.

8. Develop multiple educational tools and know when and how to use them. Don't be the person who, only having a hammer, uses it on everything from nails to glass to skin. Use the correct tool for the situation, knowing that there are differences between people and situations.

9. End an activity on a high note. When an activity begins, student energy tends to be high and declines over time; involvement is low, increases to a point, and begins to decline fairly rapidly; and interest begins to climb and then ebbs and flows. Attempt to end the activity while interest, stamina, and involvement are all high.

10. Follow an activity with opportunities for reflection, discussion, generalization, and application. These are the times when learning occurs.

• **Stage 4—Reflection and discussion.** Stage 4 is analogous to the reflection, discussion, and generalization stages of the experiential learning cycle, but in the teaching cycle the teacher reviews how the experience worked. It would be ideal if this stage included other teachers and their ideas.

For example, reflect on the lesson's organization, student involvement, and ways the lesson could be improved.

• **Stage 5—Evaluation.** Evaluate the success of the lesson and determine whether or not the objectives were actually accomplished.

For example, have students make four different metabolic analogies to fire by drawing or listing the three essential requirements or how they are supplied.

• **Stage 6—Adaptation.** Adapting the lesson for future use as well as deciding how the next experience can best be structured for the class.

For example, think about changes that can be made to improve the student's fire-building success, such as changing locations for protection from prevailing wind and having multiple small piles of wood for students to access.

This six-stage approach to teaching is certainly not new. Most teachers regularly follow this process or something similar. The purpose of putting it into a cyclical diagram is to show the importance of planning and implementation.

Two key terms describe the first three stages and add further explanation: intentional and vigilant. They are especially important for effectively teaching toward curriculum standards using outdoor education.

• **Intentional.** You should be intentional about looking for ways to connect curriculum areas and then planning how to put your ideas into action. Being aware of the importance of making connections is half the battle, because awareness leads to ideas that otherwise you might not recognize. Intentional planning means organizing your lessons to make sure you know what you are trying to accomplish beyond simply doing the activities and how you intend to get it done. For example, just because you are doing one or two initiative games that will require the class to work together to solve a problem does not mean that you are teaching problem solving. Unless you *intend* to teach problem solving and have a plan for accomplishing that, you cannot claim to be teaching problem solving or group cooperation. One of the unique features of this book is that the lessons are intentional in bringing to the students' attention the connections among diverse curriculum areas and character qualities.

• **Vigilant.** A teacher who is vigilant and engaged during the implementation of the intentionally planned lesson will be much more effective than a teacher who is less engaged in finding opportunities to make comments and ask questions. Comments and questions are two of the main ways to help students make connections among different subjects, and they guide students in analytical and creative thinking. Vigilant implementation means actively observing the class while it is participating in an activity so you can make comments and ask questions while the activity is happening and after it has ended. The belief that reflecting on an experience occurs only after the activity is over is misleading. A lot of thought, questioning, and insight can happen during the activity and can be guided and encouraged by a vigilant and engaged teacher. With this type of vigilant implementation, the reflection time following the activity will be more natural and meaningful.

Once a teacher understands and values the outdoor education method, additional components of teaching must be considered before actual application. For example, teachers must know their students, something about their backgrounds, and any special needs they may have. Other components are what program or unit contents might be most conducive to the teacher's objectives, location, and skills; what curriculum standards can be included; and what logistics may be involved.

Students

Adolescent students are difficult to describe because they embody so many dichotomies. For example, they are very self-centered yet capable of impressive altruistic acts. "Their attention wanders like a butterfly, yet they can spend hours concentrating on seemingly pointless involvements. They are often lazy and rude, yet, when you least expect it, they can be loving and helpful" (Csikszentmihalyi and Larson, 1984, p. xiii). The greatest difference between adolescents and adults, other than physical maturation and experience, is motivation. Feeling less free in choosing their goals can be a significant reason

The best way to reach adolescent students is to pull them out of the classroom and into the subject matter.

why some students do not use their mental capacities to the fullest. They are less involved in what they are doing. This lack of involvement has sent teachers searching for ways to reach their adolescent students. The search has led some teachers to dramatic theatrical devices; others to wild language, flamboyant dress, or affect; and still others to game show or entertainment themes; yet "the most impressive approaches are the ones that directly pull students into the subject matter itself" (Csikszentmihalyi and Larson, 1984, p. 215).

A teacher's genuine interest in the subject is always more effective than clever stunts. When teachers are excited about the subjects they are teaching, the chances are good that the students' curiosity will be aroused. They will want to know why this person is so interested in the subject, which improves the teacher's chance to create an environment that leads to the students being intrinsically motivated. When students find classes intrinsically rewarding, they learn more. To make the educational experience enjoyable and therefore intrinsically motivating, students need opportunities for active physical, sensory, and cognitive participation. Additionally, these participation experiences must offer increasing challenges as the skills of the students develop: "Only when going to school becomes a flow activity [where the challenge is equal to the students' interest and potential skill] will students be motivated to learn on their own, and grow in the process" (Csikszentmihalyi and Larson, 1984, p. 259).

Content

The content for outdoor education may include the ecosystem and its relationships. In fact, that is probably what most people would think of when they hear the words *outdoor education.* However, the content of the outdoor education lessons presented in this book focuses on outdoor recreational activities that are often associated with residential camp programs. The rationale for focusing on such activities is that they are not the typical sport activities found in a school setting and can serve as motivators and offer opportunities for cognitive, physical, and sensory involvement. The actual content focus

is on the concepts and skills that the outdoor activity requires.

Curricular Standards

Curricular standards have been developed to guide teachers in planning the content to be learned at various grade levels. Yet when teachers become too focused on only their own content standards, context can become fuzzy and opportunities to incorporate other subject areas are lost. One of the unique features of this book is that the lessons are designed with multiple purposes, one of which is to present lessons that are intentionally interdisciplinary. The lesson plans go beyond the listing of curricular areas that the lesson touches on and actually give curricular standards and techniques for reinforcing them.

Each lesson includes concepts and skills from at least two subject areas. The main interdisciplinary emphasis of this book is on the following subjects: the social studies topics of civics, economics, and geography; health; language arts; math; physical education; and science (see appendix A for a complete list of standards). The interdisciplinary standards used in this book are generally applicable for students in kindergarten through 12th grade (ages 5-18). The National Association for Sport and Physical Education (NASPE) has provided physical education standards for such students. The Mid-Continent Research for Education and Learning group (McREL) has provided the remaining subject standards. Teachers can browse the standards provided at www.mcrel.org to find more specific standards for different age groups.

Class Organization and Management

This section is included for new teachers and is intended to reinforce basic management practices. Many teachers are hesitant to take students outside for fear of losing control. If going outside is new for students in a particular class, the novelty can result in an initial rowdiness. However, with specific behavior instructions and a teacher's ability to be flexible with conduct expectations for outside activities, students will acclimate and the teacher will have control indoors or out. This can be an extremely intimidating prospect for teachers, and the vision of chaos can prevent a teacher from attempting to use the outdoors. But with agreement between the students and the teacher on acceptable behavior and with appropriate organizational structures, learning can flourish. The following three sections offer structure suggestions for organizing student behavior and communicating with students when using the outdoors as a classroom.

Activity Teams

The lessons in this book are designed for activities in small groups, which include three, four, or five students per group. The teacher cannot be everywhere at once, so the groups must be organized to function with indirect supervision rather than direct supervision. Indirect supervision is the ability to visually scan groups to check for safety and on-task activity, and direct supervision is the ability to see and hear every face and every word that is said, such as sitting in a circle for a group discussion. To facilitate indirect teacher supervision, select one student per team to be a team leader. Team leaders then get directions and a little instruction before class so they can help their team during that class period. Team leaders can be changed frequently, as can the makeup of the various teams.

Pledge of Respect

A class pledge of respect should be made before using activity teams. A pledge of respect is an agreement between the teacher and students to respect themselves and each other so they can make class an enjoyable experience for everyone. It works best if you hold a class discussion about what the pledge means and then write it up and have everyone sign it. You initiate this process, but the students are closely involved in the wording. In general, the topics for discussion include the following:

- What is the purpose of school?
- What is the teacher's job?
- What is the student's job?
- How does everyone like to be treated?

The discussion should lead to the definition of *respect*, which is defined by Character Counts as "being considerate of the feelings of others

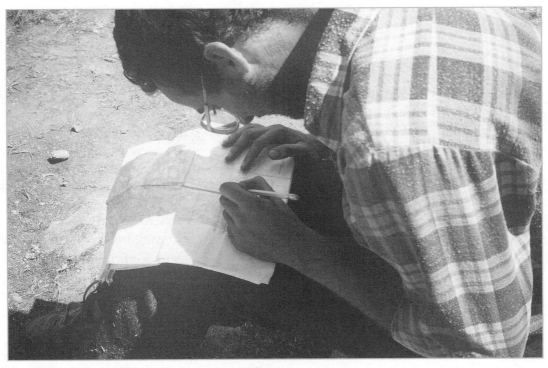

Team leaders can be utilized to help manage small groups.

SAMPLE PLEDGE OF RESPECT

We, the undersigned students in Mr. Miller's math class, along with Mr. Miller, pledge to

1. honor the equal value of everyone in the class,
2. talk and act toward others as we would want to be treated,
3. make allowances for individual differences and accept the value of diversity, and
4. make every effort to resolve disagreements peacefully and with a willingness to work toward a positive class atmosphere.

(think of how you would feel); refraining from insulting and discounting language and actions toward yourself and toward others; being tolerant of individual differences; and dealing peacefully with anger, insults, and disagreements" (www.charactercounts.org). Following the discussion about respect, have a discussion about the definition of *pledge*. Pledge can be defined as a promise, or giving your word that what you say is true. This process could take a whole class period.

Student Behavior Instructions

If students know your expectations and your class structure, they are much more likely to cooperate. The following instructions are structures that you can teach to your students. They are divided into two types: organization instructions and instruction signals.

- Organization instructions are rules that students are instructed to follow at specific times, such as when going from the classroom to the outdoors or when class is taking place outside.
    - Walking quietly in the hallway without talking is a requirement for the privilege of going outside.
    - Each student has a partner, and each pair has a buddy pair. Students are responsible for their own attitudes and actions as well as for reminding their partner and buddy pair of their responsibilities and pledge of respect.

- Instruction signals provide a basic means of communication between teacher and students when the students are doing activities outside in small groups and are not all within easy hearing distance from the teacher, or when the teacher would otherwise have to use a whistle. All signals are made overhead, and a designated class meeting place should be noted at the beginning of class.
    - The teacher's hand going up overhead signals students to put one of their hands up, quit talking, and listen for more instructions. This should be used when the teacher wants to address the group as a whole.
    - Hand signals are also useful for getting students to arrange themselves into a particular configuration for instruction or activity. For example, the teacher's arms extended overhead with the thumb and forefinger of both hands touching each other creates a circle. The students signal back as they see the signal and get into a circle. A semicircle or horseshoe is signaled by touching the thumbs from each hand while holding the forefingers straight up.
    - Pointing the forefinger of one hand straight up and moving it in a hat-sized circle can indicate that it is time to return to the classroom. Again, students respond with the signal to indicate that they understand and to help spread the instruction to other class members. At the signal, the students begin walking back to the classroom.
    - A hand overhead with two fingers held up means students should pair up with their partner, and four fingers means to join with their partner and buddy pair.

Hand signals are not magic, but they can be more effective than yelling or blowing a whistle. However, they do need to be introduced, practiced indoors, and used with consistency. It will take about a week for the students to adjust and understand your expectations. There is nothing sacred about these hand signals, so feel free to make up your own. Just remember to be consistent.

Basic Teaching Formations

Specific teaching formations that everyone understands can also be an asset for outdoor instruction. When teaching in the outdoors there are no desks or chairs that tell the students where to sit or stand. Three basic teaching formations for students will aid the communication process when teaching outdoors.

- Circle. A circle is the ideal configuration for a class discussion. Teachers should stand as a part of the circle rather than standing inside the circle with their back to a few students. (See figure 1.3a.)
- Semicircle. This configuration gives more room for demonstrations. The teacher stands at the opening. (See figure 1.3b.)
- Small groups. The third configuration has the class divided into small groups and scattered throughout the designated activity area. (See figure 1.3c.)

The first two configurations are best when the whole class needs to be involved in a presentation or discussion, and small groups are best when the teacher does not need to give instructions to everyone at the same time. Teaching and consistently using these or similar organizational structures, signals, and formations can make a significant contribution to an effective outdoor learning environment.

The method, students, content, curricular standards, and class organization are components of teaching outdoor education that require a bit of conceptual adjustment from traditional teaching. Another way to think about outdoor education is in terms of what is fundamental to its method. Four fundamentals are presented here in an attempt to summarize the essential elements of outdoor education.

Fundamentals of Outdoor Education

The outdoor education teaching method can be implemented within a variety of subject areas, with different populations, and for diverse objectives. But there are four fundamentals that are essential. First, outdoor education is primarily experiential. The students must be actively engaged in the learning process through participation in structured experiences that will facilitate student learning. Second, there should be some connection with the natural environment. Humans are a part of the natural environment, we are dependent upon it for our survival, and there are too many analogies and correlations between the environment and various subject areas to pass them by. Third, outdoor education consistently encourages reflection, generalization, and application. And fourth, it is intentionally interdisciplinary. The outdoor educator knows that students understand best when they can see or experience connections between

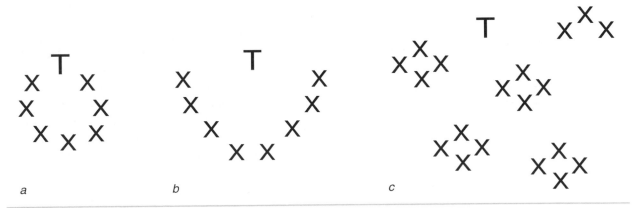

Figure 1.3 The three basic teaching formations: *(a)* circle, *(b)* semicircle, and *(c)* small groups.

subject areas. An understanding of these fundamental elements will provide a foundation for understanding the structure and details of the lesson plans in chapters 3 through 9.

Structured Experiences

The experiences must be structured, meaning they must be well-planned and well-prepared activities for the purpose of illustrating, expanding, investigating, practicing, or discovering information, skills, questions, or emotions regarding the topic. It is not a matter of taking students into an outdoor environment and letting them play. The term *experience* refers to hands-on activities that allow students to be directly engaged in the activity. Most of the time, this includes some degree of psychomotor activity.

Environmental Connection

All outdoor education need not take place in an outdoor environment, but there must be a clear connection to it. This involvement with the natural environment could take the form of activities that either are best accomplished in a natural outdoor environment because the activity requires it or depends on some type of cooperation with it (such as canoeing, rock climbing, backpacking, and fishing) or are focused on learning about the environment, its relationships, and its significance to human life. Simply using an object, animal, insect, or plant as an illustration of something can be valuable in capturing interest and furthering understanding.

Reflection and Discussion

Reflection on the experience, followed or fueled by discussion, is an integral element of the outdoor education method. Experience does not automatically yield learning. For learning to result from even the most carefully planned experiences, reflection upon that experience must occur. As we reflect on what occurred, discuss our thoughts with others who shared the experience, and generalize from the experience to a real-life focus or a different curricular focus, the likelihood of finding meaning and increased understanding is amplified. Research into the brain function for learning has shown us the importance of reflection and making personal meaning in the learning process. In the last 10 years conventional classroom education has begun to focus on guided reflection, but it has been an important part of the outdoor education method for many years. Figure 1.1 on page 5 illustrates the role of reflection in the experiential learning process.

Interdisciplinary Connections

The idea that a lesson or unit is interdisciplinary means that more than one discipline, for example math plus science, music plus social studies, or physical education plus language arts plus science, is woven into the learning experience with the objective of realizing their connections. By its very nature, outdoor education is interdisciplinary, but too often exploring the connections between disciplines is not an objective of the lesson. Without the teacher planning for students to see and understand the connections, the connections are often missed. The interdisciplinary connections that are so readily available in outdoor education are one of its greatest strengths as an educational method, and the importance of making connections has been documented by neurological research. Periods of guided reflection are excellent opportunities for thinking about, discussing, and understanding interdisciplinary connections.

With these fundamental elements all functioning in an integrated fashion, the significant correlation with the findings of brain-function research is quite evident. However, this is not to say that learning does not and cannot happen with other teaching methods, because some things—perhaps multiplication tables, for example—are more effectively taught via different methods.

Success with outdoor education requires being aware that it can be done, being intentional about planning for these additional objectives, and being vigilant while implementing the lesson. The outdoor education teaching method also requires the teacher to be courageous, since teaching outdoors can be intimidating for teachers acclimated to the indoor classroom. However, with an appropriate structure for class organization and the willingness to be flexible and give students time to adjust to having class in the outdoors, outdoor education can enliven the teaching and learning experience and hopefully increase learning.

Highlighting an Embedded Curriculum

Outdoor education has been described as a method for highlighting embedded, interdisciplinary curriculum concepts as well as character qualities within the teaching of outdoor recreational activities. The lessons in this book encourage teachers to look for connections among various subjects, outdoor activities, and character qualities and to plan how they can highlight those connections, thereby increasing their students' understanding. The interdisciplinary and character connections to outdoor education are referred to as an embedded curriculum.

Concrete can be a metaphor for the embedded curriculum. On the surface, concrete is smooth and uniform. But when it is broken up and observed more closely, you can see small stones of varying size and shape. Another metaphor might be a three-dimensional, random-dot stereogram in which you initially see only different colored dots and some degree of repeated pattern. But as you look more closely and adjust your vision, images begin to emerge. In this metaphor, the easily seen picture with its colors and pattern represent the outdoor recreational activity. It has attraction in its own right, but a closer look brings out things that are less obvious. These images represent embedded connections to other areas, whether they are life skills or subject matter concepts and skills. By relating these connections to the larger picture, they hold more interest and meaning than if they were presented in isolation.

This book uses the term *embedded curriculum* to refer to learning objectives beyond the main focus of the lessons. In most cases, it will consist of two types of objectives: concepts and skills related to the outdoor environment or other subject areas, and the understanding and exercise of character qualities. Teachers regularly encounter students who are not interested in math or science or what it means to be diligent or trustworthy. However, when students are engaged in fun activities and the relevance of another subject to that activity becomes apparent, progress can be made toward interest and understanding.

Embedded implies that something is below the surface and thus not readily obvious. Therefore, the embedded connections must be highlighted so the students know they are present. Highlighting means making something stand out. Think of a teacher asking a question that stimulates thinking in a particular direction or making a statement that reinforces positive behavior or a student comment. Both techniques serve to highlight a connection that may otherwise go unnoticed.

Highlighting Interdisciplinary Connections

The examples given for stages 1 and 3 of the experiential teaching cycle (see pages 6 to 8) illustrate one way to plan and implement interdisciplinary connections. We must remember the reasons for this type of teaching and why outdoor education is an excellent venue for making connections among subject areas.

Since we know that context, movement, and variety of stimuli enhance the learning process, and we know that the outdoor education method capitalizes on these ingredients, then it follows that interdisciplinary teaching is ideal for outdoor education. See the sidebar When Will We Reach Camp? (page 16) for an example of a math problem that could be included in a canoe camping trip.

When you want to reinforce concepts or skills that connect with different curriculum areas, structure your questions or comments in a way that requires the students to combine information from different sources and then apply it in the context of the activity. Information for the sake of information is usually forgotten, but if the students experience an application of the information, it becomes useful knowledge. For example, the canoe camping situation in the sidebar is an obvious application for math skills. Algebra or the specific formula for calculating speed might have been presented in a math class, but if students are actually learning to canoe and camp they will be more likely to retain or understand the calculation.

Outdoor education also provides opportunities to highlight and integrate concepts or

WHEN WILL WE REACH CAMP?

Calculate how long it will take you to get to your destination: S(peed) = d(istance)/t(ime).

If you know that you can travel in a canoe at a rate of 4 miles (6 kilometers) per hour, can you make it to your campsite before dark? It is dark by 9 p.m. and it is currently 2 p.m., so you know you have 7 hours until dark. According to the map, there are 15 miles (24 kilometers) yet to travel. Can you make it there before dark?

You need to know how long it will take to get to the campsite, so leave *t* for time unknown and fill in the rest of the equation.

$$S = d/t$$
$$4 \text{ mph} = 15\text{mi} /t \text{ or } 6.5 \text{ kmh} = 24 \text{ km}/t$$

Cross multiply and divide to get *t* alone.

$$t = 3.75 \text{ hours}$$

This tells us that it will take you 3.75 hours to go 15 miles (24 kilometers) at a speed of 4 miles per hour (6 kilometers per hour). Since you know you have 7 hours until dark, and it will only take you 3.75 hours to travel, you know that you will be able to reach the campsite before dark.

skills from other curriculum areas that are not as obvious as the canoeing math problem. For example, if a class is learning how to set up tarps for sleeping shelters and needs to know the best configuration for the most sleeping space, you can highlight the Pythagorean theorem ($a^2 + b^2 = c^2$). Set up two tarps differently and give the students the problem of which provides the most usable space and why. In situations such as this, you must decide whether to use an indirect method for encouraging the students to think in a particular direction or a more direct method.

The indirect method uses comments and non-specific questions to help focus student observations. The direct method uses questions that are directed specifically toward the bottom line of the problem. An indirect comment to aid the students' observation and assist with making the connection to the Pythagorean theorem could be, "Look carefully at the top angle of each tarp and the influence it has." Direct questions are, "Which of these tarps best represents the Pythagorean theorem?" and then, "What does that tell us about the sleeping space?" In this scenario, the indirect comment allows the students to make the connections and figure things out with less guidance. You can always move on to questions if no one makes the connection.

Real-life application of math skills during a canoe trip can help students retain information.

Also, don't always think that the answer must be reached in the same day. It is affirming for a student to have time to think and consider and then to experience the "light bulb" coming on. To reinforce concepts and skills from across the curriculum, you must intentionally plan for reinforcement and be vigilant about following through with your plan. Otherwise, it is easy to go on with the activity and forget about the embedded curriculum.

Some students will be resistant to subject matter from classes they do not like or do well in, but with patience, consistency, and time they will learn to look for connections themselves and begin to feel more competent. On the other hand, connections to character qualities tend to be less threatening and should always be introduced from a positive point of view.

Highlighting Character Qualities

Character development has natural connections with outdoor education activities. The term *natural connections* in this context is not referring to the natural environment and its ecosystem, but to behaviors in outdoor activities that illustrate either positive or negative character qualities. For example, most activities work best when students cooperate, and when cooperation is not present success is usually more difficult or diminished. Rather than just talking about and role-playing positive character qualities, outdoor education activities use real demonstrations and practice sessions.

New Horizons for Learning is a nonprofit international network of educators focused on identifying, communicating, and implementing the most effective teaching and learning strategies for all ages and abilities. The Center for the Advancement of Ethics and Character is a part of the New Horizons organization and has developed a Character Education Manifesto. This manifesto is essentially a series of statements on the importance of character education and its centrality to overall education. It states, "Character education is about developing virtues—good habits and dispositions which lead students to responsible and mature adulthood"(Center for the Advancement of Ethics and Character, 1996). It is not about teaching the "right" views or beliefs. Character is defined by what people do, not by what they say or believe. Character qualities are actions and therefore can be taught along with activities that will naturally bring out positive or negative character traits. Many character education lessons are similar to traditional classroom lessons and are viewed by students as just another subject. However, outdoor education provides opportunities to practice positive character qualities in the context of activities. Such activities are not designed specifically for character education, but it becomes obvious that positive character traits are important to the success and enjoyment of the activities.

The character qualities that programs actively pursue can vary. The Character Education Partnership (CEP) suggests that "character education holds that widely shared, pivotally important, core ethical values—such as caring, honesty, fairness, responsibility, and respect for self and others—form the basis of good character" (www.character.org). Individual programs or teachers can use the CEP's list of traits, or they can develop a list of traits they feel are important, such as trustworthiness or citizenship. The following eight character qualities chosen for this book's lessons are highlighted in the lessons to help you see how each lesson helps students develop certain character qualities.

- **Caring**—Being kind and compassionate; expressing gratitude and forgiveness; helping people in need.
- **Citizenship**—Doing your share to make your school and community better by cooperating, protecting the environment, and being involved.
- **Courage**—The steadfastness to commit yourself to what is good and right and actively pursue it, even if it is not convenient or popular.
- **Patience**—Being able to wait or slow your pace without becoming irritable.
- **Perseverance**—Continuing steady action or effort toward an undertaking in spite of counterinfluences, opposition, or discouragement.
- **Respect**—Being considerate of the feelings of others; dealing peacefully with anger,

insults, and disagreements; being tolerant of differences.

- **Responsibility**—Thinking before you act by considering the consequences; being accountable for your choices; using self-control; doing what you are supposed to do.

- **Trustworthiness**—Being honest and reliable (doing what you say you'll do).

Since character is demonstrated through action, and since outdoor education involves action, the connections are easy to make. But once again, it requires intentional planning and vigilant implementation. Character qualities are exhibited any time students do a project, whether it is designed for individual or group work. Although the main focus of the lesson is outdoor activity concepts and skills, if the teacher has planned to intentionally highlight selected character qualities, there will be many opportunities for doing so. If, however, there is no planned intention, the opportunities are often not recognized. The best way to become aware of the connections with outdoor activities is to read through the definitions of the seven character qualities in the preceding list and then read a few of the lesson plans. It will become clear that although the main objective of the lessons is not to teach character, character can be learned through highlighting the embedded curriculum.

Using language that attributes positive qualities to people can be an empowering and positive influence in behavior and self-perception. A technique for encouraging positive character qualities is verbal recognition and appreciation that attaches the action to the student's innate nature. This is called *attribution language* and can be quite effective in helping students understand positive character qualities. The emphasis is not on teaching all the nuances of the character qualities but on recognizing them when they are exhibited and setting up situa-

tions that will allow students to benefit from them. For example, you might say, "Gene, you are a thoughtful young man. It was very caring of you to help Ryan with his heavy backpack." In that statement, the first sentence attributes to Gene the innate characteristic of thoughtfulness, saying that being thoughtful is who he is. The second sentence describes the action that illustrated that characteristic. Attribution language can help students perceive themselves as capable and thus increase their willingness to be active learners. As an aid to character development, putting up a poster, such as the ones found in Appendix C, with specific character qualities and their definitions will help students become familiar with them.

At first glance, it can seem that using embedded curriculum is simple because all that is required is a few questions or comments. It is true that questions and comments are excellent highlighting techniques, but it is not always that simple. What makes the highlighting more difficult is the planning. Without planning ahead, you may miss opportunities for highlighting and making positive attributions. To be consistently effective with an embedded curriculum, the teacher must first become aware of it and then be willing to weave those highlights into the activities of the main content focus.

Summary

Integrating outdoor education into your curriculum paves the way for deeper learning for the whole child. Knowledge can be transmitted in a manner that intrigues and encourages exploration and involvement. Skills are presented that are interesting and readily applicable, and emotions are tapped that can facilitate meaning and connections. Through the simultaneous engagement of the cognitive, psychomotor and affective domains, students are poised for successful learning experiences.

Foundations for Teaching Outdoor Education

Chapter 2

© M Holmes

The foundation of outdoor education comes from history, philosophy, and science. To help you gain a sense of context, this chapter contains a brief history of outdoor education and its evolution. It also discusses some of the goals and benefits of school-based outdoor education programs. This information can be critical when preparing a proposal to start an outdoor education course or program, and it is very helpful for lesson planning. The chapter also presents social psychology theories and neurological research relevant to outdoor education, which provides a foundational support upon which to build an effective program.

History of Outdoor Education

Many educators throughout history have emphasized the importance of firsthand experience in the natural environment. Jean-Jacques Rousseau (1712-1788) was a philosopher who advocated learning from direct experience rather than indirectly from books. He also emphasized the importance of physical activity. Johann Heinrich Pestalozzi (1746-1827) was an educator who advocated direct experience, specifically in practical living skills such as farming, housekeeping, spinning, and weaving: activities that many residential outdoor education programs now incorporate. William James (1842-1910) got a medical degree from Harvard and went on to become the father of American psychology and an acclaimed philosopher. He lectured on the psychology of teaching, advocating the importance of capitalizing on the student's interests. John Dewey (1859-1952) holds an important place in American education for his writings about moral development, or what he called the "hidden curriculum." He advocated the importance of teaching morals, how to cooperate in a community, and how to think. For Dewey, thinking was problem solving, and to learn problem solving there had to be direct experience.

Of course, when people are left to learn on their own, experiential learning is the method of choice. However, when children are crowded together in cities, the available experiences are different. Furthermore, access to the natural outdoor environment and its health benefits is limited. This was the situation in the 1930s during the Great Depression, when many children lived in crowded, slumlike conditions and suffered from malnutrition. The children needed to get outside in the fresh air and sunshine of the countryside. It was during this time that Lloyd Burgess Sharp became executive director of Life Camps, which was sponsored by *Life* magazine and targeted underprivileged children. There, he developed a philosophy and program for *camping education,* a term he coined while writing his dissertation.

Camping Education

L.B. Sharp became known as the father of public school camping due to his advocacy for school camps. He talked about how school camps were used mostly during the summer months, which he saw as "an educational waste. . . and the public school camp should be open all year" (Rillo, 1980, p.23). According to Hammerman and Hammerman (1964), "one of the selling points of early school camping was that the outdoor environment provided healthful outdoor living in the fresh air and sunshine" (p. 7). In addition, after World War II social problems

existed that camping education could address more effectively than a classroom education. Such problems were congested slum areas, a lack of playgrounds, nutrition, and opportunities for activities in fresh air and sunshine. Citizens needed to understand the importance of soil conservation and the reality of the physical world and its web of interdependencies. Thus the growth and development of camping education, which came to be called school camping, evolved and eventually became one form of outdoor education. This form primarily consisted of residential camp experiences, but through the years programs developed that focused on one or two dimensions of outdoor education on the school campus. Many schools developed gardens or ponds for ecology and biology study, others developed physical education programs that taught lifelong outdoor activities. Some had interdisciplinary programs taught in teams, and a few went a step further and offered field trips with opportunities for more extensive experience. Many educators saw the benefit of extended trips, and with the influence of the Outward Bound schools, adventure education began to influence outdoor education programming.

Adventure Education

Two influential programs in the expansion of outdoor education are Outward Bound and Project Adventure. The first North American Outward Bound school was started in Colorado in 1962. In this program, outdoor adventures are used to give young people the opportunity to discover that they can accomplish far more and withstand more hardship than they had imagined. Although the school began with trips for boys only, it has since expanded to include girls as well people of diverse ages. Project Adventure is an outgrowth of Outward Bound in that the ropes challenges were adapted for use in schools rather than as preparation for weeks in the wilderness. The purpose is similar, but it does not include the outdoor living skills and wilderness travel component. Project Adventure has been so successful in spreading the philosophy of ropes-course participation that ropes courses have been built around the world. Many schools even have a ropes course on campus. Since ropes courses are viewed as similar to an Outward Bound course and since they are usually an outdoor adventure, ropes courses have become synonymous with outdoor education for many teachers. However, there is much more to outdoor education than ropes courses. It is just one activity that may be a part of an outdoor education program. In fact, the concept of ropes courses has expanded beyond individual challenges and ropes attached to trees. A more accurate term now is *challenge course*. This term encompasses the individual challenges that often use more steel cable than rope and that offer group development activities and challenges.

Why Teach Outdoor Education?

The foundations for teaching outdoor education are relevant for meeting the needs of a diverse population. However, 5th-grade students through high school students go through so many physiological and emotional changes that they can lose interest in school if motivation diminishes. Outdoor education with a focus on adventure activities can serve as both a motivator and a lens through which the relevance of other subject areas can be experienced. Additionally, outdoor adventure activities are typically less familiar to students than traditional sports and serve as an equalizer in terms of skill levels. Starting a new activity with a more level playing field increases the possibility for different students to excel and be recognized. And of course, there are also the lifelong physical fitness benefits of learning activities that encourage physical activity.

In the mid-20th century, during the early days of the school camping movement, professionals in the field of outdoor education listed seven needs that outdoor education can meet. These needs are essentially the same as the goals of outdoor education that today's outdoor educators would list. The following seven needs are quoted from the classic, *Teaching in the Outdoors*, by Hammerman, Hammerman, and Hammerman (1964, p.13-16).

1. The need for effective learning. Extending the learning process into instructional settings beyond the classroom provides the opportunity for bringing greater understanding, deeper insight, and clearer meaning to those areas of knowledge which, all too often, are merely read and discussed and are seldom experienced.

© DigitalVision

The benefits of adding outdoor education to the classroom can last a lifetime.

2. The need for basic concepts. Outdoor education provides teachers with a vehicle for bringing real meaning to abstract concepts. Those students who go out into the playground or to a nearby park to collect a soil sample and then test it and analyze the results will have a far different concept of soil than those students who merely read about it in their science textbook.

3. The need for realism in education. Lessons of life are to be found at every hand in the outdoor classroom. Students don't need to rely on words alone—symbols of reality—when they can see, touch, taste, smell, and hear living lessons that change with the seasons. Real understanding comes through doing, or experiencing.

4. The need for awareness. Modern young people are missing a basic aspect of their own existence—acquaintance with the earth upon which we depend for our livelihood and survival. One of the greatest contributions outdoor education can make to this generation is to reestablish the fast-disappearing bond between humankind and the natural environment.

5. The need for appreciation of the natural environment. Because so much of our lives center on the acquisition and use of material objects, there is a need to counterbalance this devotion to things with the inner renewal that can be derived from enjoying the simpler things in life. The intricacies and inner workings of the natural environment tend to bring things into proper perspective.

6. The need for environmental literacy. Human survival may well depend upon our ability to control the pollutants with which we despoil the land. Schools, as societal institutions, are in the prime position to ultimately influence behavior, change attitudes, and develop guidelines and principles that will affect the masses.

7. The need for recreative experience. Outdoor activity can be a major contributing force toward improved physical fitness and better health. The pressing need for wise use of leisure can be met in part through outdoor recreational pursuits.

Hammerman, Donald R.; Hammerman, William M.; Hammerman, Elizabeth L., *Teaching in the outdoors*, ©1964. Adapted by permission of Pearson Education, Inc., Upper Saddle River, NJ.

The following and last need was not in the original list, but it is a significant concern for every teacher today.

8. The need to relate well with others. The development of skills and attitudes necessary to understand and appreciate the interrelatedness among people and their individual differences, along with the ability to communicate effectively, are crucial in our shrinking world. Outdoor activities can provide a forum for learning such skills and practicing them in real situations while also learning about environmental interrelatedness.

Introducing students to a variety of outdoor recreational skills is a valuable goal in itself since one important educational goal is to encourage students to engage in positive physical activity throughout their lives. Outdoor recreational activities provide opportunities for such physical involvement without the necessity of being athletically coordinated. Physical fitness is valuable for optimal health, and even physical activity below the level of intensely strenuous exercise can be health enhancing. Often an emphasis on physical fitness and sport skill development discourages people from physical activity rather than encouraging them toward it. Outdoor recreational activities can inspire an active lifestyle by providing positive personal rewards for physical involvement without the fear of stigma for poor coordination.

Supporting Theories

Because outdoor education is presented in this book as a teaching method rather than a subject area, we need evidence to support its use along with guidance for using it effectively. The social psychology theories in this section are not new and have been used by experiential and adventure educators for years as the foundation of their methodologies. However, the theories continue to be relevant and are supported by emerging information on how the brain functions during learning. Brain research validates what highly successful teachers have known for years and provides encouragement for teachers to use certain methods in their professional practice.

Social Psychology Theories

Social psychology theories pertain to the psychology associated with social actions and interactions. In other words, why do people choose certain behaviors in certain situations? The theories discussed in this section offer some explanation for behavior and why outdoor education methodology is effective. Teachers can use these theories to enhance their teaching practice. For example, knowledge of attribution theory can help teachers understand the effect their reinforcement language can have on a student, while optimal arousal can inform the necessity for offering various levels of challenge.

These theories are represented by icons that appear in a lesson if the lesson presents a situation where the teacher can apply that particular theory.

Maslow's Hierarchy of Needs △

Maslow's hierarchy (1970) reiterates the old adage, "Don't put the cart before the horse." This theory holds that people must have basic needs met before they are able to attend to higher-order needs. For example, if the main objective of your

lesson is to teach multiplication, you want your students to be free to think about multiplication rather than worrying about being too cold.

Figure 2.1 illustrates that basic needs must be met before a person is able to attend to the needs of the next level. For example, if a person cannot breathe, she will not be concerned about staying safe from lightning. If she finds herself in an intense storm with lightning striking all around, her desire to be accepted by her peers will not be relevant. If she does not have an accepted place in a group of peers, she will not be inclined to explore direction for her life or believe in her self-worth. As educators, aiming for the higher levels of the hierarchy is futile without first planning for and meeting the lower needs. Analogous to this hierarchy is the concept of teaching skills in a proper sequence, such as teaching how to hold a canoe paddle correctly before teaching the correct way to do a forward stroke.

Theory of Optimal Arousal ⌂

The theory of optimal arousal (Duffy, 1957) is essentially the philosophy of most adventure education programs. It is the scientific equivalent of "No pain, no gain," with the recognition that at some point there are diminishing returns (see figure 2.2). If arousal or challenge continues to increase, the positive benefits will decline and may even become negative or detrimental.

In this theory, arousal means challenge or stress. Optimal arousal theory suggests that some level of arousal is necessary for performance to reach its optimal level or for optimal benefits to be gained. Using the optimal arousal theory in teaching is a way of motivating or challenging

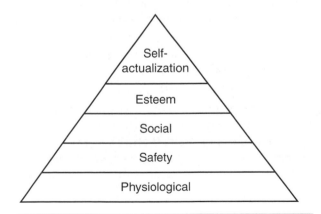

Figure 2.1 Maslow's hierarchy of needs.

MASLOW, ABRAHAN H; FRAGER, ROBERT D, (EDITOR); FADIMAN, JAMES (EDITOR), MOTIVATION AND PERSONALITY, 3rd Edition, © 1997. Reprinted by permission of Pearson Education, Inc., Upper Saddle River, NJ.

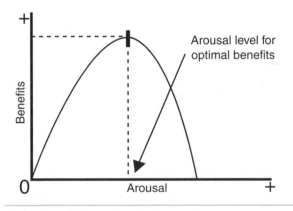

Figure 2.2 Theory of optimal arousal.

your students by presenting them with tasks that have a recognizable risk. This risk is not one of life and limb, but a perceived risk that will yield a sense of accomplishment when completed. The teacher may help the students' perception of the challenge by discussing it and its associated risks before the students begin. If they do not perceive the challenge, their sense of accomplishment upon completion will be greatly diminished or lost. For example, when teaching rock climbing and rappelling, it is important to offer climbs of varying degrees of difficulty and rappels from different heights. If only one option is available, it might be too much of a challenge for some and not enough of a challenge for others.

Theory of Competence-Effectance ⌐

The theory of competence-effectance (White, 1959) is an elaborate title that has become better known as flow theory. The hypothesis is that people have a need to demonstrate their abilities and that those abilities can affect their circumstances or environment. Imagine a comedian doing a standup routine on a stage for two consecutive nights. On the first night the audience is happy, laughs easily, and the comedian can tell that he is "in the zone." But on the second night his audience seems distracted, inattentive, and generally unhappy. This situation presents a greater challenge. If he is a highly competent comedian, he will be able to rise to the challenge. If his competency is only enough to entertain an already happy audience, he will probably have a bad experience. Csikszentmihalyi (1975) has built on this hypothesis and proposes that individuals actually pursue opportunities that will

challenge their competence to affect a situation (see figure 2.3). The point of seeking such challenges is to experience the satisfaction resulting from demonstrated competence and its effect, or to be in the zone or flow. This is very closely related to the theory of optimal arousal.

As ability increases, challenge must increase to maintain interest. However, if the challenge far surpasses ability level, failure is almost certain. The consequences of failure vary depending upon the task, but as the challenge or task difficulty is decreased for the same skill level, the probability of a positive experience increases. As skill level increases, task difficulty must increase. Navigating a rapid that you perceive as more difficult than the rapids you typically paddle is an example of testing your competence.

A primary application of competence-effectance theory is to sequence activities to gradually increase the challenge as skill and knowledge levels of the students increase. However, too much challenge may serve as a demotivator. This means that, similar to optimal arousal theory, challenges will often need to be different for different students, depending on their varying knowledge and skills. An important way to make the most of this theory is to commend students for their individual increases in understanding and skill rather than making comparisons between students.

Theory of Self-Efficacy ☺

Bandura's theory of self-efficacy (1986) defines self-efficacy as an individual's belief in her ability to accomplish a specific task. It is probably one of the best known psychosocial theories in the field of outdoor adventure education. The theory hypothesizes that efficacy expectations are weighted by an individual's perceived ability; the task difficulty, effort needed, and aid he expects to receive; the situation and the transferability of his perceived abilities; and his persistence and patterns of success. An individual's efficacy expectations can be affected by four basic processes:

• Experiences of success. The most influential process, offering experiences of success, is critical to planning outdoor experiences. Skills must be taught in an appropriate sequence so they can be mastered incrementally. By sequenc-

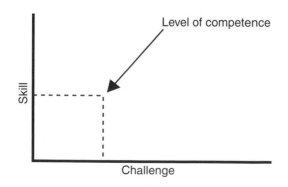

Figure 2.3 In flow theory, individuals seek opportunities to exhibit their competence.

ing, students can experience success and gradually gain confidence in their abilities.

- Verbal persuasion. Verbal encouragement is addressed in the following section on attribution theory.

- Vicarious experience. Vicarious experience is important because students need to be able to identify with others' positive accomplishments. For example, a teacher demonstrating a skill is less effective than another student demonstrating a skill. Students need to see themselves doing the task and can more often identify with a peer than the teacher. A teacher demonstrating a rappel will be less empowering than another student demonstrating the rappel.

- Emotional arousal. The process of emotional arousal, such as excitement or anxiety, has to do with the feelings a person has in relation to a particular task. If students have an experience with a task, whether it is a direct experience, a vicarious experience, or an experience through being told about the task, their excitement will tend to increase their efficacy in relation to the task. On the other hand, if the elicited emotion is negative, efficacy will generally decrease. Teachers can potentially affect the first three processes through good planning and hope that positive emotions, the fourth process, will result.

By looking back at the theory of optimal arousal and flow theory, you can see the close relationship of both theories to self-efficacy. The desired end result is some type of enhanced performance or personal satisfaction resulting from a test or challenge. It is important for the teacher to help the student recognize the challenge, accomplish the task successfully, and recognize the student's success. This is done by

- properly sequencing tasks,
- introducing the tasks to highlight their challenges, and
- discussing the accomplishments upon completion of the task.

However, tasks are not always successfully accomplished nor are the successes or failures always attributed to the appropriate causes. The following theory addresses this issue.

Attribution Theory

To what do you attribute your success? This question relates directly to attribution theory (Weiner, 1972). The theory refers to the process by which an individual makes assumptions about the cause of certain events. In other words, it is about how people explain why things happen. In general, there are two types of explanations, or attributions. The first is external explanations, which claim that some outside factor caused the outcome; the second is internal explanations, which claim that the person was directly responsible. For example, students can explain their failure to complete an assignment by claiming that poor instructions from the teacher (external) or their own lack of effort (internal) was responsible. They can attribute their success on a test to the attention they paid to the teacher's instructions for studying (internal) or luck (external), or they can explain their poor test results as a result of the tricky test questions (external). Teachers can help students increase their academic performance when they offer comments that encourage internal attributions, which differ from persuasive and reinforcing comments (Miller, Brickman, and Bolen, 1975). Table 2.1 shows examples of the three different types of positive comments.

Table 2.1 Attribution Language

Attribution	Persuasion	Reinforcement
• You seem to know your arithmetic assignments very well. • You really work hard in math. • You're trying more, keep at it! • Larry, I don't know if you realize it, but you've been sitting here quietly working alone on your project. You must be a very hard-working person.	• You should be good at math. • You should be getting better grades in math. • You should be doing well in math.	• I'm proud of your work. • I'm pleased with your progress. • Excellent progress.

Attribution language attributes desired qualities to students, letting them know that the teacher discerns qualities in them that the students know are not always evident. The effect seems to be one of motivation for the student to consciously try to demonstrate those qualities. Persuasive language tends to reinforce the student's own negative self-talk, and reinforcement language is overly focused on the teacher.

There are two key steps to effectively using attribution language. First, it must be applied in a situation where people are thinking about why things are happening. Second, the explanation must be an internal attribution that focuses on the student. Teachers should use these types of comments regardless of the setting. However, because outdoor education can be so oriented toward activity and cooperation, it is an excellent medium for internal attribution comments. Positive internal attribution comments from teachers do not even need to be fully true to have positive effects on student performance. Focus on and encourage the students' strengths rather than encouraging them to focus on their weaknesses.

Taking the Brain Outdoors

There has been considerable excitement and discussion over the past several years about research on brain function and the learning process. Workshops and books on brain-based learning have been abundant. What is really meant by the terms *brain-based* or *brain-compatible* is that the teaching methods facilitate brain functioning and therefore facilitate learning.

This research into how the brain functions during information processing has contributed significantly to our understanding of learning principles. Some of these principles can be summarized as follows (Caine and Caine, 2001):

- The brain is constantly searching for meaning and connections.
- The brain learns from peripheral as well as focused attention, and it performs simultaneous functions.
- The brain performs best with complex and meaningful challenges in the absence of threat.
- Learning engages the entire physiology.

© DigitalVision

Teaching methods affect the learning process.

These basic understandings substantiate many previously held beliefs regarding good teaching practices. For example, we know the practice of getting students involved in activity rather than passively sitting and listening is much more likely to result in learning. Research has discovered that this is because activity engages more of a person's physiology. Emotions tend to be stirred when the body is moving along with cognitive processing, which engages more areas of the brain and yields a greater likelihood for understanding. Table 2.2 gives some examples of how these research findings can affect teaching. The methods common in outdoor education are naturally "brain friendly."

Neurological research has also given support to the theories that have been used as foundations for outdoor adventure and education methodologies. Maslow's hierarchy of needs is supported by the finding that the brain is constantly searching for meaning and relevance. If individuals do not feel they belong or have a sense of security, it is difficult for them to search for meanings apart from trying to fulfill that need. The optimal arousal theory and the theory of flow are both related to the need for appropriate challenge without the perception of threat. Bandura's theory of self-efficacy is supported by the finding that learning engages the entire physiology because experiences of success, the main contributor to increasing self-efficacy, are experienced by the whole body. Attribution theory is supported by the finding that the brain learns from focused and peripheral attention, and the language of teachers, peers, administrators, and parents can greatly influence self-perception.

Summary

Familiarity with the history of outdoor education, related social psychology theories, and the results of brain-function research will help you use the outdoor experiential education methodology more effectively. A heightened awareness of these foundational theories, followed by intentionally using them in lessons, will enhance the students' learning experience as well as your own teaching experience.

Table 2.2   Brain Functioning and Teaching Implications

Learning principles	Teaching implications
The brain is constantly searching for meaning and connections.	Present activities in a way that provides relevant context. During the activity, make comments that contribute to an awareness of connections beyond the activity itself, and ask questions that will encourage the students to consider connections that may not be readily apparent.
The brain learns from peripheral as well as focused attention, and it performs simultaneous functions.	What is peripheral during an activity? 1. You, the teacher. They're watching what you are doing. Are you engaged in their activity? Are you being supportive? Students can tell if the activity has a purpose beyond filling time. 2. The environment. Is it messy? Is it safe? Has it been set up with a purpose? Are visual aids used to reinforce objectives? 3. The other students. Is there an organizational structure? Do you attend to student issues?
The brain performs best with complex and meaningful challenges in the absence of threat.	Present activities at age-appropriate levels of challenge. There should be options for everyone to participate and be successful. The activities should be structured to be relevant and interesting. If activities are structured so that people of all abilities can participate at a meaningful level, the perception of threat will be diminished without doing away with challenge.
True learning engages the entire physiology.	If all of the previous teaching implications have been met, participation will engage the whole person: emotionally, physically, and intellectually.

Part II

Outdoor Adventure Activities for Schools

Challenge Initiatives—
No Ropes Course Needed

Challenge initiatives are activities that can enhance a student's ability to process information, interact more effectively with others, and practice problem solving. Plus, they're fun. People often think that such activities require a ropes course built out of poles or trees, cable, and rope. However, the challenge initiatives in this unit don't require much equipment. The term *challenge* in this context refers to a situation that inspires interest because the solution is not initially obvious. *Initiative* refers to a person's prerogative to confront the challenge or to encourage the group to act in an enterprising manner. The activities are adventures that create a sense of excitement and wonder at the unknown outcome. Incorporation of this educational format can promote student growth and development.

Project Adventure is to be credited with the introduction and spread of the ropes course phe-nomenon. In 1970, Jerome Pieh, the principal at Hamilton-Wenham Regional High School in Massachusetts, and Gary Baker, the curriculum coordinator of the Hamilton-Wenham Regional District, succeeded in acquiring funding from the U.S. Department of Education for developing innovative educational programs. Their proposal was to pilot a program that would apply some of Outward Bound's educational concepts to public education. The staff developed and implemented innovative experiential programs in physical education and academic subjects. After three years of implementation and evaluation, the program was validated by the U.S. Office of Education and was designated as a National Demonstration Site. With this status, other schools could then write proposals to adopt the Project Adventure model and receive funding for their own program. From that time forward the concepts of learning through adventure began to spread throughout the United States. The most familiar of these concepts is that human development, especially intra- and interpersonal development, can be enriched through group and individual experiential play and challenge. A less familiar concept is that academic achievement and learning can be enhanced by using gamelike challenges in the classroom and connecting them to the curriculum.

Most teachers associate Project Adventure with ropes courses since that was one of the highlights of the program. School ropes courses are associated most often with social skill development that is not directly linked with other subjects. Social skill development is definitely a major benefit of a ropes course, but what about academics? In addition, most teachers do not have ready access to a ropes course. Although Project Adventure is most closely associated with ropes courses, the concept of learning through adventure is not limited to activities on a ropes course. Many games and group adventures, or challenge initiatives, can be used in a classroom or on the school grounds with limited equipment. These are the types of activities that are discussed in this unit—no ropes course needed.

Unit Focus

The Challenge Initiatives Unit Plan is the first unit of the book because its challenge initiatives serve to introduce the character-quality terms and definitions. All of the character qualities listed and defined in chapter 3 will come up naturally in the course of this unit. Therefore, the objectives for this unit involve character and social development. It will provide the opportunity to introduce the character qualities and begin moving students toward an understanding and appreciation of those qualities. The activities provide excellent opportunities for exercising good character in a fun and playful environment. The activities are different from role-play scenarios because they get students involved in real experiences that naturally lead to character exploration. The atmosphere of fun reduces resistance and captures students' attention, but the teacher must remember that the activities are secondary to the learn-

ing objectives of positive character and social development.

These activities are not to be used as "time fillers." It would be negligent to have fun as the only objective when fun does not have to be sacrificed in order to accomplish objectives such as learning communication skills, respect for individual differences, problem-solving skills, and how to transfer learning to other areas of students' lives. The key to using activities in this way is planning and implementation; therefore, this unit is designed to provide guidance for planning and implementation.

Teacher's Role in Presenting Initiatives

There are several ways to introduce an adventure initiative. The method you select should be based upon your objective for the activity. The following four presentation styles illustrate how objectives can influence your choice.

• **Direct approach.** This approach simply states the problem, gives the rules or limiting factors, and raises awareness of safety issues.

• **Fantasy story.** This approach provides make-believe context for the activity. An example that might be used for the Team Skis initiative (see pages 43 to 44) is:

> You are all on an expedition on the island of Twowalkiewalkie. Your mission is to bring fishing equipment and medicine to the local people of the island who have been invaded by mutant robots from a sunken ship of toxic waste. Since you parachuted onto the island, you do not have transportation or a means of escape. The only chance you have to get off the island is to cross the alligator canal to the mainland. Since the alligators are anything-eaters, your group's only chance for crossing the canal is to walk on the backs of two dead alligators who died from eating long sections of rope, which can be seen protruding from their bodies. Naturally, if anyone falls

off or even a foot slips off, an alligator immediately devours that individual. The object is to deliver the equipment and medicine, then get your entire group safely to the mainland.

This story provides a fantasy context and has the rules woven into it. This type of presentation is fun for all ages. Just remember, the longer the story, the more difficult it is to keep everyone's attention.

• **Metaphor.** There are many ways to use metaphors to present initiative adventures. Two examples follow that again use the Team Skis activity:

  • One way to use a metaphor is to focus the group's attention on the main objective for the activity. Let's say that objective is effective group work that achieves a goal. Present the activity and its rules directly, and then say that the distance the students must travel represents the various steps in the group projects that have recently been assigned. Tell the students that project work is challenging in a group and you want them to use this activity as a trial run for working on their projects to see if they can identify things that could become stumbling blocks as well as things that will be necessary for success.

  • Another way to use a metaphor is to present the initiative directly, have the group do it, and then ask how this task could relate to the projects that have been assigned. What ingredients or behaviors of the group will they want to keep and what will they want to change?

• **Written directions.** Written directions can be used in different ways. For example, you can write different parts of the directions on several cards. This requires the group members to share their piece of the directions so they understand what they are to do. Or all directions could be on one sheet of paper that they have to all work from. Either method requires the group to begin working together from the very beginning of the activity by sharing instructions. You could even combine written instructions and an appropriate metaphor.

Teacher's Role During Initiatives

One of the things that makes initiative games adventurous is that there are usually many ways to solve the problem and the teacher does not give out any answers. The teacher's role during the activity includes the following:

• Monitor safety, remind the students about it, and be ready to stop the activity if there is a safety problem.

• Step in to assist with spotting (be in a position to catch a person or protect from injury) if needed.

• Listen to the dialogue and observe the group dynamics, noticing things that might be useful discussion topics because they relate to the current objective or elements of the embedded curriculum.

• Ask questions if the group is getting bogged down or make comments that can reinforce appropriate behavior.

• If the group is not making any progress toward their objective, stop the activity and instigate a discussion about what is happening.

Again, the teacher's role does not involve telling students how to complete the initiative. There are many ways to complete each initiative, and the main objective is the collateral learning, not how well a group can walk on pieces of wood or turn over a sheet of plastic.

Teacher's Role Following Initiatives

The teacher's role following an activity is to guide the group through the other steps of the experiential learning cycle (see figure 1.1, page 5). Reflection and discussion are crucial for developing understanding and should not be ignored. A lesson plan could be designed to have a group discussion following each separate activity, or the design might group a few activities together before having a reflective group discussion. As with presentation techniques, there are different techniques for aiding student reflection and awareness.

- **Class circle with teacher-directed discussion**. This is probably the most common method for reflective discussions. The teacher asks leading questions that encourage students to become aware of the activity's purpose and what they can take from the experience that could help them in other areas of their lives.
- **Small group discussions**. These allow for involvement from more students. Groups of three, four, or five students get together and designate one person as the group leader. Written questions are given to each small group for discussion. The small groups can then share their thoughts with other groups by getting together with two or three groups or with the whole class.
- **Small group skits**. These are similar to small group discussions, but the outcome is something the students act out in skit form.
- **Individual drawings or paragraphs**. Two or three starter questions or comments can be written on a board or handed out on paper for the students to consider. They then have the choice of making a drawing that illustrates something they thought about the activity or writing a paragraph about what they thought.

Whatever method is used, reflection is essential to the learning process. The teacher is responsible for designing the whole experience, not just the activity.

To use adventure initiatives, a basic understanding of different initiatives and their typical rules is important, so general guidelines are given for the initiatives in this unit. It is vital, however, to understand the value of adapting the structure and rules of these and other activities to best fit a specific situation.

Challenge Initiatives

The initiative activities in the unit plan have been selected because they require minimal equipment yet offer fun challenges for groups. The activity descriptions include materials, challenge instructions, and often variations for the activity. Most of the activities in this chapter are original with the author, but have been learned from many people over the past 30 years. People such as Karl Rohnke, Tom Smith, Jim Cain, and many other professionals have shared in the development of ideas. A few activities in this chapter have been in use for so many years that it has been impossible to verify their origin. However, when an activity has been presented in a previous publication with a different name and varied directions, every effort has been made to reference that source.

The activities presented in this chapter have been named and directions have been written to fit the unit objectives. The following unit plan shows a suggested sequence of initiatives. The specific directions for each initiative can be found in order of mention after the unit plan. The Cooperating Groups lesson plan involves a megainitiative, which is a combination of several previous initiatives. This allows students to remember the different activities and attempt to improve on their previous performance.

Unit Objectives

Students will:

- experience the importance of clear communication, cooperation, and creative problem solving;
- experience the value of positive character qualities;
- learn the definitions of positive character qualities; and
- learn how to choose positive actions that exhibit sound character.

Character Focus

Courage, patience, respect, responsibility, trustworthiness

Curriculum Areas

Civics, language arts, math, physical education

Activities

Activities such as the ones in this book are somewhat similar to games. In fact, they are sometimes referred to as initiative games. One difference between these and more traditional games is that there does not have to be a winner and a loser. Occasionally, it is good to have competition between groups when doing initiatives, but the teacher must be careful that it does not become a negative situation that will adversely affect students' motivation to develop cooperative skills.

Challenge Initiatives Day Planner

Day	Topic	Concepts and skills	Teaching activities	Standards
1*	Cooperation and trustworthiness	Requirements for cooperation (patience, respect, responsibility); define trust and trustworthiness	Introduce Rainbow Circle. Do Circle of Fun, Trust Circle, Circle Down and Up. Discuss cooperation, respect, responsibility, and trustworthiness. Do Yurt Circle.	Civics: 24 and 27 Language Arts: 8 Physical Education: 5 and 6
2	Working in a group to make decisions and solve problems	Appropriate and effective communication (speaking one at a time, listening, clarifying, getting everyone involved); identify possible results of a decision	Begin with Rainbow Ball, then do Flying Cape. Discuss communication process, the need for facilitator, options for group process, and do Flying Cape again. (To use this initiative on day 2, the size of the carpet should be larger than normally recommended. A smaller size increases difficulty.)	Civics: 24 and 27 Language Arts: 8 Physical Education: 5 and 6
3	Cooperation and responsibility	Requirements for responsibility (courageous communication for clarity and trustworthiness)	Do Sicky Fishy. Discuss cooperation and responsibility.	Civics: 24 and 27 Language Arts: 8 Physical Education: 5 and 6

(continued)

Challenge Initiatives Day Planner *(continued)*

Day	Topic	Concepts and skills	Teaching activities	Standards
4	Patience and self-control	Listening carefully and following directions (it takes coordination to be good followers)	Introduce the Team Skis. Alternate doing the activity and talking about how to improve.	Language Arts: 8 Physical Education: 1, 5, and 6
5	Respect and communication	Requirements for respect (patience, responsibility, caring)	Do Life Ring Golf and Sicky Fishy. Discuss respect and communication.	Civics: 24 and 27 Language Arts: 8 Physical Education: 5 and 6
6	Communication and decision making	Requirements for group decision making (communication, respect, courage, patience, trustworthiness)	Do Spell by Numbers and Life Ring Messaging. Discuss communication and decision making.	Civics: 24 and 27 Language Arts: 1 and 8 Physical Education: 5 and 6
7*	Group problem solving	Requirements for group problem solving (all character qualities and skills previously discussed in this unit)	Do Straw Strength, an adaptation of Stickles.	Civics: 24 and 27 Language Arts: 8 Math: 1 Physical Education: 5 and 6
8*	Megainitiative: cooperating groups	Review of all character qualities and skills previously discussed	Megainitiative: divide class into groups to do Spell by Numbers, Sicky Fishy, and Stickles.	Civics: 24 and 27 Language Arts: 1 and 8 Math: 1 and 4 Physical Education: 5 and 6

* Has a corresponding lesson plan.

FLYING CAPE

Materials

For this activity you need a cape made of a flexible material, such as a piece of plastic, canvas, tarp, tablecloth, or shower curtain. It is best if the two sides are different colors, but it is not imperative. The number of people in a group determines the size of the cape. For example, groups of at least 6 and no more than 10 could use a 4-by-6-foot (122-by-183-centimeter) cape. A group of 12 could also use a cape of this size, but it would be more difficult. A group of 12 could start with a 6-by-12-foot (183-by-366-centimeter) cape and move to a smaller size for greater challenge.

Challenge

With the cape laid out on the ground and all group members standing on it, the challenge is for the group to turn the cape over so that everyone in the group is standing on the opposite side (the side that started out touching the floor) and no one has stepped off the cape at any time during the process of turning it over (see figure 3.1).

Figure 3.1 In the Flying Cape activity, the objective is to turn the cape over without anyone stepping on the floor.

Variations

- Begin with only two or three group members on the cape and have them turn it over. Then add the rest of the group and have them turn the cape over.
- Space several tarps of varying sizes within 2 to 3 feet (61 to 91 centimeters) of each other. Everyone stands on a tarp. Once everyone is on

a tarp, give instructions to turn the tarp over without stepping onto the floor. Nothing is said about not stepping on other groups' capes in the introduction, so it is legal, but don't say anything about it unless they ask. If students do ask, have them repeat the instructions they were given and discuss the instructions among themselves. They will probably figure out that it is okay to cooperate with other groups.

Adapted from TEAMWORK & TEAMPLAY by Jim Cain & Barry Jolliff. Copyright © 1998 by Jim Cain and Barry Jolliff. Adapted by permission of Kendall/Hunt Publishing Company.

LIFE RING

Materials

For this activity you need a life ring. A typical life ring is made from a metal ring with a 1.5-inch (40-millimeter) diameter, which can be found in hardware stores. The ring has multiple strings or cords tied to it that are approximately 8 to 10 feet (2 to 3 meters) long (see figure 3.2).

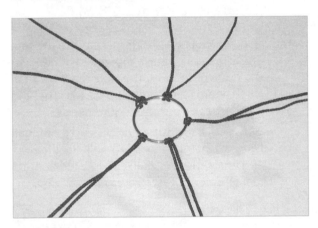

Figure 3.2 Life ring.

A life ring can be anything that is a circle, has a hole through the middle, and has multiple strings tied around the ring. The purpose of the life ring is to transport an object, usually some type of ball, from one location to another without anyone getting closer than 6 feet (183 centimeters) to the ring. The size of the life ring and its hole will determine what type of object can be transported. For example, you could use a rubber ring such as one used in a ring toss game. However, you would not be able to transport a tennis ball or golf ball because they would fall through the hole. You could, however, use a playground ball or volleyball. If transporting a marble, a washer can be used as the life ring.

Other necessary equipment is a goal (i.e., tin can, bucket, cup) to receive the transferred ball.

Challenge

A group of four to eight students must transport the ball on the life ring without getting any closer than 6 feet (183 centimeters) to the ring. A transport is successful when the ball is dropped from the ring into the goal. The difficulty can be increased by placing obstacles along the route and by using a small container for the goal.

Variations

- Sicky Fishy. Float a tennis ball or racquetball in a bucket of water. The group has to allow the life ring to sink below the ball and then they have to lift the ball out of the water and transport it to a different bucket of water. Place a variety of obstacles along the route to the goal.

- Life Ring Golf. Divide students into groups of at least four but no more than eight. You will need one life ring for each group and a variety of balls, PVC pipes, can, cups, buckets, and obstacles. Set up a course similar to a golf course with a designated starting point and ending point for each "hole." The challenge is to go through each hole on the course with as few "strokes" (ball drops) as possible. Following are some examples of holes, but you can create your own course based on your space and students.

  - Hole 1—Begin with a golf ball on the life ring. The hole is a large plastic bucket on the ground, about 40 feet (12 meters) away through narrowly spaced trees or cones.
  - Hole 2—Begin with a tennis ball on the top of a vertical PVC pipe 1 inch (2.5 centimeters) in diameter and 1 foot (30 centimeters) long, pushed into the ground. The life ring starts around the pipe and on the ground. Groups

(continued)

lift the ball off the pipe and then take it to the hole, which is a large plastic cup tacked to a pole or post about 3 feet (91 centimeters) off the ground.

- Hole 3—Begin with a table-tennis ball placed on the life ring. The hole is a 2-inch (51-millimeter) horizontal PVC pipe 5 inches (30 centimeters) long, lying on the ground next to a tree or post. The ball must be placed inside the horizontal pipe without touching the ground.

- Hole 4—Begin with the life ring lying on the ground. Four vertical PVC pipes 1 inch (2.5 centimeters) in diameter and 1 foot (30 centimeters) long are located about 3 feet (91 centimeters) apart. On top of one pipe is an orange golf ball. On top of the second pipe is a white golf ball. The third and fourth pipes are empty. Students exchange the position of one of the golf balls to an empty PVC pipe. On this hole, allow students to pick up the PVC pipe where the ball starts to help get the ball onto the life ring. They can also pick up the empty PVC target pipe; they just cannot touch the ball itself. Another group may attempt the same thing with the other golf ball if two groups end up at the hole at the same time. This hole will probably produce a few strokes on the scorecard.

- Hole 5—At this station, a billiard ball or steel ball bearing is placed on the life ring. The hole is a large tin can next to a wall. Don't attempt this on a wooden floor.

- Hole 6—Begin with the life ring around a vertical PVC pipe that is 1 inch (2.5 centimeters) in diameter and 5 feet (152 centimeters) long. Push the pipe into the ground and place a baseball on the top of the pipe. Place bases (plastic cones) in a diamond formation about four feet (120 centimeters) apart. Have the group remove the baseball using the life ring; walk to first, second, and third base, and finally come back to home to replace the baseball back on the pipe.

- Hole 7—Begin with the life ring around a vertical PVC pipe 1 inch (3 centimeters) in diameter and 1 foot (30 centimeters) long, pushed into the ground. Use an ice cube as the ball. The hole is a tilted ice bucket 100 feet (30 meters) away. Better hurry on this one!

- Hole 8—This hole begins with the life ring placed over a tire that is lying flat on the ground. A tennis ball is placed on the life ring, which is on the ground inside the tire. The attached twine is allowed to drape over the edge of the tire. The hole is a 5-foot-tall (152-centimeter) water pipe standing behind some trees or outdoor equipment.

- Hole 9—The group must pick up a golf ball lying on the ground using only the life ring. The final hole is a small cup located about 5 feet (152 centimeters) away.

LIFE RING MESSAGING

Materials

- Life ring
- Large-tipped marker
- Masking or duct tape
- Rubber bands
- Popsicle sticks (optional)
- Large piece of paper secured to the floor or a table. It is a good idea to protect the supporting surface from markers. For example, several pages of newspaper could be placed under the marking paper to protect the table or floor.

Challenge

The group must attach the marker to the life ring and be able to write legibly while all group members stay at least 6 feet (183 centimeters) from the life ring using only the twine of the ring to move the marker. As in the Life Ring activity, group members must remain several feet back from the ring itself. The group works together by cooperatively manipulating the marker via the strings that are attached to the life ring.

Materials

Rainbow Circles (also called Raccoon Circles in *The Book On Raccoon Circles* by Tom Smith) are made from 1-inch (25-millimeter) tubular nylon webbing cut about 15 feet (5 meters) long. This webbing can be purchased from any rock-climbing supply store or catalog, or you could use rope. If using rope, make sure it has a large enough diameter to support the weight and not injure students' hands. A 1.5-inch (12-millimeter) diameter should be adequate.

To make a circle out of the webbing, tie it with a water knot, leaving 3- to 4-inch (8- to 10-centimeter) tails on each side of the knot. A water knot is made by tying a loose overhand knot in one end of the webbing. Trace the first knot with the untied end of webbing. Start tracing at the tail of the first overhand knot and continue going backward through the knot until that end of the webbing extends at least 3 inches (8 centimeters) past the knot (see figure 3.3). The ends of the webbing should extend from the knot in opposite directions.

Challenge

With the class divided into groups of 8 to 10, group members hold the rainbow circle with both hands shoulder-width apart and slowly move backward until the webbing is in a tight circle.

Sequenced Variations

1. Circle of Fun. While all group members hold the webbing with both hands, the challenge is to keep the webbing in the shape of a circle and pass the knot around the circle as fast as possible until it gets back to its starting spot. This can be repeated a few times to allow each group the opportunity to improve its time.

2. Trust Circle. Everyone slowly moves backward until the webbing is in a tight circle. To create a trust circle, all group members slowly lean backward, keeping the elbows slightly bent, and let the tension of the circle support everyone's weight. It is called a trust circle because group members have to trust all the other members to lean back. If not everyone cooperates, people who are leaning will not be supported and may fall. A discussion about trust and trustworthiness is important before doing this activity.

3. Circle Down and Up. After the group can hold their balance in the trust circle, they can try to bend their knees and lower themselves to the floor while leaning back, allowing the circle to support them. Then on a signal they move back to a standing position with the circle as their support. From there, they sit down and stand up again with no verbal signals. If all goes well, they can close their eyes and repeat the activity without talking.

4. Yurt Circle. This is similar to the trust circle but with alternating leans. Have group members count off by twos. With everyone holding at the wrists or the webbing with both hands almost shoulder-width apart, have all of the 1s slowly lean back while all 2s slowly lean forward. Once the circle is balanced and stable, have

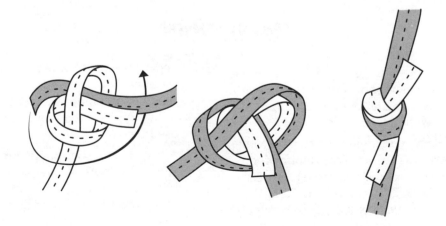

Figure 3.3 How to make a water knot.

Reprinted, by permission, from J. Stiel and T.B. Ramsey, 2004, *Climbing walls* (Champaign, IL: Human Kinetics).

(continued)

Figure 3.4   Yurt circle.

the 1s and 2s slowly switch their positions. The group can practice with the goal of being able to smoothly and rhythmically switch positions back and forth. The name *yurt* comes from a round, tent-type structure used by Mongolian nomads. It has sides that use poles leaning in opposition like a lattice for support (see figure 3.4).

5. Rainbow Ball. With all group members holding the webbing with both hands, the group must pick up a ball (a playground ball or volleyball is easier than a tennis ball) with only webbing touching the ball (no hands) and transport the ball to a designated goal. For this activity, the webbing is pulled tight in parallel lines to support the ball, but remember, teachers never tell the solutions.

SPELL BY NUMBERS

Materials

- Paper plates or vinyl spots numbered on one side from 1 to 26 and lettered on the opposite side A to Z (see figure 3.5).

- Additional spots continuing up from 26 with letters repeated as needed. For example, if you need three more Ns and one more E, you can have spots 27-N, 28-N, 29-N, and 30-E. The actual letters you will need depends on what you want to spell. You can change the letters

and numbers to be able to spell out a particular message. All numbered squares do not have to be used, and there should always be several in the playing area that are not going to be used.

- A long rope to designate a boundary within which the spots will be placed and a shorter rope to indicate the line behind which the group must stay (should be far enough away from the spots that the numbers or letters cannot be read).

Figure 3.5 Squares or spots that could be used for Spell by Numbers. The number is printed on one side and the letter on the opposite side.

Challenge

Each small group receives an ordered list of letters and numbers and sends one member at a time to pick up the items in the order of the list. You can time them to see how fast they can complete the task and then allow them two or three more tries to improve their time. The challenge could also be to spell out words or decipher a code. Only one person can be in the game area at a time and may only pick up one spot per trip to take back behind the starting line.

Sequenced Variations

1. The group can stand around the game area for 10 to 15 seconds and look at the numbers or letters and where they are placed. Then everyone must go behind the starting line and remain there the rest of the time except for the person who is picking up a letter or number.

2. Spots can be arranged in game area so that only numbers are showing. The group is given a specific order of numbers. They bring the spots out and turn them over. The correct order of numbers spells a word or words.

3. With spots in game area showing numbers, the group is given math problems and they must go pick up the numbers that are the answers to the problems.

4. With spots showing letters, the group is given questions and they must pick up the letters to spell the answers to the questions.

Materials

- 10 to 15 one-inch (2.5-centimeter) styrofoam blocks
- 20 plastic soda straws
- 5 to 8 Popsicle sticks (optional)

Challenge

The objective is to build a structure with specified dimensions, such as a three-point base that is half as wide as the height of the structure. At the tallest point, the structure must be able to support a ball. The type of ball (weight and size) will determine how strong the structure must be (see figure 3.6).

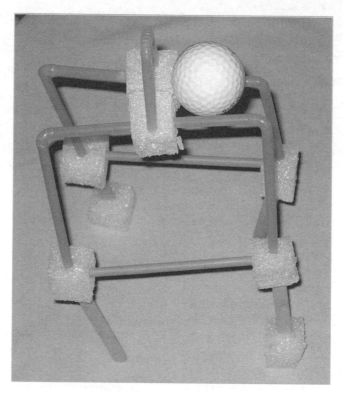

Figure 3.6 Straw strength structure.

STICKLES

Materials

- Approximately 18 feet (5 meters) of 5/16-inch (7-millimeter) dowel rods cut into various lengths for each group. There should be 15 to 20 pieces, cut into lengths ranging from 6 to 20 inches (51 centimeters in length).
- Ten golf-ball-sized perforated plastic practice balls 1.5 inches (4 centimeters) in diameter with a 5-inch (13 centimeter) circumference.

- Four baseball-sized perforated plastic practice balls 3 inches (8 centimeters) in diameter with a 9-inch (23 centimeter) circumference.

Challenge

The goal is to build a structure (see figure 3.7 *a*) that complies with specifications given in the instructions. Specifications could include the following:

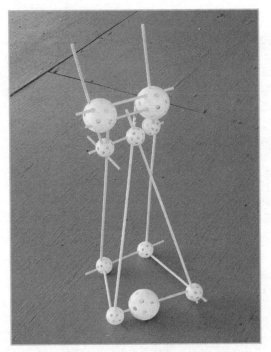

a

b

Figure 3.7 Stickles challenges: tower *(a)* and slide *(b)*.

- Certain measurements for the structure's width and height, within 2 inches (5 centimeters)

- A structure whose height must be three times the diameter of the base, within 2 inches (5 centimeters)

- Certain measurements as in the previous suggestions, but with one moving part

- A structure that can support a PVC trough on which a marble can roll (see figure 3.7 *b*)

- A structure that can span a 4-foot (122-centimeter) distance off the floor

TEAM SKIS

Materials

Team skiing can be constructed out of various materials depending upon budget and availability. Skis can be constructed out of 4-by-4-foot (122-by-122-centimeter) wood ranging from 8 to 12 feet (2 to 4 meters) in length. The longer they are, the more difficult they are to store. Holes can be drilled through the wood about 18 inches (46 centimeters) apart so rope can be run through the holes for use as handles. Ropes should be cut about 4 inches (10 centimeters) in length and a knot should be tied close to one end of the rope. Larger holes should be drilled on the bottom of the 4-by-4 to allow the knots to be countersunk after the rope is pulled through the holes.

There should be a separate 4-foot (122-centimeter) rope for each hole (see figure 3.8).

Another option for creating rope handles is to screw large eye screws into the wood for holding the rope rather than drilling holes. However, the screws can pull out if users are large and the screws are too small. Make sure the screws do not go all the way through the wood and extend out the other side.

It is also possible to make skis that have loops of rope for feet to slide under rather than using the rope as handles.

(continued)

Figure 3.8   Negotiating on team skis.

Wooden 2-by-4s can be used in place of 4-by-4s, but they will eventually break if used on uneven ground. A more elaborate design is to use 2-by-4s cut into 18-inch (46-centimeter) sections and joined together with another section by eye screws in the ends of the wood. Lengths of 4-inch-wide (10-centimeter-wide) carpet can also be used with cord tied to the carpet for handles.

From K. Rohnke, 1984, *Silver Bullets* (Hamilton, MA: Project Adventure) pp. 118-120.

Challenge

The challenge is to traverse a specified distance without having a member of the group step off the skis. The distance can be as simple as a 10-foot (3-meter) straightaway, or it could include a course with turns and obstacles.

COOPERATION AND TRUSTWORTHINESS

Lesson Objectives

Students will:

- experience the concepts of cooperation, trust, and trustworthiness;
- practice those qualities during activities; and
- be able to define patience, respect, responsibility, and trustworthiness.

Character Focus

Patience, respect, responsibility, trustworthiness

Curriculum Standards

Civics 24 and 27; Language Arts 8; Physical Education 5 and 6.

Materials

- Rainbow circles, one for each group (see page 39)
- One lighter per group
- Bucket of water
- Posters with character words and definitions (see appendix C)

Preparation

1. Teach a few students to tie a water knot before the class period and let them practice.
2. Teach a few other students how to melt the ends of nylon to prevent unraveling and let them practice.
3. Position water bucket in the area where students will make the rainbow circles.
4. Place posters around the area. Each poster should contain one of the character words and its definition. Make the lettering large enough to be read from 20 or 30 feet (6 or 9 meters) away.

Lesson Sequence

1. Introduce the idea of the rainbow circle.
2. Read the rainbow story (see the rainbow story sidebar on page 47). At the end of the story, mention that the act of completing the rainbow can be illustrated by making and using rainbow circles.
3. Divide class into small groups of 8 to 10 students. Each group should have one or two students who have been taught how to tie the water knot and one who has practiced using the lighter to sear the ends.
4. Demonstrate how to tie the knot to make the rainbow circle.

Activity 1

1. Give each group of students a length of webbing and have them make their rainbow circle. ⌂
2. Check each group's knot and webbing ends.

Questions

- What made it difficult for some of you to be patient while the knot was being tied and the ends burned?
- What were the assigned responsibilities?
- Who in your group showed respect for the people doing their assignments and how did they show respect?

Possible Character Affirmation ☺

You were trustworthy in completing your task of burning the ends of the webbing in a safe manner. I knew I could depend on you.

Activity 2

1. Remind the class of the pledge of respect (see page 12). Ask, "Toni, will you read the definition of respect for me please?" Then ask, "Will someone now tell us an example of respect?"

2. Have groups do Circle of Fun. Each group has a designated timer. They repeat twice more, trying to improve their time. Sound effects of race cars can be added. If each member of a circle pulls equally on the webbing as the knot is being passed around, their time will improve. Unequal tension slows them down. This teaches cooperation. ⌐ ☺

Activity 3

1. Explain the Trust Circle activity on page 39 and have one group demonstrate. ⌂

2. All groups do the activity, with balance and stillness as the goals.

3. If all goes well, progress to Circle Down and Up and from there to Yurt Circle if students are cooperating and being trustworthy.

Comments ⤶ ☺

- This group is being trustworthy and successful. I am proud of you. Because you were being trustworthy no one lost their balance.
- This group is struggling. Stop for a minute and think about what you can do differently that might help. (Wait for thinking, then ask for ideas.)
- I like the way this group is being patient and talking one at a time, showing respect and patience.

Discussion and Review

- What was the most fun part of these activities?
- What was the hardest thing for you to do?
- Describe something that someone in your group did that illustrated one of the words that is on a poster.
- How were the character words we learned today used or not used in the activities we did?
- Let's review all of the character words that are written on the posters in our area and read the definitions. Starting with this one, who will read the word and its definition for us?

Teaching Tips

- Have everything set up and ready to go when class begins.
- Do not let the groups spread out far apart from each other.

Safety Tips

- Have each group try the Trust Circle slowly, one group at a time. When they all have the idea, the groups can practice simultaneously and several times so they become accustomed to how it feels, gradually finding their balance.
- Make sure the students begin by leaning back from a position with both feet directly under them and with their elbows slightly bent.

References

The Book On Raccoon Circles by Tom Smith, Learning Unlimited.

STORY OF THE RAINBOW

One day long ago, the grandfather of a Native American tribe was talking to the children about how things in nature are connected in relationships to each other. When something disrupts the natural flow of energy within the environment, other entities are affected because of their connections. An example he used was the circle. He said, "Look at things in nature. Pick up a stone, a leaf, a stick, or a flower and look at it carefully. All things in nature are related to a circle, which represents completeness. Each circle may not be perfectly round, but if you trace around the edge you return to your starting point, making a complete circle."

The children went and gathered natural objects and discovered this to be true. Then one child said, "But Grandfather, what about the rainbow? It's in nature and it's not a complete circle." Grandfather replied, "Oh, that is a very good question. It is our responsibility, the people of the Earth, to complete the circle of the rainbow on Earth. Just as things in nature are connected through their interrelationships, we are also part of nature, and to function in harmony with the natural flow of energy, we must honor our connections and interdependency with each other. If we do that, the rainbow will be complete."

GROUP PROBLEM SOLVING

Lesson Objectives

Students will:

- develop an understanding of the concepts and skills for successfully working as a team toward a common goal, and
- demonstrate skills for effective group problem solving.

Character Focus

Patience, respect, responsibility, trustworthiness, cooperation

Curriculum Standards

Civics 24; Language Arts 8; Math 1, 3, and 4; Physical Education 5

Materials

- 15 1-inch (3-centimeter) squares of Styrofoam per group
- 20 soda straws per group
- 5 Popsicle sticks per group
- Character word posters
- A ball

Preparation

Lay out materials in separate stacks, one stack of materials per group. The number of Styrofoam squares, straws, and Popsicle sticks depends upon the size requirements of the intended structure. Prepare posters and make them visible to students.

Lesson Sequence

1. Introduce the idea of building a structure to certain specifications and sharing ideas and skills with a partner to get it built.
2. Ask, "What skills have we discussed and practiced that will be good to use in completing this assignment?"

Activity 1

1. Divide the class into pairs. Each pair gets a stack of materials. ◠
2. Instructions for the activity are to spend 10 to 15 minutes designing and building a structure using the Styrofoam squares, straws, and Popsicle sticks that is
   - 2 feet (61 centimeters) tall,
   - twice as tall as its base is wide, and
   - able to support a tennis ball at its highest point.

Questions

- How did you and your partner begin your assignment?
- How did you decide what design to build?
- What was the hardest part of this assignment?
- How could that part have been made easier?

- If you got a new partner and had to build a different type of structure, what would you do differently to make the process better than the last time? (Have students identify some specific actions and write them on a dry-erase board or chalkboard.)

Possible Character Affirmation

- Thank you for being a patient person. You waited for your teammate to express his whole idea before you started your response.
- The both of you cooperated very well together. You each were willing to try each other's ideas and kept thinking of how you could blend your ideas together. That is good cooperation.

Activity 2

1. Have each pair take its structure apart. Then combine pairs to get groups of four.
2. Each group of four gets the materials used previously by both pairs.
3. Groups use the materials to design and build a chair that can support a softball.

Questions

- What did your group do differently this time compared to last time?
- Name something your group did that illustrated respect.
- Was the structure easier or harder to build this time?
- What do you think made it easier or harder this time?
- What does respect have to do with this type of process?
- What size group do you think would be ideal for this type of project?

Possible Character Affirmations

- This group is working well together and doing a good job of talking one at a time and listening to what is being said.
- Grace, you showed your trustworthiness by carefully placing the ball on the chair.
- It is good to do what you say you will do.

Discussion and Review

- What was the most fun part of these activities?
- What was the most difficult thing for you to do?
- Describe something that someone in your group did that illustrated one of the words that is on a poster.

Teaching Tips

- The Stickles activity (page 42) has helpful information for organizing and leading this activity.
- Ask questions and make comments to pairs or groups that seem to be experiencing the same problems.
- Avoid the temptation to give solutions.
- A variation of this sequence is to let each student construct a structure and then put students in pairs and tell them they cannot use all of one person's design. Their design must be new or a synthesis of their individual designs.

Safety Tips

Let students know that the straws and Popsicle sticks are not clean and they should not put them in their mouths.

Lesson Objective

Students will:

- practice skills for successfully working as a team toward a common goal,
- demonstrate skills for effective group problem solving, and
- demonstrate the ability to extend group skills beyond their individual group.

Character Focus

Patience, respect, responsibility, trustworthiness, cooperation

Curriculum Standards

Civics 24; Language Arts 8; Math 1, 3, and 4; Physical Education 5 and 6

Materials

- Spell by Numbers materials (see page 40 for setup and instructions)
- Life ring and marble (see page 37 for setup and instructions)
- Stickles set and plastic cup (see page 42 for setup and instructions)
- Instruction cards for the megainitiative (see page 52)

Preparation

1. Set up Spell by Numbers with numbers showing.
2. Position the life ring at least 10 yards (9 meters) away from Spell by Numbers setup, with the marble on the ring.
3. Have stickles at least 20 to 25 yards (18 to 23 meters) from the life ring and inside a circle with a 10-foot (3-meter) diameter.

Lesson Sequence

Inform the class that today is the day to see how well they have learned to work together. Divide class into three, four, or six groups depending upon class size, and assign one student in each group to be the facilitator for that group. Get all of the facilitators together and give them the instruction cards found in the megainitiative instructions. △ ◠

Activity: Megainitiative

1. This megainitiative combines three initiatives students have done previously into one challenge for the whole class. Assign one group to do Spell by Numbers. The numbers they are to retrieve are in the correct order to spell out instructions for where the Life Ring group is to deposit its marble. One word in the instructions will have to be unscrambled. ◠ ◡

2. Assign one group to the Life Ring activity. The route that the carriers of the life ring must travel is as follows: All carriers must climb onto a bench and down to the other side, go under the rope that is stretched between two trees, and go outside of the poles or trees marked with flagging tape. The life ring and marble must go between the poles or trees. After successfully navigating this route, the life ring and marble should be maneuvered into the area with the stickles.

3. Assign one group to Stickles. When the group is in the Stickles area, the Spell by Numbers group tells them what to do with the marble. (The stickles are to be built into a structure that has a base that is three times wider than it is tall, and its highest point is an open tube that ends in a cup on the ground. The marble must go through the tube and into the cup.)

4. Make activity modifications if more than three groups are needed. For four groups, have two life ring groups. Each group must transport their marble to the stickles structure. For six groups, have two groups do each of the activities simultaneously.

Discussion and Review

- What is the hardest thing for you to do in group work situations?
- I would like for you to think about the person on each side of you and come up with a character quality that you think they have exhibited in this initiative.

Teaching Tips

- Ask questions and make comments to pairs or groups who seem to be experiencing the same problems repeatedly.
- Avoid the temptation to give solutions.

Safety Tips

- Use secure obstacles for the Life Ring group. For example, if using chairs, make sure they are sturdy and that you are watching when people are stepping up and down.
- Don't use folding chairs. Stacked tumbling mats, balance beams, park benches, and side horses are good obstacles to go under or over.

Possible Character Affirmations ⮌ ☺

- Jennifer, you were very patient in waiting to explain your idea.
- I'm proud of the both of you for being respectful with each other when you disagreed on how to build the marble chute. That was a good way to come to a peaceful resolution.
- Josh and Jessie, you communicated well with the other group by letting them know what might work best for your part of the initiative.

Megainitiative Instructions: Spell by Numbers

- Bring numbers out one at a time and in the following order:

_____ .

- Keep the numbers in this order to read the message.
- Use the message that is spelled out to tell the Life Ring group where they must take their marble.

Megainitiative Instructions: Life Ring

- The Spell by Numbers group will discover the destination for your marble.
- While they are breaking the code, you must follow the usual directions for Life Ring and your group must complete some obstacles in the path along your route.
- Route: Each carrier must step up onto a bench and then back down, go under the rope or string, and go outside of the trees (or poles) while the life ring goes between the trees or poles. Each obstacle must be accomplished while carriers are maintaining contact with the life ring support string.

After the last obstacle is completed, you will get the marble's destination from the other group.

Megainitiative Instructions: Stickles

- Build a structure that has a base that is three times wider than it is tall, within 2 inches (5 centimeters).
- The tallest point of the structure must be the top of a tube that has its other end pointing down into the cup.
- A marble must be able to roll from the top of this tube down into the cup.

You may not tell the Life Ring group where they must deposit the marble.

Frontcountry Camping

The natural environment is an important part of our lives. Many pictures on the walls of offices and public places are of beautiful nature scenes. But even though most of us enjoy looking at pictures of nature, not everyone likes spending whole days and nights in the outdoors. They say, "I'm just not the outdoorsy type." But how can they know without having the experience?

It's likely that most of those nonoutdoorsy folks have never learned to make themselves comfortable in the outdoors. A unit on camping that includes some of the important concepts and skills for being comfortable in the outdoors provides an introduction to a leisure activity that is well suited for families and groups as well as individuals.

There are two types of camping, frontcountry and backcountry. Frontcountry camping involves camping in a planned campground relatively close to a vehicle, certain amenities (i.e., showers, toilets, stores), and emergency aid. These sites include national, state, and local parks and other such accessible areas. Backcountry camping is much less accessible or is inaccessible by motorized vehicle and no such amenities or emergency aid are readily available. Because of the time it would take to get help if a problem arose, the need for good camping skills becomes much more critical in backcountry camping.

Frontcountry camping is where we will begin, with the realization that many of the skills overlap with backcountry skills. First we will identify the general locations of frontcountry camping. Then we present some basic concepts and skills for making yourself comfortable while camping. In the frontcountry, these concepts and skills fall into three areas:

- Shelter (proper clothing, tents and tarps, and sleeping systems)
- Food and water (preparation and storage)
- Campfires (situationally appropriate)

Locations

Frontcountry camping is often referred to as car camping because you are in close proximity to a vehicle. For many people, this can include travel-trailer camping as well as tent camping. For our purposes, however, frontcountry camping will refer to tent camping in a campground with designated campsites. Campgrounds can be quite varied in the services that they provide. Private campgrounds such as KOA (Kampgrounds of America) typically have electricity, bath houses with hot showers and flush toilets, and other types of services like washers and dryers. Many national and state parks also have these types of amenities, but they vary. National Forest Service campgrounds are usually very basic. There are typically picnic tables at each tent site, a specified location for a tent, a designated fire ring, latrines located around the campground, and a water hydrant. However, many of the remote campgrounds have no running water.

Each state typically has various guidebooks to its campgrounds, and the National Park Service also has many references in print and on the Internet for national park campgrounds. For a guide to U.S. national forest campgrounds and U.S. Army Corps of Engineers recreation facilities, go to http://gorp.away.com/gorp/activity/camping/cam_place.htm.

Shelter

Shelter comes in many forms. It is not just a house or a tent, but includes everything you use to help your body maintain a normal temperature.

Clothes

Clothes are your first line of shelter. They play a significant role in allowing your body to maintain an appropriate core temperature. To understand the importance of the proper clothes, you must have some knowledge about the mechanisms for heat transfer and their relationship to clothing. When it's hot, your body must be able to rid itself of excess heat. Without that ability, your core temperature will begin to rise and heat exhaustion or heat stroke can occur. When it's cold, you must be able to conserve your body heat to prevent hypothermia, a life-threatening drop in the body's core temperature, and to protect exposed skin to prevent frostbite.

The specifics of how heat is exchanged between the body and the environment are covered in the Backcountry Camping Unit Plan. In this unit, the basics of clothes layering are discussed. Everyone has probably worn a sweater or jacket at the beginning of some activity and then decided to take it off after doing the activity for awhile. You started the activity comfortably dressed, and then to remain comfortable (not too warm or too cold) you took the outer layer off. You "warmed up." In fact, that's why sweat suits are also called warm-ups.

Layering enables people to gradually adjust the amount of insulation they are wearing rather than only having one thick layer. There are three primary principles for dressing in layers.

• **Layering principle 1.** Fabric makes a difference. If you are dressing to stay cool, the fabric should be thin and not block the wind. If you are dressing to stay warm, the fabric should allow your perspiration to pass through and prevent the wind from blowing away the warm air next to your body. In general, cotton is best for warm to hot conditions while synthetics, wool, or silk are best for cool to cold conditions. The reason for this is discussed in the Backcountry Camping Unit introductory information.

• **Layering principle 2.** Insulation is trapped air that your body warms up. Multiple layers are able to trap air, as long as there is an outer layer that blocks out the wind. Without a "windbreaker," the air your body has warmed will be replaced by fresh cold air.

• **Layering principle 3.** Layering enables you to gradually adjust the amount of insulation you wear. If you are in a cool environment and begin to hike, your body will produce heat as a result of the exercise. The more heat you produce, the warmer you will feel and the fewer layers you will need. You warm up slowly, so it is best to adjust the layers gradually. The opposite is also true. When you stop and sit down to eat lunch while hiking, your body will stop producing heat and you will begin to feel cooler. This is the time to begin adding layers. If you cool off too fast or get too cold, your muscles get tight and beginning to hike again will be more difficult and could even lead to an injury.

In addition to layering, the type of shoe that is appropriate for camping depends upon the types of activities you will be doing and the weather conditions. Athletic shoes are generally fine unless it is really wet, in which case a shoe or boot that can keep your feet dry longer would work better. It is always a good idea to take two pairs of shoes so you have a dry pair in case one gets wet. If hiking is on the agenda, leather-soled shoes are not a good choice because they lack traction.

Sleep Systems

The weather usually gets colder at night so more shelter is often required. The term *sleep system* is used rather than *sleeping bag* because a conduction barrier, or pad, is used along with a sleeping bag. A sleep system includes a pad, sleeping bag, and a means to stay dry inside the sleeping bag in case of rain.

A pad serves two purposes. The main purpose is to block the conductive heat exchange between the body and ground, and the second purpose is to provide cushioning. There are two types of pads. One is a closed-cell foam pad that cannot absorb water, and the other is a combination foam and air pad enclosed in a water- and airproof cover (see figure 4.1). Either way, a pad must be impermeable to water to insulate the bag from the ground. A sleeping pad is an integral part of a sleep system.

Sleeping bags come in several styles. In general, bags filled with goose down are warmer than synthetic-filled bags. Each bag has an advantage and disadvantage (see table 4.1).

- Down-filled bags tend to be warmer for the weight, depending on how much down is used. However, down will compress when wet, much like cotton, and can lose its insulating ability.

- Synthetic-filled bags can provide insulation even if they get wet. However, usually they are not as warm as down-filled bags.

Each of these bags can come in the shape of a body (mummy bags) or in a rectangular shape with more room inside the bag. The larger the bag is compared to your body size, the more air you have to warm up. Thus mummy-shaped bags tend to be warmer than rectangular bags (see figure 4.2).

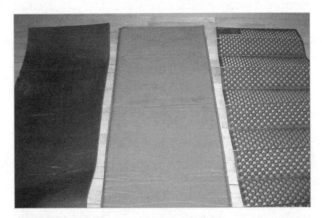

Figure 4.1 Sleeping pads.

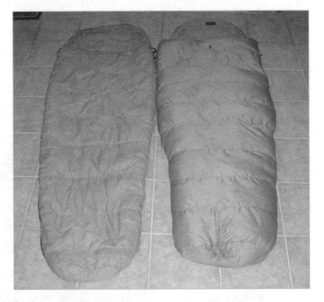

Figure 4.2 Sleeping bags

Table 4.1 Sleeping Bags

	Advantage	Disadvantage
Down	Warmer than synthetic fill.	Has no insulating ability when wet.
Synthetic	Retains some ability to insulate when wet.	When insulating ability is equal, a synthetic bag will weigh more and be larger when compressed.

Tents

Next in the line of shelter is a tent or tarp (see figure 4.3). The purpose of a tent is to protect you from the rain, wind, and bugs. A tarp will protect you from rain and wind but not from bugs. Tents come in many styles, shapes, and sizes. For frontcountry camping, a large tent is generally preferred for ease of entry and exit and to accommodate more than two or three people. However, the size should be selected to accommodate your needs. There are three things to look for in a tent:

- It should be easy to set up with the help you'll have.

- It should have a waterproof rainfly that protects the top of the tent and extends well down the walls. The walls of the tent itself should not be waterproof; they should be breathable to allow moisture from respiration and evaporation to escape.

- A ground cloth should be used under the bottom of the tent to protect the floor from abrasions and punctures. Don't allow the ground cloth to extend out past the sides of the tent because rain will collect on it, run in between the tent floor and ground cloth, and leak inside the tent if the seams are not sealed well.

Food and Water

In frontcountry camping, water is usually provided via plumbing or pump, so treating your water is not necessary to make it safe to drink. Food, on the other hand, must be furnished by the campers. Frontcountry cooking is typically done on a portable two-burner stove or with charcoal. In frontcountry campsites, fire rings or charcoal grills are often found. Your menu and the amount of time you have will help determine the cooking method.

Food Storage

Whether camping in frontcountry or backcountry, your food must be stored in a manner that will not attract animals or be accessible to them. For example, leaving food in a cooler outside with a rock on it may keep chipmunks out, but not a bear. The safest place for food storage during frontcountry camping is in your vehicle, even if you're not in bear country. Raccoons can be big and will overcome much to get at your

Figure 4.3   Tent with ground cloth and rainfly.

food. When in bear country, the campground or agency responsible for camping area may have specific requirements for food storage, such as special containers. Always check regulations for the area in which you will be camping.

Washing Dishes

Washing dishes while at a campground that provides garbage cans is fairly easy. Heat some water on your stove or fire and use three plastic wash pans. One pan is for washing, one is for rinsing, and one is for sterilizing (see figure 4.4). If you use soap, make sure it is biodegradable. Scrape dishes and pots and throw the scraps into the animal-proof garbage can. Wash dishes in one dishpan with a small amount of hot water (less than half full), starting with the cleanest dishes and working toward the hardest to clean. This will help you use less water. After washing, rinse the dishes in the second dishpan with warm water. Then move the dishes to the third wash pan for sterilizing. This can be done by pouring hot water over the dishes or by using a bleach and water mixture in the third pan (approximately 1 tablespoon of bleach to 1 gallon (4 liters) of water). The final step is to dry the dishes and store them in a bin to keep everything together and organized.

If the campground does not have animal-proof trashcans, the preferred place to keep your scrapings and any leftover food is in a container in your vehicle. Do not try to wash scraps down a sink, scrape them onto the ground, flush them down a toilet, or drop them into a latrine. None of those actions is considerate of other campers or the animals.

Safety

Safety is an important topic for all activities, both indoors and outdoors. Although safety considerations are essential for each activity presented in this book, the frontcountry camping unit is a good place to introduce a basic safety concept: the accident equation.

In 1984, Alan Hale developed the accident equation: human hazards + environmental hazards = accident potential (see figure 4.5). It is still one of the best conceptual models for evaluating situational risk and elevating participants' awareness of their responsibilities. Hale identified human hazards as attitudes, behaviors, knowledge, or lack of knowledge on the part of participants, instructor, supervisor, and others. Environmental hazards are things such as location and the

Figure 4.4 Dish-washing procedure.

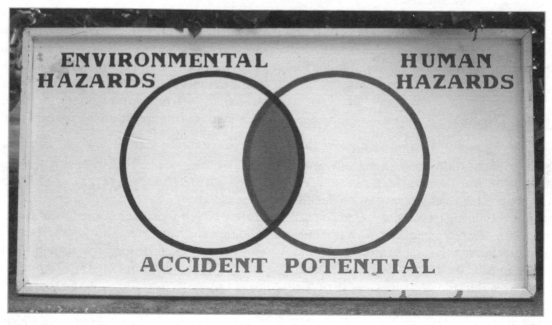

Figure 4.5 Accident potential.

actual features of the place, activities, equipment, and philosophy of the environment or program. The equation says that if human hazards are in the presence of environmental hazards, there is potential for an accident to occur. The more the two types of hazards overlap, the greater the accident potential. For example, if all participants in a group are unaware of certain risks or safety precautions, there is a greater chance for an accident than if only one participant is unaware. Carelessness is a big human hazard, but it can be greatly reduced through a safety briefing.

An activity safety briefing is the time to go over activity rules and hazards associated with the activity. A briefing that discusses specific environmental hazards as well as potential human hazards can be quite effective in reducing accident potential. In general, participants are empowered by environmental knowledge and awareness, which raises their safety consciousness. Such briefings also set an appropriate tone for the activity and encourage participants to accept ownership of program safety. They are given the tools for self-care and for caring for others in their group.

Campfires

Fire is always a hazard, but it can be managed safely. However, it is important to be aware of the fire restrictions in the area, follow them closely, and teach your students to do the same. When drought is prevalent, open fires may have to be deleted from the lesson plan. Contact the local fire department for current regulations.

At campgrounds with designated open-fire containers, typically called fire rings, it is fun to have a fire even if you don't choose to cook with it. Anyone can start a fire by pouring lighter fluid on some wood. However, in a spirit of developing environment-friendly skills, it is good to know how to start a fire without using liquid fuel or a whole newspaper. Using liquid fuel or lighter fluid is an unsafe practice.

Sitting around a campfire in the evening telling stories, singing, or just enjoying the warmth and atmosphere is a longtime camping tradition. However, as an increasing number of people are enjoying camping, concerns have grown regarding the environmental damage caused by campfires. Most parks allow campfires only in designated campfire rings and some parks only allow fires in charcoal grills.

If campfires are allowed, most people enjoy having one, so the ability to get a fire started is valuable. One method is stacking wood in the fire ring, pouring on some fuel, striking a match, and jumping back after dropping the match on the fuel-covered wood—not a good choice.

A more satisfying fire-starting technique incorporates the use of carefully selected tinder and kindling as well as an understanding of the chemical requirements for fire and its physics. The following list includes some of the essentials of successful fire building without using liquid fuel.

- Requirements—Fuel, heat source, and oxygen.
- Tinder—Fuel for getting a fire started. A more descriptive name for tinder is twiggies. Twiggies are no larger in diameter than a wooden kitchen match and are about three times longer. They should be dead, dry, and brittle and snap when broken. If there hasn't been any rain and the ground is dry, you can usually find tinder lying on the ground under dead bushes or trees that have lost some limbs. The dead branches of bushes and small trees often provide good tinder, but breaking them off is against the rules in some camping areas. In most campgrounds, gathering firewood of any kind is prohibited to lessen the human effect on the natural environment. If that is the case, you must be prepared and bring your own wood. Tinder can be made by chopping small slivers of wood from split wood for fireplaces.

- Kindling—Fuel for adding to a tinder fire that is burning well. Like tinder, it should be dead, dry, and brittle. Kindling is larger in diameter than tinder and can range from the size of a pencil to a thumb in diameter. Its purpose is to gradually increase the size of the fire's flame and to increase the amount of heat. The thicker a piece of wood, the more heat is required to get it to burn. For example, a stick the size of a tennis-racket handle cannot be started by the flame of one match, but several twigs each the size of a match can be started by that flame.

- Fuel—Wood ranging from the diameter of a forearm on up. The diameter of wood determines the time it will take for it to burn all the way through.

- Oxygen—If wood is positioned so that oxygen cannot flow under and between the wood of a fire, it may not light or continue to burn.

- Heat source—Match, lighter, or candle.

- Right combination and configuration of wood—See figure 4.6 for types of firewood. Figure 4.7 shows how to light a twiggy bundle to start a fire.

Figure 4.6 Three types of wood for fires: tinder, kindling, and fuel.

Figure 4.7   Lighting a twiggy bundle.

The most common reasons for not getting a twiggy fire started are using twiggies that are too large in diameter, not having enough twiggies in your bundle, or not holding the lighter or match flame correctly under the twiggies.

Give it a try. It is fun and exciting to start a fire with one match or a "flick of a Bic" to a bundle of twiggies held in your hand or carefully placed on the ground.

FRONTCOUNTRY CAMPING UNIT PLAN

Unit Objectives

Students will:

- safely light a two-burner stove, mix and cook pancakes, and wash their dishes in an environmentally friendly manner;
- select appropriate clothing for different weather situations as well as appropriate sleep systems;
- determine which heat-loss or heat-gain method would be most likely to occur in different situations and how to protect against it; and
- identify positive and negative qualities of different campsites.

Character Focus

Respect, responsibility

Curriculum Areas

Health, Language Arts, Physical Education, Science

Assessment Activity

Have each student make two drawings, one illustrating a Leave No Trace (LNT) "happy" campsite and one illustrating a "sad" LNT campsite. See appendix B for a list of the Leave No Trace principles.

Frontcountry Camping Day Planner

Day	Topic	Concepts and skills	Teaching activities	Standards
1	Introduction to different types of campgrounds; camping equipment	Different types of campgrounds (RV, tent, trailer); different types of camping equipment	Show slides of frontcountry campgrounds. Show camping equipment and types of camping.	Physical Education 6
2	Tents	Types of tents, parts, setup, and care	Have one tent set up and talk about parts and care. Divide class into groups and have each group set up a tent.	Language Arts 8; Physical Education 1 and 5
3	Sleeping systems	Types of sleeping bags and pads; outer materials and stuffing; types of sleeping pads and their purposes	Show pictures. Demonstrate compressibility, the weight different bags, and the insulating ability of pads.	Math 1; Science 8
4*	Camping safety	Accident potential model; identifying human and environmental hazards	Show pictures of different camping locations and camping-related activities. Small groups identify possible hazards for each picture.	Health 5; Language Arts 8; Math 1; Physical Education 5
5*	Fire building	How to start a fire in a campground fire ring	Demonstrate selections of wood, twiggy bundles, and starting a fire. In small groups students each start a twiggy bundle.	Physical Education 5 and 6; Science 8 and 9
6	Campground cooking	How to safely operate a camp stove; food preparation guidelines; cooking cleanup; LNT practices	Demonstrate use of a stove. Small groups mix pancake mix, cook, eat, and clean. Discuss LNT application.	Civics 3; Physical Education 1, 5, and 6
7	Leave No Trace for frontcountry campgrounds	Setting up, using, and leaving a car campsite using LNT practices	Have an LNT poster prominently displayed and in another area have the seven LNT practices clearly listed. Divide class into small groups and have each group go through the actions of setting up or dismantling a campsite and then list LNT applications.	Civics 27; Health 5 and 8; Physical Education 5 and 6

* Has a corresponding lesson plan.

CAMPING SAFETY

Lesson Objectives

Students will:

- draw and label the accident potential model,
- analyze the hazards associated with different locations and activities, and
- identify ways to reduce accident potential.

Character Focus

Responsibility

Curriculum Standards

Health 5; Language Arts 8; Math 1; Physical Education 5

Materials

- Several pictures of frontcountry camping locations
- Several pictures of frontcountry camping activities
- Paper and pencils or dry-erase boards and markers for each group

Preparation

1. Display camping and camping activity pictures.
2. Have the writing and drawing materials readily available.

Lesson Sequence

Introduce the idea of safety issues and the fact that hazards can be both similar and different in different locations and activities.

Activity 1

1. Begin class by putting students into small groups and asking each group to go to at least three different pictures and list all the hazards they can think of that could be associated with that location or activity.
2. When the groups finish with three pictures, each group combines with another small group to share its answers.
3. Bring the class back together for discussion. Point out a picture and ask a group to name the hazards it listed for that picture. Repeat this process for three different pictures. Give the class an opportunity to add hazards the group may not have listed. After three pictures, lead a class discussion. For example, you might say, "Let's look back at some of these pictures and their list of hazards and identify things that could reduce the risk of accidents."

Questions

- If we group the hazards that have been listed into two general categories, what might we name those two categories? (Human hazards and environmental hazards)
- What character trait can greatly reduce the human hazards? (Responsibility)

Possible Character Affirmation

Madison, that was very responsible of you to encourage your group to stay on task while looking at the pictures.

Activity 2

1. Have each group draw two circles side by side on their drawing surface. (This can be done in groups or individually.) Label one circle *Environmental Hazards* and the other circle *Human Hazards*.

2. On another part of the paper or dry-erase board draw two circles that overlap, as in figure 4.5. Follow with class discussion.

Questions

- If one of these overlapping circles represents human hazards and the other represents environmental hazards, what label could we apply to the overlapping parts of the circles? (Accident potential)

- If our class were on one end of the playing field and there were several beds of ants on the opposite end of the field, would there be accident potential for ant bites? (No)

- Would there be accident potential if our class were on the same end of the field as the ant beds? (Yes, if we were not careful about where we stepped.)

- How could the accident potential be reduced? (By noticing the ants beds were there and warning everyone to look out for them)

- Would the accident potential be completely gone? (No, because we are depending on humans to be very careful, but the accident potential is reduced by the warning.)

Activity 3

1. Draw a large version of the accident potential model and illustrate that the purpose of being aware of hazards is to reduce the potential for accidents. Two different colors of hula hoops can also be used to illustrate the model.

2. Ask students to list situations they normally experience and identify the environmental and human hazards associated with them.

Discussion and Review

- What are the most hazardous environments you experience?
- What things can you do to reduce the accident potential in those environments?

Teaching Tips

Have the pictures set up and ready to be viewed when class begins.

Possible Character Affirmations ☺

- This group is being very responsible by working together and following the instructions.

- Casey, thank you for doing the drawing and writing for your group. That was a responsible thing to do.

FIRE BUILDING

Lesson Objectives

Students will:

- demonstrate that they can light a fire with one match,
- demonstrate appropriate fuel selection and arrangement, and
- demonstrate responsibility and caring while building fires and extinguishing them.

Character Focus

Caring, responsibility

Curriculum Standards

Physical Education 5 and 6; Science 8 and 9

Materials

- Heavy-duty aluminum foil or sand
- Matches (4 per student or 1 lighter per group)
- Firewood sorted into piles of three diameters (matchstick, little finger, thumb) representing tender, kindling, and fuel
- Several buckets of water

Preparation

1. Locate a safe area for fires, such as a parking lot at least 100 feet (30 meters) from any vehicles or outdoor walkways.
2. Cut 2-foot (61-centimeter) squares of foil so that there is one square for every three students in the class plus one for a teacher demonstration.
3. Place several buckets of water around the perimeter of the fire-building area.
4. Arrange firewood piles outside of the fire-building perimeter.

Lesson Sequence

1. Introduction: Have two very small fires burning when class arrives. Ask, "What can we remove from the fire that would cause it to quit burning?" (Fuel—wood or oxygen)
2. Demonstrate covering one fire with an airtight cover to remove oxygen, and then separate wood in the other fire to remove the fuel source. The demonstration should cover
   - positioning two or three pieces of kindling in shape of a lean-to or A-frame that will provide oxygen access to burning tender and provide a base of support,
   - selecting tinder (diameter of a matchstick and 6 to 8 inches or 15 to 20 centimeters in length),
   - bundling tinder in hand (a fist full) at least 3 inches (8 centimeters) in diameter so there is adequate fuel in a size (diameter of a matchstick) that will ignite easily (see figure 4.7),

- holding the bundle for lighting with match or lighter under middle of the bundle, and

- holding the tinder together while placing it on the support.

3. Emphasize the importance of small-diameter tinder 6 to 8 inches (15 to 20 centimeters) in length and placing the match or lighter under the middle of bundle.

Activity

1. Divide the class into groups of three.

2. Give each group three wooden matches (one per person) and have each student attempt to start a bundle of tinder burning in the same manner as the demonstration.

3. Ask students to watch and try to figure out why some people got their tinder to burn and others didn't. (Tinder too big in diameter, not enough tinder in bundle, match flame went out before tinder started burning, not enough pieces of tinder caught on fire, and so on)

4. Discuss why some students got their bundles started and others didn't.

5. Give everyone a second match and have each group try to have all three members get their tinder bundle started.

Questions

- What is needed for starting a fire and keeping it going? (Fuel source, heat source, oxygen)

- If you wanted to build a fire to cook on, what would be the next size of wood to add to the burning bundle of tinder and why? (Gradually increase the diameter of the wood. The larger the diameter of wood, the hotter the fire must be to ignite it. If the heat source is not hot enough, it will not ignite a larger piece of wood or a wet piece of wood. If no one can answer the question, wait until the next day to see if someone comes up with the answer.)

- How is a fire similar to our body's metabolism? (Both need oxygen and fuel and both produce heat.)

- How does the use of fire require the characteristics of caring and responsibility? (When we care about the safety and well-being of other living beings and property, we must accept the responsibility to use fire wisely and protect against harm.)

Tips

- Hold the match close to the striking end.

- Strike the match close to the tinder bundle.

- Have other students provide a windshield.

Safety Tips

- Have students keep their hair tied back securely.

- Appoint one student in each group to be the safety monitor.

- Warn students to keep loose clothing away from fire.

- If students are acting unsafely, have them sit in the center of the circle with you.

- Make sure all fires are completely out without getting the ground soaking wet. All fires should be kept small so they can be smothered out. Place partially burned wood in a metal bucket.

Possible Character Affirmations

- Pat, you demonstrated excellent caring when you caught Jamie's hair and held it back.

- Thank you for coming back to check a second time to make sure your fire was out. That was very responsible of you.

Backcountry Camping

Chapter 5

The backcountry can be defined as locations that cannot be explored with a motorized vehicle and that require some means of physical exertion for traveling through them. This could include hiking with a backpack, cross-country skiing, canoeing, sea kayaking, and off-road bicycling. Such modes of travel naturally limit the amount and type of clothing, equipment, and food that you can take because your muscles and bones are the means of getting from one place to the next.

It is a wonderful thing to see beautiful sights from a car, truck, or bus. But it is totally different to actually be in and experiencing those beautiful sights. As the great environmentalist John Muir said in 1898, "Thousands of tired, nerve-shaken, over-civilized people are beginning to find out that going to the mountains is going home; that wilderness is a necessity." The knowledge and skills of backcountry camping allow people the opportunity to experience environments that most will only see on television or in calendar pictures. However, without adequate knowledge and skills, venturing into the backcountry can be harmful to both people and the environment.

This unit does not teach all the knowledge and skills necessary for backcountry camping, but it does present a basic introduction that hopefully will inspire further interest.

Locations and Types of Travel

Backcountry camping can be found in many different types of locations, and the location you choose is often based on the type of travel you want to do (see figure 5.1). For example, if you want to do a backcountry canoe trip, you choose among paddling down a river, on a lake, or down a series of lakes and rivers. Campers should first check the availability of public camping spots. If hiking is your choice, then accessible public areas include national wilderness areas, national parks with backcountry areas, national forests, and backcountry areas in state parks or forests. Many of these same areas can be used for bicycle trips, but you must inquire whether bicycles are permitted. Regardless of your travel choice, the availability of drinking water is of the utmost importance. If you will not have access to suitable water sources or chemical treatment for drinking, then you will have to carry water. This will limit your trip simply because water weighs 8 pounds (4 kilograms) per gallon (4 liters) and you should plan on carrying at least 3/4 gallon (3 liters) of water per day per person.

It doesn't take very many days to make a pack much too heavy!

Keep in mind that more and more backcountry areas are requiring permits for camping. Be sure to check with the appropriate agency to learn about their regulations.

Following are a few Web sites on backcountry areas for camping:

- National Park Service—www.nps.gov
- USDA Forest Service—www.fs.fed.us
- Bureau of Land Management—www.blm.gov
- Wilderness.net—www.wilderness.net

Figure 5.1   When traveling in the backcountry, you want your equipment to be as small as is functional, as light as possible, and always dependable.

Planning a Backcountry Trip

Much goes into planning a trip into the backcountry. The three plans are called *control plans* because the goal is to control and prevent potential problems. The three control plans are time, climate, and energy. A time control plan involves planning distances to travel within certain periods of time. This requires consideration of terrain, elevation gain and loss, and the health and physical fitness of the group. Time control planning is beyond the scope of this book and will not be discussed in this chapter. However, a conservative rule of thumb for backpacking is that a group can travel 1 mile (1.6 kilometers) in 30 to 60 minutes including rest breaks. This unit will concentrate on the knowledge and skills that go into climate control and energy control plans, plus how to care for the environment you are enjoying.

A climate control plan and an energy control plan each relate to what to take on a trip. A climate control plan deals with maintaining an appropriate climate for yourself through the clothes and other shelter options you choose. An energy control plan involves how you will expend energy and fuel (food and water) to replenish that expended energy.

An additional topic of significance for backcountry travel and camping is taking proper care of the environment through which you travel. This has become known as Leave No Trace (LNT) travel and camping. The LNT organization has an excellent Web site (www.leavenotrace.org) that provides details on the seven principles of outdoor ethics that are also found in appendix B. These seven points are:

1. Plan ahead and prepare
2. Travel and camp on durable surfaces
3. Dispose of waste properly
4. Leave what you find
5. Minimize campfire impacts
6. Respect wildlife
7. Be considerate of other visitors

Climate Control: Clothes

While traveling and camping in the backcountry, the same principles of layering apply that are discussed for frontcountry camping in chapter 4. However, since backcountry camping means being away from immediate help and access to an automobile or buildings, it is important to understand the scientific concepts behind the layering principles. The main concepts for dressing to maintain appropriate body temperature are based on how heat is exchanged between the body and the environment.

Heat is exchanged in five ways (see figure 5.2).

- **Radiation**—Heat travels from a warm object to a cooler object or place. In a colder environment the body loses heat directly into still air.
- **Evaporation**—This is the conversion of liquid to gas, or the process through which sweating cools the body. Evaporation explains why people feel cooler when they are wet.
- **Conduction**—This is the direct transfer of heat from an object or a body part to a colder object, such as when you pick up a cold soda can.
- **Convection**—Convection occurs when heat is transferred to circulating air. It explains why it is cooler outside when the wind is blowing.
- **Respiration**—Body heat is transferred to the air from your lungs when you exhale. When cooler air is inhaled, the body is required to warm it up. During normal breathing you lose heat.

In cold weather two of the main concerns regarding heat loss are staying dry and out of the wind. One saying that is often heard in camping circles is, "Cotton kills." This is because when cotton fibers get wet, they expand and all the air space in between the fibers is lost. Not only does the wet fabric speed up heat loss due to evaporation, but because there are no air spaces between the fibers there is nothing to hold warm air next to the body. It is the air next to your body that has been warmed by radiation from your body that keeps you warm. That's why a thick down jacket is warmer that a denim jacket—there's more warmed air next to your skin. Since warmed air next to your skin is what keeps you warm, it is important to keep it there. In cold weather

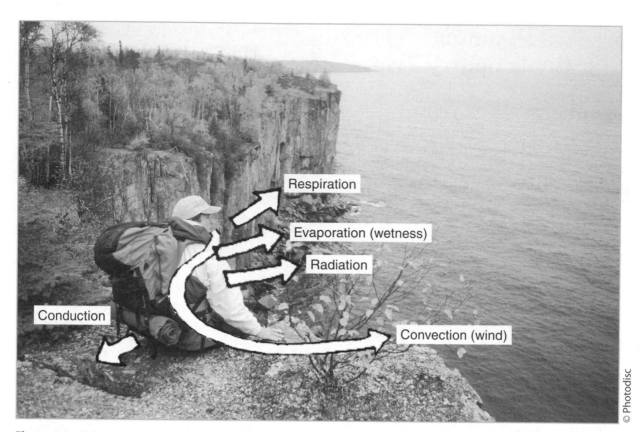

Respiration

Evaporation (wetness)

Radiation

Conduction

Convection (wind)

© Photodisc

Figure 5.2 Using proper clothing for climate control can help prevent loss of body heat from heat exchanges.

(especially if it's wet) you are better off dressed in fabric that does not absorb water and lose its air spaces. You also need some way to prevent the wind from carrying the warmed air away.

There are three types of materials that do not absorb water: wool, silk, and synthetics. To keep convection to a minimum, a wind shell should be worn. Nylon makes an excellent wind barrier. On a cool day, a person wearing a wet cotton shirt under a windbreaker will be colder than a person with a synthetic shirt and windbreaker.

For cold weather the layering system is quite important, along with the materials the layers are constructed from. Following are some basic guidelines:

- Skin layer—long underwear in synthetic material, silk, or wool

- Insulating layer—synthetic fleece, wool shirt or sweater, down jacket or vest

- Wind-barrier layer—nylon or Gore-Tex material

If it is raining, the wind-barrier layer can be rain gear, which also blocks the wind. For the extremities, the same rules for material type apply. There are an abundance of capillaries close to the surface of the head and primary loss of body heat is through the head, so a hat is important for protecting the body from heat loss.

Climate Control: Sleep Systems

Sleep systems, such as those discussed in chapter 4 on page 55, help campers exert control over their climate comfort. This control is the result of loft.

Loft is a term often used in describing sleeping bags. It refers to the thickness of the bag when it is laid out on the ground undisturbed for 30 minutes or so. During that time, the bag's fill material becomes decompressed and springs back to its intended size and shape. A bag that has 4 inches (10 centimeters) of loft will generally be warmer than a bag with 3 inches (8 centimeters) of loft because of its ability to trap more air. Refer to figure 4.2, page 55. The sleeping bag on the right carries more loft so it will be warmer than the sleeping bag on the left.

The more air is trapped around the body, the warmer you will be. The exception is when there is too much air for your body to warm. For example, if you are in a small tent without a sleeping bag, your body still has the ability to warm the air in the tent. However, there is so much air that your body probably cannot warm it enough to make you feel warm.

The same principle applies to the size of sleeping bags. You will be cooler in a large bag than in a bag that fits your body more closely because of the amount of trapped air your body has to warm. Due to this, the shape of the sleeping bag should be considered. For warm weather camping, a rectangular bag will provide adequate insulation. The cooler the weather, the greater need there is for the bag to conform to your body and cover your head with a cap or a hood that is part of the sleeping bag.

Climate Control: Tents and Tarps

Most people choose to take a smaller tent into the backcountry than they would choose when frontcountry camping because smaller tents are usually lighter to carry (see figure 5.3). Remember the tip mentioned earlier in the chapter: small, light, and dependable is the key. The same principles for a functional tent apply in the backcountry as in the frontcountry. The tent must be able to keep you dry when it's raining, snowing, or sleeting, and it must protect against

wind. Because your body is constantly giving off moisture vapor through the skin as well as through respiration, the tent must have a means for the vapor to escape. If the vapor cannot escape, it will condense on the inside of the tent and begin to drip onto the occupants. For this reason most small tents have a vapor-permeable roof and a waterproof rainfly or tarp a few inches above the tent's roof. This space allows the vapor to escape the tent and dissipate into the air between the roof and the rainfly. The floor of the tent should be waterproof and the same material should extend several inches up the lower walls of the tent. This prevents water from getting into the tent from the ground or off of the rainfly. Most tents also have waterproof door and window coverings as well as mosquito netting on doors and any windows to keep bugs out.

Many people choose to carry an extra piece of tent material or a lightweight sheet of plastic to use as a ground cloth or tent footprint. Its purpose is to protect the floor of the tent from abrasion and punctures by small rocks, pine cones, or sticks. It is not used to prevent water from seeping through the floor of the tent, and it is best if water does not collect between the ground cloth and the tent floor. To prevent this, the ground cloth should not extend out past the edge of the tent.

Tents come in a variety of shapes and sizes. When considering a backcountry tent, the main

Figure 5.3 A smaller tent will be lighter to carry in the backcountry.

considerations are how many people the tent will comfortably hold and whether it is appropriate for the weather conditions. If four people are going on a trip together, it is often better to take two separate tents that each accommodate two people rather than a tent for four because it is usually easier to find places to set up small tents.

Tarps can be used as shelters in place of tents. They are lighter since few or no poles are carried, they do not include as much material, and they have no zippers. There are no doors, windows, or floor. Tarps can be set up in a variety of configurations and are often appropriate for groups of mixed gender because the openness reduces misbehavior. Using appropriate knots is important for setting up a tarp, as is an understanding of design for shedding water and wind. The tighter the tarp, the better it will shed wind and rain. Loose sides will sag, collect rain, and make the room under the tarp much smaller. When the tarp's roof is pushed up to dump the rain, it usually runs under the edge of the tarp and onto the occupants.

Two knots are important for setting up tarps with tight sides that will shed wind and rain.

- Bowline knots are used to attach cord around the edges of the tarp (figure 5.4).

- Taut-line hitch knots are used with stakes for tightening the cords that pull the sides of the tarp out to make room for people under the tarp (figure 5.5).

Energy Control: Water

An energy control plan involves factors that affect your energy level. These factors include food,

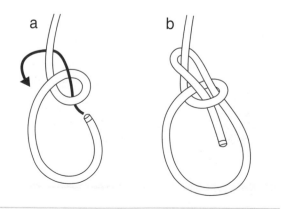

Figure 5.4   Bowline knot.

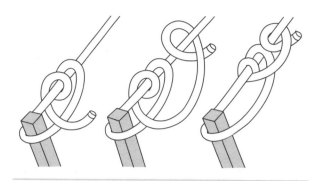

Figure 5.5   Taut-line hitch knot.

water, travel techniques, equipment, required exertion, and physical fitness. However, for the scope of this book, the energy control elements are limited to water, food, and the fitting and packing of backpacks.

Water is a necessity. We need it to drink, cook, and clean. A dry campsite does not have access to a water source and the length of your stay is determined by how much water you bring with you. A preferred campsite has a water supply, whether it is a stream, lake, river, or spring. In the past, people could safely drink from any of these sources without fear of getting sick. However, today we must be much more careful with the water we drink and take precautions to purify it.

There are different ways to treat water to increase its safety for drinking, and people often have preferences. Some pros and cons for a few of the water treatment options are listed in table 5.1, but you will have to determine your preference by experience. The options listed include filtering, iodine tablets, bleach drops, Aquamira drops, and boiling. Recently, another iodine treatment has become available, Polar Pure, which has a longer shelf life than iodine tablets.

We often forget how important adequate water consumption is for an optimal energy level. Depending upon the temperature and energy expenditure, water requirements vary. However, you should always drink at least 1 to 2 quarts (1 to 2 liters) of water over the course of a day. That amount will increase with heavy exercise and hot temperatures. Another consideration is the type of food you are eating. If you are eating primarily dried or dehydrated foods, more water consumption is suggested. A general rule of thumb is to drink before you get

Table 5.1 Water Treatment Options

	Advantages	Disadvantages
Filtering	• Does a good job of purification.	• Takes a long time to filter much water. • Filters are used up quickly and are expensive.
Iodine tablets	• Easy to carry. • Treatment takes only 30 minutes.	• Often discolors containers. • Creates a taste that is unpleasant to some people. • Does not kill giardia lamblia (an intestinal parasite).
Bleach solution	• Easy to carry. • Treatment takes only 30 minutes.	• Creates a taste that is unpleasant to some people.
Aquamira	• Easy to carry. • Treatment takes only 35 minutes. • Only slightly changes taste.	• Have to mix two solutions together and wait 5 minutes before treating water.
Boiling	• Kills all harmful organisms.	• Takes time to bring water to a boil. • Depending on altitude, must boil for 5 to 15 minutes. • After boiling, water must be allowed to cool before drinking. In warm weather this is a serious disadvantage.

thirsty—by the time you actually feel thirsty, you are already heading toward dehydration.

Energy Control: Food and Cooking

Since travel in the backcountry makes carrying an ice chest impossible, you must select food that will not readily spoil. Additional considerations are the calories and nutrients that the food contains, its bulk and weight, and its ease of preparation. Ideally, you want food that will help maintain your energy, is lightweight for ease of carrying, and requires minimal effort to cook and minimal cooking utensils. Meals that take only one pot are a favorite of tired backcountry travelers.

On the Internet, the Great Outdoor Recreation Page (GORP) offers a few examples of backcountry foods for each meal (http://gorp.away.com/gorp/activity/hiking.htm):

• Breakfast—toaster pastries, cereal (cold or hot), bagels, breakfast bars, granola bars
• Lunch—cheese, peanut butter, salami, beef or turkey jerky, crackers, nuts, other high-energy snack foods
• Dinner—boxed macaroni and cheese, packaged noodle or rice dishes, ramen soups, instant potato flakes, foil-packaged meats and sauce mixes

A variety of freeze-dried foods are available for all three meals and they require only boiling water and 15 minutes. However, the cost is high and the packages are quite bulky.

It is also a good idea to bring a few basic condiments to enhance the taste of your meals. Recommended condiments are salt and pepper, garlic powder, olive oil, powered instant milk, onion flakes, and repackaged margarine or packets of clarified butter that can be purchased from freeze-dried food distributors.

Cooking in the backcountry is most easily done on portable one-burner stoves. Such stoves come in a variety of sizes with different fuel requirements. There are stoves that burn white gas or butane. There are also higher priced stoves that can burn various types of fuel, even regular gasoline. As always, there are pros and cons to each stove type, some of which are highlighted in table 5.2.

Be sure to follow the instructions carefully for the stoves you are using. It is advisable to practice lighting the stoves several times before teaching your students this skill. There are also some general safety rules you should follow regardless of the type of stove you are using.

Table 5.2 Camping Stoves

	Advantages	Disadvantages
White gas	• Can burn very hot flame and some models offer a fair amount of flame adjustability. • Gas is readily available in most locations.	• Requires pumping and priming to light. • Requires maintenance of fuel jets. • In general, cannot burn consistently with low flame for simmering.
Butane canister	• Easy to light and requires no priming. • Flame is adjustable from low to high. • Easy for beginners to use.	• Fuel is generally found only in specialty outdoor stores. • Flame does not burn as hot as white-gas stoves.

Stove Safety Rules

- Hair should always be tied or held back from the face.
- Long, loose sleeves should be pushed up away from the hands.
- Keep your head back from the stove when lighting it.
- Place the stove on a level surface that will not be harmed by heat.
- Cook 200 feet (61 meters) away from your tent and any water source.

When traveling in the backcountry, the weight you carry is an issue and the fuel for your stove adds to that weight. Therefore, you should follow two guidelines for conserving fuel so you will not have to carry as much: always cover the pot with a lid when cooking, and do not light your stove until you are ready to put a pot on.

Food Storage

Many critters in the backcountry will be interested in eating your food. It can be fun to feed wild animals, but it is also unhealthy for them and could be dangerous for you and other campers who come after you. To be a responsible backcountry traveler, don't feed the wildlife, either intentionally or unintentionally.

Animals will often smell your food and come to see what they can get. Because of this instinct, you must take precautions that will make it less likely for them to get to your food. Here are some guidelines for food storage:

- Never have food in your tent, and especially don't eat in your tent.
- Do not leave food in a pack unless you are in the process of traveling from one campsite to another.

Use strong cord to hang your food in a bag from a tree limb high enough to discourage animals on the ground or in the trees. Figure 5.6 illustrates one way to hang a food bag.

Washing Dishes

To clean your dishes in the backcountry, use the same procedures that were introduced in the last chapter's discussion on frontcountry camping. Since there will not be animal-proof garbage cans in the backcountry, cook only as much food as you will eat. Any uneaten food must be scraped from the dishes and pots into a plastic bag and carried out with the rest of your gear. Another exception is that you will not have a dishpan for your wash and rinse water. Use a pot to hold hot water and clean your dishes in order from cleanest to dirtiest.

Dish Cleaning Progression

1. Eat all food, or scrape remaining food into a plastic bag for carrying with other gear.
2. Move 200 feet (61 meters) away from the cook site, campsite, and water source.
3. Dig a sump hole about 8 inches (20 centimeters) deep at an appropriate wash site.
4. Wash dishes, utensils, and pots in warm water using your fingers. Use biodegradable soap only if dishes are greasy.
5. Rinse water becomes wash water for the next dish or pot.
6. Strain wash and rinse water for any food particles to add to the plastic bag (see figure 5.7).
7. Broadcast strained water onto the ground by flinging it out in a wide arch.

Figure 5.6 This method of hanging food will help keep your food safe from animals looking for a meal.

a   *b*

Figure 5.7 Strain the wash water *(a)*, then add to the plastic bag *(b)*.

8. Scald rinse with very hot water.

9. Allow dishes to air dry.

Backpacks

Two types of backpacks are currently used—external- and internal-frame packs (see figure 5.8). As with other equipment, they each have their pros and cons (see table 5.3).

For the most part, packing a backpack is a matter of personal preference. However, there are a few important guidelines:

- Keep heavier items close to the back and midline of the body.
- Do not pack fuel containers (including stove) among the food.
- Make water easily accessible.
- Large, bulky items work best in the lower part of the pack.
- Distribute weight as evenly as possible from right to left.

Table 5.3 Backpacks

	Advantages	Disadvantages
External frame	• Can carry heavier weight more comfortably because majority of weight is carried on the hips • Tend to be less expensive than internal-frame packs. • Cooler in warm climates because it is held away from the back.	• Relatively bulky and does not easily conform to a boat's hull for canoeing trips. • Because it is held away from the back, may result in balance problems when going over, under, or around obstacles.
Internal frame	• Wide variety of choices available. • Conforms to the back of the carrier. • Improves balance.	• Hot in warm climates because it hugs the back. • Weight must be carried on both the hips and the shoulders.

Figure 5.8 The backpack on the left has an external frame, while the backpack on the right has an internal frame.

Steps of Trip Planning

A lot of preparation goes into planning a back-country trip. It is beyond the scope and purpose of this book to cover the details of planning, but to provide an idea of the types of things to consider, the following list contains 13 steps for planning a backcountry trip.

Six Questions to Ask

1. Who is going? (Names, contact information, health information)

2. What are you going to do? (Itinerary and activities)

3. When are you going? (Date and time of year)

4. Where are you going? (Destination)

5. How are you going to get there? (Mode of transportation and travel routes)

6. Why are you going? What are the group and individual goals?

Three Control Plans

7. Time control plan—Factors that influence how fast you can travel (terrain, distance, elevation, environmental conditions, physical fitness, health)

8. Climate control plan—Factors that allow you to be comfortable and safe in the environment and weather

9. Energy control plan—Factors that affect your energy level (water, food, travel techniques, physical fitness)

Four Miscellaneous Areas

10. Emergency procedures—Leave itinerary with a responsible adult; take police and ambulance numbers with you; plan emergency routes out of the backcountry

11. Expenses—Transportation costs, permit fees, fishing licenses, equipment purchases

12. Group gear—Equipment that group members share, such as tents, stoves, pots, food

13. Pretrip group meeting—Discuss individual expectations and expedition behavior

Traveling through the backcountry is an inspiring experience. With the knowledge from this chapter, you should be able to travel away from human conveniences for a few days and try out your skills. The wonders of nature await you!

BACKCOUNTRY CAMPING UNIT PLAN

Unit Objectives

Students will:

- identify possible places for backcountry travel,
- use basic backcountry equipment safely and correctly,
- identify health and safety issues and how to manage them, and
- explain the rationale for LNT travel and camping.

Character Focus

Respect, responsibility

Curriculum Areas

- Physical Education, Science, Language Arts, Health, Math

Assessment Activity

Divide the class into 5 to 10 small groups depending upon the number of students in the class. Have each group draw a topic that has been covered in the backpacking unit and create a charades skit that communicates the most important concept or skill from that topic. Have other class members guess the topic from the charades. Then have each student list one or two other concepts or skills from that topic on a sheet of paper.

Backcountry Camping Day Planner

Day	Topic	Concepts and skills	Teaching activities	Standards
1	Introduction to backcountry travel: places, activities, types of travel, and equipment carried	Weight consciousness: necessities versus comfort; human anatomy, and carrying a backpack	Show slides of backpacking places and activities. Unpack a loaded pack and show different types of backpacks.	Physical Education 6
2	Leave No Trace principles	Climate control (clothes); Leave No Trace skills for minimizing effects	Show pictures of messy and clean campsites and collecting litter; discuss human effects on the environment.	Health 2; Physical Education 6; Science 6, 8, and 9
3*	Climate control (how to dress)	Layering and wind protection; methods of heat exchange	Demonstrate layered dressing; match clothes with climate; identify heat transfer using stations and pictures.	Health 7; Physical Education 5; Math 1, 6, and 7; Language Arts 4 and 8; Science 12
4*	Climate control (clothing fabrics)	Cotton versus synthetic material; insulation	Use microscopes to identify material best for insulation and climate control for different climates.	Health 2; Physical Education 5; Math 1, 6, and 7; Language Arts 4 and 8; Science 12
5	Climate control (sleeping bags)	Down versus synthetic bags; closed- versus open- celled foam versus air versus Thermarest	Identify which bag is down and which is synthetic. Discuss the difference between fills and types of pads and the purpose of a pad.	Physical Education 6; Language Arts 4 and 8
6	Climate control (tents)	A-frame versus dome; single wall versus double (rainfly) material	Demonstrate tent setup and have students practice. Explain tent features.	Physical Education 1, 5, and 6; Language Arts 4 and 8
7	Climate control (tarps and knots)	Uses and how to configure; how to tie bowline and taut-line hitch knots	Demonstrate tarp setup; demonstrate and explain bowline and taut-line hitch. Students practice knots and setting up tarps.	Physical Education 1, 5, and 6; Language Arts 4 and 8
8	Energy control (food and cooking)	Types of food to carry; nutrition and energy requirements; weight considerations	Show and explain appropriate and inappropriate backcountry food. Heat water for soup and freeze-dried food sample.	Physical Education 6
9	Energy control (stove safety for backcountry cooking)	Stoves; safety; organization for cooking	Demonstrate lighting a stove. Student groups light two different types of stoves and heat water for hot chocolate.	Health 2 and 7; Language Arts 8; Physical Education 1, 5, and 6; Science 6
10*	Energy control (backcountry cooking)	Following cooking directions and safety procedures while cooking.	Student groups cook assigned food on single-burner stove, eat what they made, and clean up.	Health 2 and 7; Language Arts 8; Physical Education 1, 5, and 6; Science 6
11	Trip planning	13 steps of trip planning	Groups act out the steps of trip planning.	Language Arts 8; Physical Education 5 and 6

* Has a corresponding lesson plan.

CLIMATE CONTROL, PERSONAL SHELTER, AND HOW TO DRESS

Lesson Objectives

Students will:

- demonstrate the concept of layering for various environmental conditions, and
- apply the thermal principles of evaporation, conduction, convection, and radiation as they dress for the outdoors given different situations.

Character Focus

Responsibility

Curriculum Standards

Health 7; Language Arts 4 and 8; Math 1, 6, and 7; Physical Education 5; Science 12

Materials

- Extra clothes
  - Several large pairs of cotton shorts or long pants
  - Several large cotton shirts
  - Several large windbreakers and nylon pants
  - Wool or synthetic shirts and pants
  - Wool or fleece hats
  - Straw hats
  - Cotton caps
- Poster pictures
  - Pictures of locations that have obviously different climates
  - Pictures depicting heat transfer via radiation, conduction, convection, and evaporation
- Heat transfer stations
  - Cups of ice
  - Fan
  - Two space heaters, one with a blower fan
  - Two 2- to 5-gallon buckets

Preparation

1. Dress yourself in layers for hiking in a cold climate.
2. Lay the extra clothes out randomly.
3. Set up pictures of different climates and heat transfer methods.
4. Set up the heat transfer stations at least 20 feet (6 meters) apart.

Station 1

Several paper cups filled with ice are on a table or bench.

Directions: Hold a cup of ice in one hand for 1 minute. What type of heat transfer is taking place? Identify the type of heat transfer from one of the pictures that is displayed. (Conduction)

Station 2

A space heater is running without a fan.

Directions: Stand 2 to 3 feet (61 to 91 centimeters) away from the heater for 1 minute. What type of heat transfer is taking place? Identify the type of heat transfer from one of the pictures that is displayed. (Radiation)

Station 3

A fan is running.

Directions: Stand 4 to 6 feet (122 to 183 centimeters) away from the fan for 1 minute. What type of heat transfer is taking place? Identify the type of heat transfer from one of the pictures that is displayed. (Convection)

A space heater is running that has a blower fan.

Directions: Stand 2 to 4 feet (61 to 122 centimeters) in front of the heater for 1 minute. What type of heat transfer is taking place? Identify the type of heat transfer from one of the pictures that is displayed. (Convection)

Station 4

Two buckets are filled with water.

Directions: Dip both arms into the water. Walk around for 1 minute with your arms held out away from your body while they are wet. What type of heat transfer is taking place? Identify the type of heat transfer from one of the pictures that is displayed. (Evaporation)

Station 5

Exhale on the inside of your dry forearm. Does your breath feel warm or cool? What type of heat transfer is taking place? Identify the type of heat transfer from one of the pictures that is displayed. (Respiration)

Lesson Sequence

Introduce the idea of clothing as a person's first line of shelter and an important part of a climate control plan.

1. Begin class dressed for backpacking in cold weather.
2. Explain each layer of clothing you have on as you remove each layer (down to long underwear).

Activity 1

1. Divide the class into groups of three.
2. Have each group look at the pictures illustrating various climates.
3. From the clothes you laid out randomly, let groups choose what would be appropriate to wear for hiking in each climate.

Questions

- If you are cold and the wind starts blowing, how does the wind make you feel?
- What about if you are hot and the wind starts blowing?

Possible Character Affirmation ⤴

Madison, that was very responsible for you to put the clothes back so other people could see them.

Activity 2

1. Have each group identify the clothes they have selected for one of the locations. ⌐

2. Rotate through all student groups, being sure to cover each climate at least once.

Questions

- Pat, tell us how your group made the decision to wear a windbreaker and nylon pants for the cold climate.
- Which sweater do you think would be the warmest?
- What makes that sweater look warm?
- What difference does the type of material make?

Possible Character Affirmation ⤴ ☺

Jose, thank you for helping your group stay on task. That shows you are a responsible person.

Activity 3

1. Set up the six heat transfer stations. Direct student groups to begin at different stations and rotate around to each station. ◿ ⌐

2. As a class, ask each group to identify the heat transfer method associated with one of the stations. Cover all stations.

Discussion and Review ⌐ ☺

- Which methods of heat loss do you notice the most?
- Which method of heat loss does the pad for a sleeping bag prevent?
- Which method of heat loss does a tent prevent?
- Why is layering a good method of dressing for a climate control plan?
- Think about going camping in the backcountry. How does the concept of responsibility relate to dressing properly? How could it affect other people if you are not dressed properly?

Teaching Tips

- Have everything set up and ready to go when class begins.
- Use clearly written directions and signs.

Possible Character Affirmations ◿ ☺ ⤴

- This group is being very responsible in working together on the stations.
- Jennifer, thank you for picking up the ice. That was a responsible thing to do, because someone could have slipped on that ice and gotten hurt.

CLIMATE CONTROL, PERSONAL SHELTER, AND CLOTHING FABRICS

Lesson Objectives

Students will:

- evaluate the pros and cons of cotton, wool, synthetics, and silk; and
- be able to apply the thermal principles of evaporation, conduction, convection, and radiation to dressing for the outdoors.

Character Focus

Responsibility

Curriculum Standards

Health 2; Language Arts 4 and 8; Math 1, 6 and 7; Physical Education 5; Science 12

Materials

- Extra clothes
  - At least four cotton t-shirts
  - At least four synthetic t-shirts
  - At least four windbreaker jackets without a lining
- Poster pictures of different climates
  - Pictures of locations that have obviously different climates
  - Pictures depicting heat transfer via radiation, conduction, convection, and evaporation

Fabric Testing Stations

- Six microscopes
- Slide of dry cotton cloth
- Slide of dry wool cloth
- Slide of dry fleece cloth
- Slide of wet cotton cloth
- Slide of wet wool cloth
- Slide of wet fleece cloth
- Twelve extra slides of dry (six) and wet (six) nylon cloth (windbreaker type)

Preparation

- Set up the microscopes at six different stations with each holding a different slide for viewing.
- Set up pictures of different climates along with pictures of heat transfer methods.

Lesson Sequence

Introduce the concept that different types of material have different insulating abilities. Ask the students the following questions: ⌐

- What is insulation? (Trapped air the body can warm by radiation.)
- Why do different types of materials have different insulating abilities? (Some materials are better able to trap and hold air next to your body (more loft) without absorbing moisture from your body or the environment.)

Activity 1 △ ☺

Ask for 12 volunteers who would be willing to change into different clothes.

- Have two students put on a dry cotton t-shirt (i).
- Have two students put on a dry synthetic t-shirt (ii).
- Have two students put on a wet cotton t-shirt (iii).
- Have two students put on a wet synthetic t-shirt (iv).
- Have two students put on a windbreaker only (v).
- Have two students put on a wet synthetic t-shirt with a windbreaker over it (vi).

    • Volunteers partner up as follows: i with ii, iii with iv, and v with vi.

    • Have volunteers wear their assigned clothes for 10 minutes during activity 2, and then switch clothes with their partner and wear those clothes for 10 minutes.

Questions ☺

Ask each group to report on which clothes were the warmest and which were the coolest. Ask, "Who can explain scientifically why there was a difference?" (Evaporation; insulating ability of different fibers when wet; windbreaker without shirt has less insulation)

Character Question ⌐ ☺

On a backcountry trip, what does how you dress have to do with being responsible?

Activity 2

1. Divide the class into small groups (pairs or triads). ◠ ⌐ ☺
2. Have each group move through all six stations and look at the samples under the microscopes.
3. Have students identify what type of material is at each station and whether it is wet or dry. (See climate control worksheet on page 85.)

Questions

- How was wet cotton different from wet wool and wet fleece? (Wet cotton didn't have much space between the fibers like the others had.)
- What was the difference between the different materials when they were dry? (Wool and fleece fibers are fuzzier.)
- Why is cotton not a good insulator if it is dry? (The body gives off water vapors and will make cotton slightly damp.)

Activity 3

1. Place the windbreaker slides at each station. ◠ ⌐ ☺
2. Have each group look at the new slide through a microscope and attempt to identify the material.

Questions

- How is this material different from the others? (Tight weave, no airspace between fibers)
- What piece of clothing would probably be made from this? (Windbreaker)
- What piece of equipment might be made from something like this? (Tent and tarp)

Possible Character Affirmation ☺ ᕲ

Yung, thank you for encouraging your group to think about what they were looking at under the microscope. That shows you are a responsible person.

Discussion and Review

- When wet, which fabric held the most water?
- Which type of fabric would contribute most to keeping you cool in a hot and dry environment if the fabric were wet?
- What differences did you notice between the nylon and the other fabrics?
- Which fabric do you think would be most helpful in preventing heat loss from convection?

Teaching Tips

- Have everything set up and ready to go when class begins.
- Use clearly written directions and signs.

Possible Character Affirmation

This group shows respect for each other by letting everyone have an opportunity at each microscope. I appreciate your respect and responsibility.

Climate Control Worksheet

Group _____

	Circle correct one			Circle one	
Station 1	Cotton	Synthetic	Windbreak nylon	Wet	Dry
Station 2	Cotton	Synthetic	Windbreak nylon	Wet	Dry
Station 3	Cotton	Synthetic	Windbreak nylon	Wet	Dry
Station 4	Cotton	Synthetic	Windbreak nylon	Wet	Dry
Station 5	Cotton	Synthetic	Windbreak nylon	Wet	Dry
Station 6	Cotton	Synthetic	Windbreak nylon	Wet	Dry

From *Interdisciplinary Teaching Through Outdoor Education,* by Camille Bunting, 2006, Champaign, IL: Human Kinetics.

ENERGY CONTROL AND BACKCOUNTRY COOKING

Lesson Objectives

Students will:

- safely light a backcountry stove and cook food appropriate for backcountry travel, and
- show responsibility during the cooking process.

Character Focus

Respect, responsibility

Curriculum Standards

Health 2 and 7; Language Arts 8; Physical Education 1, 5 and 6; Science 6

Materials

- Several small backcountry-type stoves (ideally, enough for the class to be divided into groups of three and for each group to have a stove)
- Cooking pot for each group (use one 1-gallon or 4-liter can per stove; ask the school cafeteria to save them for you)
- Lids for pots made out of a doubled sheet of aluminum foil
- Food for cooking (see Backcountry Cooking sidebar on page 88)
  - Ramen noodles (one package divided between two groups)
  - Cheese quesadillas (flour tortillas, butter, grated cheese)
  - Macaroni and cheese (one package divided between two groups)
  - Quick cooking oatmeal (not instant) with brown sugar and cinnamon
- One plastic bowl and spoon for each student
- Roll of paper towels
- Screen wire or bandanas for straining out food particles from dishwater
- Plastic baggies

Preparation

1. Arrange stoves outside about 15 feet (5 meters) apart on a durable surface.
2. Have plastic bowls and spoons available for students.
3. Have water available for cooking and cleaning.
4. Have extra cans available for heating wash and rinse water.
5. Have plastic baggies ready to collect all uneaten food.
6. Have screen wire or bandanas to strain out food particles.

Lesson Sequence

Remind students about the concepts of respect and responsibility by discussing the following questions:

- How can you demonstrate respect and responsibility while cooking?

(All students get to be involved, talk one at a time, follow safety rules, be careful around stove so nothing is knocked over; all cooked food is eaten; pots and dishes are washed well without wasting water; and so on.)

- What are the safety rules for cooking? (Long hair is tied back; loose sleeves are pushed back; all faces are back away from the stove when it is lit; at least one person is always monitoring the stove; the stove is not lit until the pot is ready for cooking.)

Activity 1

1. Divide the class into small groups and hand out the food they are to cook along with the directions.
2. Groups go to a stove and begin cooking preparations.
3. While the food is cooking, have one member from each group get a bowl and spoon for each member of the group.

Activity 2

1. Groups eat what they have cooked and offer to let other groups taste their food.
2. Groups should attempt to eat all of what they cooked.
3. While eating, students put water on the stove to heat it for washing the dishes.

Activity 3

1. Any food that cannot be eaten is scraped into a plastic bag. Each group tries to have the least food left over.
2. When water is hot enough for washing, the stove should be turned off.
3. Pots and dishes are washed and rinsed, with water transferred from one washed dish to another dirty dish. Any food particles should be strained out and rinse water should be broadcast across the ground.
4. Any strained food particles are placed in a plastic bag to be carried out of the backcountry.

(See figure 5.7 on page 75.)

Discussion and Review

- How much food did your group leave uneaten?
- Now let's compare the amount of food you strained out of your dishwater.
- Why do we strain the dishwater?
- What does Leave No Trace mean? (To take care of our environment, it is important not to have a negative effect on it.)
- How would you cook differently in the backcountry as compared to the frontcountry?
- What things did you observe someone else doing that demonstrated respect or responsibility?

Teaching Tip

Hand out cooking directions with the food.

Possible Character Affirmation ☺ ⤴

Ramad, thank you for respecting John while he was asking his question by waiting until he was finished to ask your question. That was an excellent example of respect.

Ramen Noodles

- Follow directions on package.
- Serve into bowls with cup designated for dipping.

Cheese Quesadillas

- Need one tortilla, 1 teaspoon of butter, and 1 ounce (30 grams) of shredded cheese per group member.
- Melt the butter in a pan and place the tortilla in melted butter for a few seconds to warm.
- Turn the tortilla over with tongs or spatula and sprinkle the cheese on top.
- Cover pan with lid for approximately 30 to 60 seconds.
- Fold tortilla over and serve.

Repeat process for each person's quesadilla.

Macaroni and Cheese

Follow directions on box.

Oatmeal, Brown Sugar, and Cinnamon

- Follow directions on box.
- When oatmeal is done, serve into bowls. Each student adds sugar and cinnamon to own bowl.

From *Interdisciplinary Teaching Through Outdoor Education,* by Camille Bunting, 2006, Champaign, IL: Human Kinetics.

Outdoor Cooking Techniques

Cooking brings together skills from many disciplines. Reading comprehension, measuring, exact and specific movement, and scientific concepts all are combined in the process of cooking. The value of presenting various cooking methods is that it motivates student interest and provides a fun and rewarding means for comparing the principles of heat transfer and changes of properties in matter. Plus, there is a great reward—food to eat!

This unit is not about typical backyard barbeque cooking. The methods it presents can be used in frontcountry camping using wood or charcoal fires. Some methods will be familiar while others will be less well known. Although probably none of us would choose to use these methods exclusively after becoming accustomed to electricity or gas, they are fun cooking methods that use open wood fires, charcoal, or some other source of heat, and all can produce delicious results.

Many regular campers choose to cook with a portable stove, as discussed in the frontcountry camping unit in chapter 4. For other campers, however, much of the fun of camping comes from cooking with a wood or charcoal fire and with heat from the sun. This unit will present cooking techniques and recipes for stick roasting, tin-can cooking, Dutch ovens, foil packets, and solar funnels. It will also discuss the economic and environmental effects of cooking around the world.

Stick Roasting

This technique is both the most simple and the most difficult of the methods presented in this chapter. It is very "low-tech," using only a green stick. The difficult part is that it requires patience and attention to cook the food on the stick without burning it or leaving portions of it raw.

The stick should have enough life left in it that it won't catch on fire easily. It should be approximately 1 inch (3 centimeters) in diameter and 3 feet (91 centimeters) long. The diameter of the stick creates a hole in the food that can be filled with other ingredients after the cooking is completed. The length allows the cook to not get too hot while cooking. It is best to remove the bark from the end of the stick where the food will be placed. Another option is to cover the cooking end of the stick with heavy-duty aluminum foil.

The fire can be either wood or charcoal, but is best if the roasting takes place over glowing coals rather than a flame. Flames tend to burn food on the outside while leaving the inside raw.

Following are recipes for green-stick roasting using ingredients ranging from meat to bread dough.

Stick Biscuits

These are known to most Boy Scouts and Girl Scouts as dough boys.

- The simplest method is to open a can of biscuit dough, squeeze the dough for one biscuit around one end of the stick, and spread it out so that it is not too thick.

- Roast the dough over coals, turning it frequently to prevent burning.

- After cooking, put butter and honey in the middle after the bread is removed from the stick.

- Any bread dough, not just biscuit dough, can be used for making stick biscuits.

These can also become cinnamon rolls or whatever your imagination allows.

Stick Burgers

- Mix ground meat with an egg and then mold enough for a patty around the stick.

- Follow the same cooking procedure for stick biscuits.

- When the meat is done, stuff burger ingredients like cheese, pickles, and tomatoes inside. Eat the stick burger in a hot-dog bun.

Note of caution: Stick burgers take longer to cook than hot dogs.

Stick Fish

- Roast freshly caught and cleaned fish on a green stick.

- Follow the same cooking procedures as for the biscuits and stick burgers.

Tin-Can Cooking

Girl and Boy Scouts know the equipment for this type of cooking as buddy burners and vagabond stoves. As with stick roasting, you construct the equipment yourself.

The equipment for tin-can cooking consists of a burner as a source of heat and a separate cooking surface. The burner has three parts: a can (such as a tuna can), paraffin, and cardboard. The can should be empty, cleaned, and dried, including the lid that has been removed. Cardboard strips should be no wider than the height of the tuna can and long enough to be rolled up into three or four coils and placed inside the can. Leave some space in between each coil. Melt paraffin in a coffee can and pour the liquid paraffin into the tuna can containing cardboard coils. Do not fill the can with paraffin; leave about 1/8 to 1/4 inches (3 to 6 millimeters) of cardboard above the top of the paraffin. When the paraffin has solidified, the cardboard will act as a wick. Make sure the cardboard does not stick up higher than the top of the can because this makes it difficult to reduce the heat while cooking and put out the flame when finished. The heat can be reduced by covering part of the can with the lid that has been removed. See figure 6.1.

The cooking surface or stove is constructed out of a 1-gallon (4-liter) tin-can (see figure 6.2). Most school cafeterias can easily provide these cans since vegetables are usually packed in them. To make a stove, completely remove one end of the can and crimp down any rough edges with pliers. Turn the can upside down with the open end on the ground. The top of the can (unopened end) will be the cook surface. With a punch-type can opener, punch about five holes in the side of the can, close to the top and only on one side. At the bottom of the can (open end) and on the side opposite the holes, cut a flap in the can's side that is as wide as the tuna can. Use tin snips to make the two cuts and then fold the flap up.

Figure 6.1 Buddy burner.

Figure 6.2 Tin-can or vagabond stove.

Figure 6.2 illustrates the cuts and punches for the stove.

Recipes for tin-can cooking include the following.

Bacon Pancakes

- Any pancake batter will work fine.
- Light the burner and place it under the stove, allowing a couple of minutes for the top to get hot.
- Place half a piece of bacon on the stove and fry it.

- When you have turned the bacon over and cooked it on the second side for a minute, pour pancake batter over the bacon.
- Use a spatula to turn the pancake and let it brown on both sides.
- If the stove gets too hot, use metal tongs to move the burner from under the stove for a few seconds and then back again.
- Be careful not to knock over the stove.
- The grease from the bacon keeps the pancake from sticking.

Fruit Pancakes

- Spray the top of stove with cooking oil, heat the stove, and pour pancake batter on it.
- Place fruit (such as blueberries or banana slices) on the uncooked pancake top.
- As the pancake begins to bubble, use a spatula to turn it over.
- The pancake is done when it begins to steam.

Instant Soup or Hot Cereal

- Heat or boil water in a small pan on top of the tin-can stove.
- The pan containing water should be small enough in diameter that its bottom is in contact with the flat surface of the stove.
- When heating water, always cover the pot. This will conserve fuel and water.

Foil-Packet Cooking

This is another Scout standby cooking technique, and it is a favorite for its easy cleanup. All you have to do is fold up the used foil packet and throw it away or recycle it—there's nothing to wash!

Equipment needs are heavy-duty aluminum foil, food, and seasonings. The fire requirements are enough hot coals of wood or charcoal to bury the packets in the coals. To construct a foil-packet dinner, lay out a sheet of foil approximately 18 by 18 inches (46 by 46 centimeters). Place the uncooked food in the middle of the square, season it, and fold the edges of the foil together over the food to make a leakproof packet.

Place the packet in the coals with a tool such as a shovel and cover it with coals. About every 15 minutes, turn the packet over to avoid burning one side of the dinner.

Recipes for foil-packet dinners are limited only by your imagination and food preferences. Feel free to experiment, but it is best to combine foods that have similar cooking time requirements.

Hamburger Stew

- Press hamburger meat into a patty no more than 1 inch (3 centimeters) thick.
- Slice potatoes, onions, and carrots.
- Season to taste with salt and pepper, oregano, and garlic powder.
- Cook for 30 minutes with good coal coverage (see figure 6.3, *a* and *b*).

Banana Boats

- Lay a banana on its side and cut away the top half of the peel.
- Cut out a V in the top of the banana along the top side of the banana (see figure 6.4). Eat the V.
- Break up a chocolate bar or use chocolate chips and put inside the V.
- On top of the chocolate, place miniature marshmallows or marshmallows that have been torn or cut in half.
- Wrap the whole banana in a square of foil, trying to keep the foil from touching the marshmallows.
- Place the packet carefully in the coals to allow the chocolate and marshmallows to melt.
- Cook for 5 to 8 minutes.
- Open the foil carefully and eat the warm banana and melted topping out of the bottom peel with a spoon.

Chicken Parmesan

- In an 18-inch (46-centimeter) square of foil, place chicken tenders seasoned with salt, pepper, and garlic powder.
- Spoon ready-to-eat spaghetti sauce onto the chicken, place sliced onion and mushrooms on top, and cover with parmesan cheese.

a

b

Figure 6.3 Hamburger stew in coals *(a)* and ready to eat *(b)*.

Figure 6.4 Cutting a V into the banana allows the chef to load it up with chocolate and marshmallows.

- Fold foil to make a leakproof packet and place it in the coals.
- Turn the packet over after 15 minutes in the coals.
- Cook for 30 minutes.

Dutch-Oven Cooking

This is a favorite cooking method of almost anyone who has ever eaten something cooked in a Dutch oven. A Dutch oven is actually a cast-iron or cast-aluminum pot that is designed to bake anything you can bake in your oven at home (see figure 6.5). It gets its heat from hot wood or charcoal coals.

Dutch ovens come in various sizes and often have a number imprinted on the lid that indicates the diameter of that particular oven. The most common sizes are 10 inches and 12 inches (25 centimeters and 30 centimeters) in diameter. They are most often used for baking or roasting, and the secret for success is the amount of heat on the bottom as compared to the top.

The cooking technique we are going to consider in this unit is baking. For best control of heat, it is a good idea to cook with the Dutch oven beside the fire rather than right in it. Another part of controlling the heat is putting coals on the lid instead of under the oven. Some people say the coals should be in a 1-to-3 ratio bottom to top, while others say it

should be a 1-to-2 ratio. The ratio is fairly easy to control when using charcoal, but with coals from a wood fire it is hard to be exact. Just keep the coals piled on top and keep the ash blown away. If too much ash builds up on the lid, it can act as an insulator. It is tempting to pick up the lid to check on the cooking progress. However, each time the lid is lifted it will delay the cooking by several minutes and may cause the bottom to burn.

Recipes for Dutch-oven baking include the following:

Upside-Down Cakes

This is a great first experience with baking in a Dutch oven.

- Empty a large can of fruit such as peaches into the bottom of the Dutch oven.
- Make sure that the bottom is thickly covered with the fruit and its juice.
- Open a box of cake mix (yellow cake works well) and dump the mix on top of the fruit.
- Spread out the mix so it is in a fairly even layer and place small dollops of butter on top of the mix. Sprinkle with brown sugar and cinnamon.
- Cook for the amount of time indicated on the box. You will start to smell the cake a few minutes before it is done.

Cookies

- Place a metal trivet in the Dutch oven and put cookie dough in a cake pan.
- Place the cake pan on top of the trivet and bake.
- Use more coals on top than on bottom.
- Cook for 5 to 10 minutes longer than the cookie recipe directions (due to no preheating).

Pizza

- Press heavy-duty aluminum foil onto the bottom of the Dutch oven. Foil should extend up the sides of the oven.
- Take the foil out of the oven and lightly spray with oil.
- Press out canned pizza dough onto the foil, forming the dough to the shape of the

Figure 6.5 Dutch oven.

bottom of the Dutch oven as indicated by the creases in the foil.

- Top dough with a thin coat of tomato paste, sprinkle with oregano, and top with mozzarella cheese.
- Other toppings can be added if desired.
- Arrange coals so most of the heat is coming from the top.
- Cook for 20 to 30 minutes.

Lasagna

- To make cleaning easier, use a foil pan in the bottom of the Dutch oven.
- Spray the pan with oil and lightly cover the bottom with spaghetti sauce.
- Layer cooked lasagna noodles, sauce, ricotta and mozzarella cheese, and more sauce. Repeat layering until the pan is almost full and top with mozzarella.
- Arrange coals so most of the heat is coming from the top.
- Cook for 20 to 30 minutes.

Anything that can be baked in your oven at home can be baked in a Dutch oven. Experiment and enjoy!

Solar-Funnel Cooking

Solar-funnel cooking is a unique cooking method that will not often be used when other options are available. However, it is one way to cook using heat from the sun. See figure 6.6 for an example of a solar funnel.

The materials needed to construct a solar-funnel cooker include a 2-by-4-foot (61-by-122-centimeter) sheet of cardboard or poster board (larger is okay), aluminum foil, glue, scissors or sharp knife, a glass jar with lid, black paint, and a large oven cooking bag with a twist tie.

1. Paint the outside of the glass jar and the lid black. A 1-quart (1-liter) canning jar with a lid works great.
2. In the middle of one of the 4-foot (122-centimeter) sides of the cardboard, cut out a half-circle with 6 inches (15 centimeters)

Figure 6.6　A solar funnel.

from the top of the half-circle to the edge of the cardboard to be cut out.

3. Glue aluminum foil onto the cardboard, shiny side up. Make the foil as smooth as possible.
4. Punch four holes in each short side of the cardboard so twist ties or brads can be used to join the edges together.
5. Bring the short edges of the cardboard together and secure with twist ties or brads.
6. Place the food to be cooked into the black glass jar and screw on the lid.
7. Place a 2-by-4-by-4-inch (5-by-10-by-10-centimeter) block of wood in bottom of the funnel as an insulator. Place the food jar on the block, blow air into the bag so it does not touch the jar or lid, and close the bag around the jar with a twist tie.
8. Place the entire bag and its contents inside the funnel near the bottom (see figure 6.6).
9. Place the solar-funnel cooker so that it faces the sun to capture as much sunlight as possible. Use a rock to hold the funnel in place or place the funnel inside a box that will hold it in position.

Tips for Solar-Funnel Cooking

- Wear sunglasses to protect your eyes when working with the funnel.

- Always use cooking pads or gloves when removing the jar and bag from the funnel after cooking.
- Open the plastic bag by untwisting the tie. Then carefully lift the jar out of the bag.
- Carefully open the jar, allowing steam to escape away from your face and arms.
- Avoid getting fingerprints and smudges on the inside surface of the funnel.
- Two to 3 cups of food in a 1-quart (1-liter) jar will usually cook in 1 to 1 1/2 hours on a sunny day.

There are no special recipes for this type of cooking, but there are guidelines for cooking different types of food, as follows.

Vegetables

Any fresh vegetables will cook fine without adding water. Just cut them into long slices to look like french fries. You can use potatoes, carrots, squash, beets, asparagus, and even corn on the cob. Cook about 1 1/2 hours.

Cereals and Grains

Cereals and grains include rice, barley, wheat, and oats.

- Mix two parts water to one part grain.
- To speed up the cooking process, let grain soak for a few hours before cooking.
- After 50 minutes of cooking, shake the jar to help ensure uniform cooking.
- Be sure to use gloves or thick pads because the jar will be hot.
- Cook for 1 1/2 to 2 hours.

Pasta and Dehydrated Soups

- Heat water to near boiling (50 to 70 minutes).
- Add pasta or soup mix.
- Shake the jar and cook for 15 minutes.
- Total cooking time is 65 to 85 minutes.

Bread and Cake

- Spray the inside of the jar with cooking oil to reduce sticking.
- Place dough or batter in the jar, no more than half full.

- Cooking time varies according to the amount of dough or batter but is usually 1 to 1 1/2 hours.

Cooking and Our World

All around the world cooking is happening. Although some foods are eaten raw, people have developed methods for cooking most foods. Cooking has both positive and negative effects in economic and ecological terms. This is especially true in developing countries. These countries have the common characteristics of widespread poverty, high birthrates, and economic dependence on more developed countries. Cooking is quite different from that in developed countries due to the fuel that is available. When there are limited resources, cooking methods become important.

Positive Economic Results of Cooking

- Fewer illnesses and deaths result from eating spoiled raw food.
- Jobs become available as cooks for others.

Negative Economic Results of Cooking

- In many parts of the world, women's time and energy is almost totally consumed with the search for cooking fuel. According to Solar Cookers International, many women and children carry up to 40 pounds (18 kilograms) of wood on their head and back after spending hours collecting it miles from their homes (www.solarcookers.org/basics/why.html).
- Excessive time required for collecting cooking fuel prevents other endeavors that could make positive economic contributions.
- About half of the world's households cook over open fires of wood, stubble, dung, and grass. According to McDonald (1997), this results in approximately 1.9 million deaths each year from indoor air pollution. Biomass smoke contains many harmful elements such as particulates and carbon monoxide, and coal smoke contains sulphur, nitrogen oxides, and hydrocarbons.

Positive Ecological Results of Cooking

There are no positive ecological effects of cooking.

Negative Ecological Results of Cooking

- In countries where wood is collected and used for cooking, the environment is being damaged by deforestation. This is happening in 40 of the world's poorest countries (www.solarcookers.org/basics/why.html).
- Deforestation leads to higher temperatures, lower levels of oxygen, and higher levels of carbon dioxide, which contribute to overall global warming.
- Wood gathered for cooking is not the number one reason for deforestation, but it contributes in the countries that are most at risk. Although cooking methods in developed countries primarily use means other than wood and charcoal, other fuels such as gas also come from natural resources and have economic and ecological effects.

OUTDOOR COOKING TECHNIQUES UNIT PLAN

Unit Objectives

Students will:

- be able to cook using a variety of methods,
- identify principles involved with changes of properties in matter and the transfer of energy, and
- discuss the economics of cooking for different peoples of the world.

Character Focus

Respect, responsibility, citizenship

Curriculum Areas

History, Language Arts, Physical Education, and Science

Assessment Activity

From a sheet picturing various items, have students list all items that are required for the different types of cooking. Indicate which type of cooking has the greatest total cost.

Outdoor Cooking Techniques Day Planner

Day	Topic	Concepts and skills	Teaching activities	Standards
1	Stick-roasting cooking	Equipment (green sticks, coals); roasting techniques; types of food	Show how green versus dead sticks respond to fire; students cook and eat biscuits.	Health 2 and 8; Physical Education 5 and 6; Science 8 and 9
2	Tuna-can burners and tin-can stoves	Purpose of a wick and paraffin in extended burning process; making a tuna-can burner and stove that draws heat upward	Show a completed tuna-can burner and its separate components; have student pairs make a burner and a tin-can stove. Discuss how they work.	Health 2 and 8; Language Arts 5 and 7; Physical Education 1, 5, and 6
3	Tin-can cooking	Controlling heat for cooking	Demonstrate using a lid and burner handle how to control heat; have students cook on top of the stoves they made the day before.	Health 2 and 8; Physical Education 1, 5, and 6; Science 8 and 9
4	Foil-packet cooking	Searing, steaming, baking	Demonstrate how to make a foil cooking packet and how to place it in the fire. Students make packets and cook.	Health 2 and 8; Physical Education 1, 5, and 6; Science 8 and 9
5*	Dutch-oven cooking	Principles and purposes of baking and applications for a Dutch oven	Introduce principles; allow student groups to each bake something in a Dutch oven. Discuss advantages and disadvantages of each type of cooking.	Civics 24; Geography 6; History 2; Language Arts 5, 7, and 8; Physical Education 1, 5, and 6; Science 8 and 9
6	Solar funnel	Why a solar funnel works; why a bag is needed; why black absorbs heat	Show a completed solar funnel that is cooking or has cooked something; discuss how it works. Student pairs make solar funnels and cooking jars.	Science 8 and 9
7	Solar-funnel cooking	Techniques of using a solar funnel; cost of fuel, equipment, time, effort	Student pairs cook with the equipment they made the day before. Discuss the safety issues of solar cooking and its advantages in terms of economics.	Health 2 and 8; History 2; Language Arts 5, 7, and 8; Physical Education 1, 5, and 6; Science 8 and 9
8*	Cooking around the world	Economics and ecology of cooking	Small groups of students compete in a cooking contest. Winner has lowest time, least human physical effort, least monetary cost, and least harm to environment.	Civics 24; Economics 1; Language Arts 5, 7, and 8; Physical Education 1, 5, and 6

* Has a corresponding lesson plan.

DUTCH-OVEN COOKING

Lesson Objectives

Students will:

- learn to cook in a Dutch oven, and
- identify advantages and disadvantages of each type of cooking they have experienced.

Character Focus

Patience, responsibility

Curriculum Standards

Geography 6; History 2; Language Arts 5, 7, and 8; Physical Education 1, 5, and 6; Science 8 and 9; Civics 24

Materials

- One Dutch oven per group
- Charcoal as heat source for each Dutch oven
- Fire-starter liquid or charcoal-starter chimneys
- Ingredients for fruit upside-down cakes (enough for each Dutch oven to bake a cake); see page 93 for recipe
- Ingredients for Dutch-oven pizza (one pizza for entire class); see page 93 for recipe
- One shovel for each Dutch oven
- One pair leather gloves and pliers for each oven (to use in removing lid)
- Small paper plate and spoon for each student

Preparation

1. Start charcoal for cooking pizza.
2. Begin cooking pizza early enough so it will be done in time for class. Pizza does not have to be hot; it could be done earlier and left in the Dutch oven for the class to see.
3. Set up Dutch oven as if it were cooking, even if coals are not lighted and burning, to illustrate the concept of more heat on top than bottom.
4. Have recipe for upside-down cake printed on cards for groups at each Dutch oven.
5. Start charcoal burning for each Dutch oven.

Lesson Sequence

Introduce the concept of baking, with heated air evenly surrounding the food, and discuss how a Dutch oven simulates a conventional oven inside a house. In addition to the functions of a Dutch oven, mention that these ovens were used for cooking as wagon trains made their way across the continent.

Activity 1

1. Show the class the Dutch oven set up for cooking pizza and discuss the concept of baking with more heat on top than bottom to prevent burning on the bottom. △

2. Serve each student a small piece of pizza (even if only a bite).

3. While students eat, continue the discussion of how to use a Dutch oven effectively.

Questions

- What do you notice about the number of coals used for cooking? (They're not a big bed of coals; there's more on top than on bottom.)

- What might happen to the food if there were the same number of coals on bottom as on top, or more on bottom than on top? (Food would burn on the bottom because it is hotter closer to the fire.)

- How does the concept of a ratio relate to Dutch-oven cooking? (The number of coals on bottom is compared to the number of coals on top. For example, for a 1-to-2 ratio when there are 8 coals on bottom there must be 8×2, or 16, coals on top.)

Possible Character Affirmation

This class is being patient while waiting to get your piece of pizza. Patience is very important, and I am proud of you all.

Activity 2

1. Organize students into groups based on the number of Dutch ovens available for student cooking.

2. Organize each group into subgroups by activity, such as instruction reading, coal delivery and placement control, and recipe mixing.

3. Hand out instruction cards to each group and have groups go to their Dutch oven to begin cooking.

4. Move from group to group, monitoring safety and groups' progress in following instructions. Ask questions and make comments.

Questions

- How is this cooking process different from foil-packet cooking? (Both sides of foil packets were in contact with coals; it took less time; foil is thinner.)

- What is actually happening during any cooking process? (The application of heat changes the molecular structure of the food.)

- What is heat? (Energy)

Possible Character Affirmations

- This group is doing a good job at being patient while your cake bakes by not lifting up the lid.

- Milo and Joanne, you were responsible in doing your job carefully while moving the hot coals. Thank you for being responsible. Who can tell me why it is a matter of responsibility to walk while carrying hot coals with a shovel rather than running?

Activity 3

1. Have each group tell the whole class when its cake is done so everyone can take a look before the group serves the cake.

2. Each group eats its cake. Take leftovers to the teachers' lounge.

Discussion and Review

- Which cooking method is the most Leave No Trace (LNT) friendly? (See appendix B for list of LNT principles.)
- What does it mean for a cooking method to be LNT friendly? (It has little effect on the environment in terms of getting fuel, affecting the air, affecting the ground, and leaving waste.)

Teaching Tips

- Set up cooking areas far enough apart to allow group movement around Dutch ovens without crowding.
- Put piles of sand at each cooking area to prevent fires from scarring the ground.

Safety Tips

- Always have buckets of water handy when using any type of open fire.
- Remind students of the possibilities for getting burned and the need to be aware, use gloves and pliers, and take care with shovels.

Possible Character Affirmation ⮌

It is very responsible for all of you to be careful around the hot coals and to resist the temptation to take the lid off too soon.

COOKING AROUND THE WORLD

Lesson Objectives

Students will:

- discuss the energy and economics of various types of cooking,
- consider the effects of various types of cooking on the environment, and
- demonstrate caring for classmates through language and actions as well as for people in other parts of the world by considering the requirements of different living conditions.

Character Focus

Caring

Curriculum Standards

Civics 24; Economics 1; Language Arts 5, 7, and 8; Physical Education 1, 5, and 6

Materials

- Sand
- Three sticks for stick-cooking group
- Aluminum foil
- Items for one solar funnel (see page 94)
- Dutch oven
- Charcoal and wood for fires
- Water buckets, pliers, and shovels for the Dutch oven and foil-packet groups
- Sunglasses for use with solar funnels
- Food for each group: 1 cup flour, 1 teaspoon baking powder, 1/4 teaspoon salt, and 1 cup milk per group
- Instructions for each cooking method, including biscuit dough recipe (see Cook-Off Biscuit sidebar; page 104)

Preparation

1. Have sand areas ready for building open fires.
2. Have biscuit ingredients for each group ready for measuring.
3. Have instruction and recipe cards ready for each group.
4. Have charcoal ready to light when class begins or have it already burning, depending upon the length of class.
5. Have wood for fire scattered widely around the perimeter of the area so it takes time to gather it.

Lesson Sequence

Begin class by asking students to identify all of the resources they can think of that are required for cooking. Include all types of cooking as well as all types of resources (both environmental and human).

Activity

1. Divide the class into four groups. Assign one group each to stick cooking, foil-packet cooking, solar-funnel cooking, and Dutch-oven cooking. ⌂ ⌐

2. Introduce the concept that cooking requires resources other than the food to be cooked, such as wood, charcoal, and utensils.

Questions

- What type of resources does cooking require other than food? (Time, human energy to acquire fuel, fuel from the environment, resources to construct cooking equipment)
- Present the idea that today the class will test the time each method requires and compare the resources.

Continue with the Activity

3. Hand out instruction cards with recipes to each group. Each group will cook biscuit dough equal to three biscuits.

4. Have each group pursue their cooking assignment while they keep track of the time.

Questions

- Which type of cooking is most like the cooking that happens where you live? (None, our fuel source is readily available.)
- How much additional time and energy goes into producing charcoal? (Unknown but significant)
- Why is our time measurement for using charcoal not accurate? (Charcoal has to be made, plus it had already been lighted when we got to class.)
- Why is time considered a resource? (It is useful.)
- So although the charcoal was already burning when class began, it would take much more resources to use charcoal than we saw today? (Yes, time, energy, and material go into making the charcoal bricks.)
- What about people all over the world who do not have our material resources? What type of resources do they use? (They use more time and energy; we use more fuel and environmental resources.)
- Which of these cooking methods is the most resource friendly? (Solar funnel)

Possible Character Affirmations

- Thank you, Adela and Jessie, for caring about the safety of your classmates and reminding them to wear sunglasses with the solar funnel.
- I can tell from our discussion today that some of you really care about people's needs in other parts of the world.

Teaching Tips

- When a group's food is done, they yell out that they are ready, and the time is recorded.
- Before class ends, get the whole class together to discuss the time that each cooking method required and the resources needed for each.
- Set up cooking areas far enough apart to allow freedom of group movement without crowding to improve safety conditions.
- Monitor groups closely to reinforce safety practices and reduce carelessness.

Safety Tips

- Always have buckets of water handy when using any type of open fire.
- Remind students of possibilities for getting burned as well as the need to be aware; to use gloves, pliers, and shovels with Dutch ovens; to use shovels with foil packets; and to use sunglasses and gloves with solar funnels.

Possible Character Affirmations

It is very responsible of all of you to remind each other about safety and cooking procedures.

Cook-Off Biscuits

1/4 cup flour

1/4 teaspoon baking powder

2 small pinches of salt

2 teaspoons oil

3 teaspoons milk

Mix ingredients well in a plastic sandwich bag. Place in the cooking materials for your method of cooking.

From *Interdisciplinary Teaching Through Outdoor Education,* by Camille Bunting, 2006, Champaign, IL: Human Kinetics.

Cook-Off Biscuits

1/4 cup flour

1/4 teaspoon baking powder

2 small pinches of salt

2 teaspoons oil

3 teaspoons milk

Mix ingredients well in a plastic sandwich bag. Place in the cooking materials for your method of cooking.

From *Interdisciplinary Teaching Through Outdoor Education,* by Camille Bunting, 2006, Champaign, IL: Human Kinetics.

Cook-Off Biscuits

1/4 cup flour

1/4 teaspoon baking powder

2 small pinches of salt

2 teaspoons oil

3 teaspoons milk

Mix ingredients well in a plastic sandwich bag. Place in the cooking materials for your method of cooking.

From *Interdisciplinary Teaching Through Outdoor Education,* by Camille Bunting, 2006, Champaign, IL: Human Kinetics.

Land Navigation

All outdoor pursuits require the ability to find your way from place to place, but this ability is especially important when traveling through the backcountry. The skills of navigation are important for activities such as cross-country skiing, mountain biking, hunting and fishing, hiking and backpacking, boating, climbing, caving, and canyoneering. The most easily accessible and least expensive tools for land navigation are a map and compass, but they are useless without adequate knowledge and skill. In fact, many reports from search and rescue operations show that poor navigation either causes or contributes to accidents. In these accidents, it was not that a map and compass were unavailable, but that the people involved did not know how to use them properly.

Why do you need to learn how to use a map and compass for navigation when there is a Global Positioning System (GPS) to tell you where to go? Because it's fun! It is also one of the best outdoor activities for interdisciplinary teaching. A hand-held global positioning receiver is an excellent tool for navigation and can be quite helpful and fun to use. A GPS receives signals from four satellites to indicate location in terms of longitude, latitude, and altitude. With this information, it is easier to find a location.

However, the GPS should be supplemented with a paper map and a compass. Anything that is powered by batteries is always at risk of being useless when the batteries run down, so maps and compasses have not been made obsolete by GPS. Teachers often shy away from teaching map and compass skills because of a lack of experience, so this unit is presented at an introductory level. It begins with how to use a compass, then how to use maps, and finally how to use them together. Orienteering clubs are located in most major cities and sponsor orienteering meets (races using a map and compass for route finding) several times a year. When you get to this unit, you may want to try out an orienteering meet. There are usually teaching sessions for novices before each meet, and different levels of challenge are always available.

How to Use a Compass

A compass is basically a 360° protractor that has a needle that will point to magnetic north. By referring to the north (red) end of the magnetic needle and lining it up with the orienting arrow (shed) that is imprinted on the bottom inside the compass housing, you can read the direction (or the number of degrees from north) that you are going to travel. The direction-of-travel arrow (DTA) on the base of the compass points the way. Refer to figure 7.1 to learn the parts of the compass (7.1*a*) and become familiar with the cardinal and intercardinal directions (7.1*b*).

The cardinal directions include the four main points on the compass—north, located on the top; south, located on the bottom; east, located on the right side; and west, located on the left side. Intercardinal directions are located between each of the four cardinal points.

The parallel lines on the base of the compass, called orienting lines, are used in more advanced activities.

Steps for Orienting to Magnetic North

1. Hold the compass level in your hand in front of your stomach (see figure 7.2).

2. Position the compass so the DTA is pointing straight out from the midline of the body.

3. While holding the compass securely, turn the dial until north lines up with the DTA.

4. Turn yourself and the compass, still holding it flat and in front of you with the DTA pointing straight out, until the red end of the magnetic needle points to the letter N ("put red in the shed").

5. You are now facing magnetic north and the DTA is pointing to magnetic north.

Procedure for Traveling in a Particular Direction

1. If you want to travel in the direction of magnetic north, after you've oriented yourself to magnetic north, sight a sta-

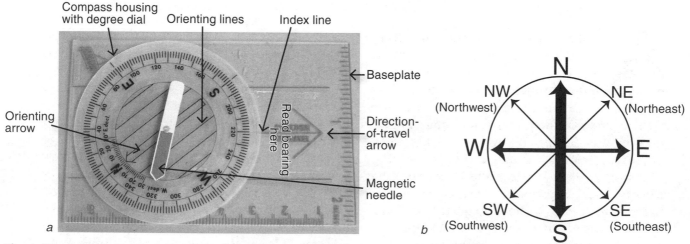

Figure 7.1   To learn to navigate, it is necessary to be familiar with the parts of a compass *(a)* and cardinal directions *(b)*.

Figure 7.2 Hold the compass flat in one hand out in front of the stomach. If you hold the compass so the arrow points off to one side, it will be difficult to walk in the intended direction.

tionary object in the distance that is in line with the DTA.

2. Keep your eyes on that object and walk toward it. You do not need to look at your compass.

3. When you get to the object, bring the compass back up in front of you. Make sure to put red in the shed, sight another distant object in line with the DTA, and move toward it.

4. If there is no object in line with the DTA, send a partner out in front of you and give directions for the partner to stop in line with the DTA.

5. Walk to where your partner is standing and repeat the previous step.

6. To travel in a direction other than magnetic north, turn the dial to line up the degree reading (bearing) for the correct direction. For example, to go in the direction of 210°, turn the dial so that 210° is in line with the DTA.

7. Turn yourself and the compass (holding it level and in front of you) until red is in the shed.

8. If you are holding the compass correctly, the DTA will be pointing straight out in front of you toward 210°.

Pace and Pace Factor

A pace is equal to two steps. When standing with your feet side by side, stepping forward with the left foot and then the right foot is one pace. Counting paces is easier than counting steps simply because the numbers do not get so high and you can count more slowly.

A pace factor is used to compute the number of paces needed to travel a specified distance, or to determine the distance between points when you do not have a measuring instrument. Pace factors are individual and must be determined by each student. To calculate pace factors, mark off 100 feet or meters. Students should start at one end of the measured distance and walk using their natural stride to the other end. To walk in a straight line, they should spot an object in the distance that is in line with them at the starting point. That object should be their focus point as they walk and count their paces. Students should walk the measured distance at least three times and count the number of paces each time. If the number varies, average them by adding them together and dividing by the total number of attempts. For example, if you walk 100 feet (30 meters) three times and get 20, 22, and 21 paces, your average number would be 21. To convert 21 into a pace factor, place a decimal point in front (.21). Your pace factor is thus .21. You can then use your pace factor to calculate how many paces you would have to take to go 75 feet (23 meters) by multiplying $75 \times .21 = 15.75$. Someone with a pace factor of .20 (20 paces in 100 feet [30 meters]) would thus take 15 paces to go 75 feet [27 meters].

Compass Course

A compass course consists of different types of activities that use a compass without a map. There are specific starting points and ending points, with distances to travel in directions designated by compass bearings, such as "From starting point 1, go 45 feet (14 meters) at 40°." The pace-factor compass course on page 127 is a sample layout. The students would not be given this sheet, however. They would be given a set of directions like the following:

Start 1

27°—30 feet (9 meters)

324°—95 feet (30 meters)

204°—40 feet (12 meters)

260°—115 feet (35 meters)

Be sure to notice the direction of north on the sample pace-factor course. If you want to use these distances and degree readings, you must have adequate room to place the starting points on the south side of the area. Different-colored hula hoops make good finish markers because they allow for a little variation as compared to a small stake. However, be sure to stake down the hula hoops to keep them from being inadvertently kicked out of position.

In addition to incorporating pace factor in a pace-factor course, pace factor can also be used when using some form of map or diagram. Number of paces per distance, area to be covered, and approximate locations can all be enhanced by the knowledge of pace factor.

How to Use a Map

There are several different types of maps, such as general building locator maps for determining where a particular building is located or where you are inside of a building (see figure 7.3), highway maps for identifying roads, and topographic maps for identifying terrain features. Whatever type of map you are using, it is important to orient the map and yourself. This means that the map is turned in the same direction as things actually exist. For example, if you are looking at a building locator map mounted on a wall, it will usually have a star that identifies where you are in relation to the map. That star helps you orient yourself in relation to the map.

The same principle is true of all maps—you must know where you are on the map. To orient a map that you can hold in your hands, turn it so the north edge or north-pointing arrow is actually pointing north. This means that the roads and trails on the map run in the same directions as they do in actuality. Sometimes the process of orienting a map is called getting it "true to the world."

On most maps, important information for interpreting the map can be found at the bottom or in the margins. A locator map often has numbered buildings or rooms and the numbers are associated with names in a legend. A highway map will generally have a publication date (road construction can make quite a difference) and a legend indicating the meaning of different road colors. A topographic map, which is designed to illustrate terrain features, has too many illustrations per map to include a legend, so the U.S. Geologic Survey publishes a separate legend that applies to the maps they produce. There is also information printed on the bottom margin of a topographic map that is important for using the map accurately (see figure 7.4).

One part of the topographic map's bottom margin is a diagram with a V, a star, and some letters and numbers. This is the indication of the difference between true North, or what is also known as geographic north, and the north that

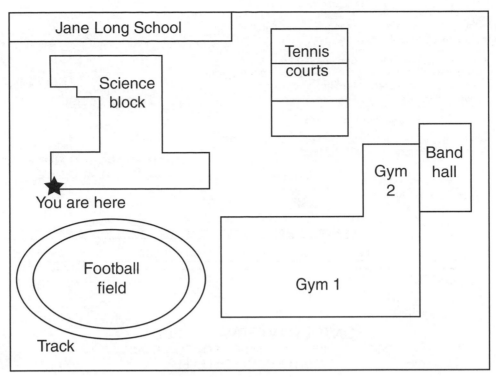

If you had a class in the Science block and then had to go to the band hall, how could you use this map to help you find the way to the band hall?

Figure 7.3 Sample locator map.

a compass indicates, or magnetic north. The two norths are different because the magnetic field of the Earth is about 11° different from geographic north, where all longitude lines come together at the top of the globe. Maps are generally drawn with the top edge corresponding to geographic north, and if the map is not drawn directly in line with both magnetic north and geographic north, there will be a difference between the two. The V on the bottom margin of topographic maps indicates that difference. For example, Madison, Wisconsin, and Birmingham, Alabama, are almost directly in line with both magnetic and geographic north. However, if you are west of that line, your magnetic compass will point to the east of geographic north. If you are east of the 0° declination line, your compass would point west of the geographic north of your location. See figure 7.5 for some general declination lines for locations in the United States. These lines are not usually printed on maps.

To use a compass and map together, you must adjust your compass for the angle of declination of the location of the map. As figure 7.5 indicates, the Salt Lake City area is approximately 15° west of magnetic north, which means that a compass in that area will point 15° east of geographic north. To accurately use a compass with a map of the Salt Lake City area, you should turn your compass dial 15° toward the east before beginning to use the map and compass together. To turn the compass dial, begin with the dial set to 360° (north), then turn the dial so that the N on the dial is moving toward where the E was located when the compass was set to 360°. This means that the compass is now actually set on 345°. This moves the direction of travel back to the west by 15° to correspond to the north of the printed map. If you were in Harrisburg, Pennsylvania, with a westerly declination of 10°, you would turn the compass dial 10° toward the W, which would set the compass on 10°.

Interpreting the colored lines, areas, and other symbols is the first step in using topographic maps. Features are shown as points, lines, or areas, depending on their size and

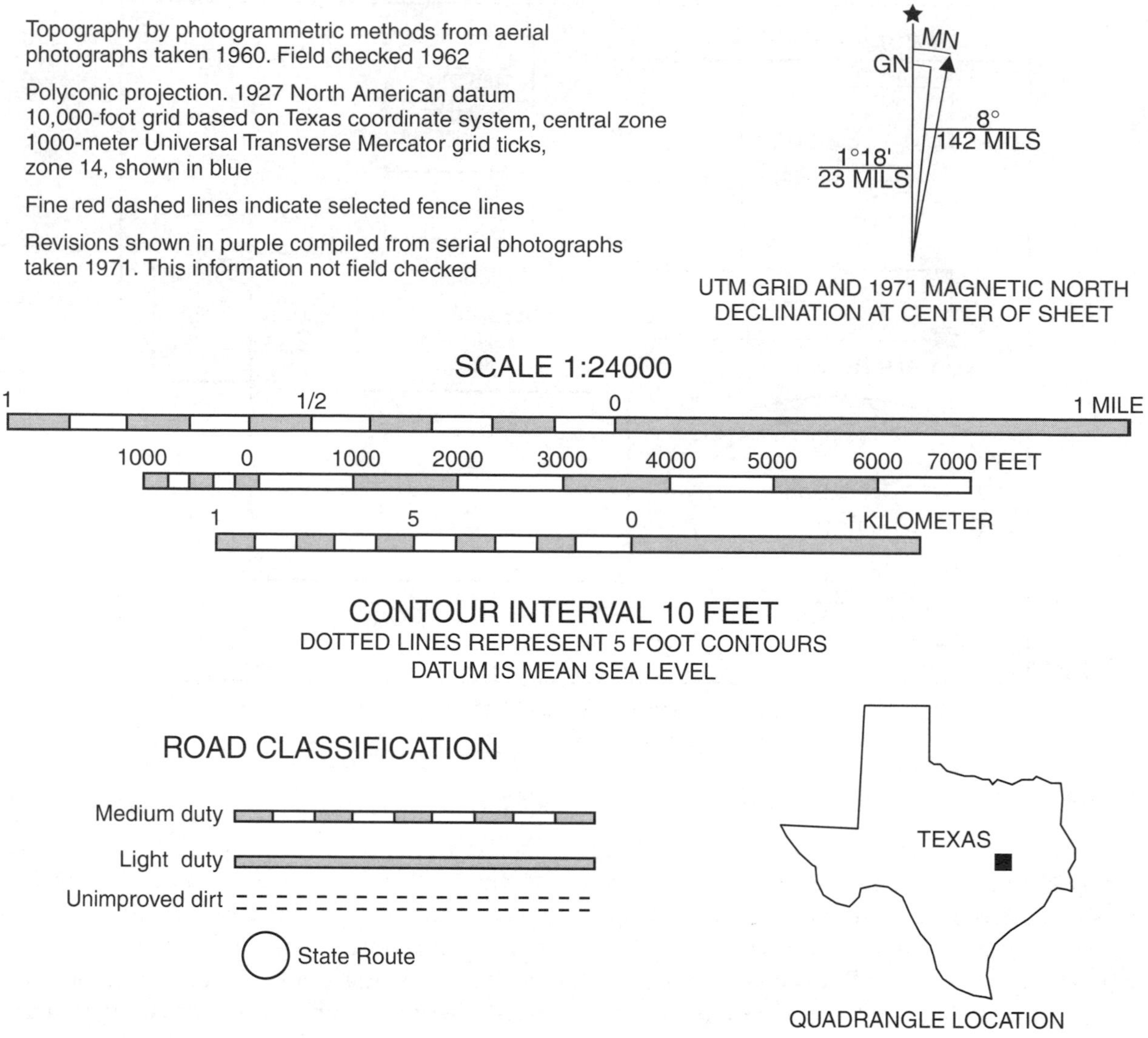

Topography by photogrammetric methods from aerial photographs taken 1960. Field checked 1962

Polyconic projection. 1927 North American datum
10,000-foot grid based on Texas coordinate system, central zone
1000-meter Universal Transverse Mercator grid ticks,
zone 14, shown in blue

Fine red dashed lines indicate selected fence lines

Revisions shown in purple compiled from serial photographs taken 1971. This information not field checked

UTM GRID AND 1971 MAGNETIC NORTH
DECLINATION AT CENTER OF SHEET

MN
GN
8°
142 MILS
1°18'
23 MILS

SCALE 1:24000

1   1/2   0   1 MILE

1000   0   1000   2000   3000   4000   5000   6000   7000 FEET

1   5   0   1 KILOMETER

CONTOUR INTERVAL 10 FEET
DOTTED LINES REPRESENT 5 FOOT CONTOURS
DATUM IS MEAN SEA LEVEL

ROAD CLASSIFICATION

Medium duty
Light duty
Unimproved dirt

○ State Route

TEXAS

QUADRANGLE LOCATION

Figure 7.4   The bottom margin of a map holds important information for properly interpreting the map.

extent. For example, individual houses may be shown as small black squares. For larger buildings, the actual shapes are mapped. In densely developed areas, most individual buildings are omitted and an area tint is shown. On some maps, post offices, churches, city halls, and other landmark buildings are shown within the tinted area.

The first features usually noticed on a topographic map are area features such as vegetation (green), water (blue), updated information (purple), and densely developed areas (gray or red). Many features are shown by lines that may be straight, curved, solid, dashed, dotted, or in any combination thereof. The colors of the lines usually indicate similar kinds or classes of information: brown for topographic contours; blue for lakes, streams, irrigation ditches, and so on; red for land grids and important roads; black for other roads and trails, railroads, and boundaries; and purple for features that have been updated using aerial photography but have not been field verified.

Various point symbols are used to depict features such as buildings, campgrounds, springs, water tanks, mines, survey control points, and wells. Names of places and features also are shown in a color corresponding to the type of feature. Many features are identified by labels, such as substation or golf course.

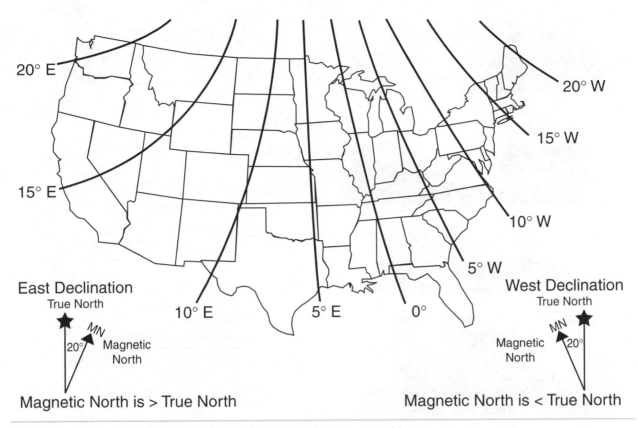

Figure 7.5 General indications of how declination differs across the United States.

Topographic contours are shown in brown lines of different widths. Each contour is a line of equal elevation; therefore, contours never cross. They show the general shape of the terrain. To help the user determine elevation, index contours (usually every fourth or fifth contour) are wider. The narrower intermediate and supplementary contours found between the index contours show more details of the land surface shape. Contours that are very close together represent steep slopes. Widely spaced contours or an absence of contours mean that the ground slope is relatively level. The elevation difference between adjacent contour lines, called the contour interval, is selected to best show the general shape of the terrain. A map of a relatively flat area may have a contour interval of 10 feet (3 meters) or fewer. Maps in mountainous areas may have contour intervals of 100 feet (30 meters) or more. Elevation values are shown at frequent intervals on the index contour lines to facilitate their identification as well as to enable the user to interpolate the values of adjacent contours. Figure 7.6 gives a side view of elevation changes with their corresponding contour lines to the side.

Being able to read, understand, and incorporate map-reading skills can be beneficial in everyday life. Reading city bus, subway, or road maps are a few examples. These skills are even more important when functioning in the outdoors. An even greater advantage for outdoor functioning, though, is the ability to use the compass in combination with a map.

Using the Compass and Map Together

There are several ways to use a map and compass together. For orienteering competitions, special maps are used that account for the declination of the area. For our purposes, we will not consider these types of map adjustments.

Most often, a compass and map are used together to find the direction of travel from one

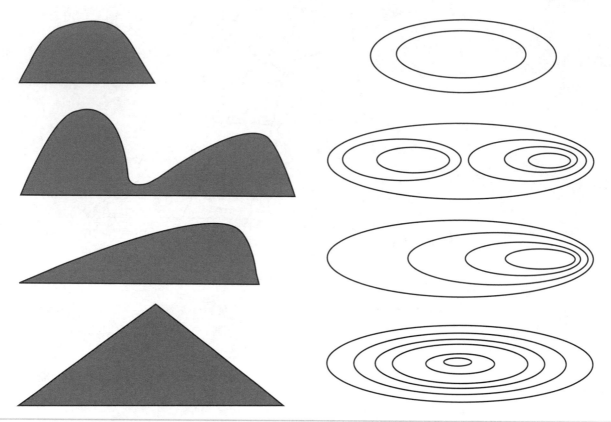

Figure 7.6 Topographic maps use contour lines to indicate changes in elevation.

point to another on the map and then determine the compass bearing to follow while traveling to the destination point. For example, using the sample map in figure 7.7, locate the trailhead at Spence Park and Moon Lake and draw a line from the trailhead to Moon Lake. Since there is no trail going to Moon Lake, you will need to use your compass to find the way. Use the following steps to determine the direction for your hike.

1. Find the angle of declination on the map and adjust your compass accordingly.

   - If the declination is toward the east, adjust the compass dial by turning it to the right (toward the east if you are facing north) the number of degrees equaling the declination. For example, if the declination is 8° east, you would set your compass to 352°.

   - If the declination is toward the west, adjust the compass dial by turning it to the left (toward the west if you are facing north) the number of degrees equaling the declination. For example, if the declination is 12° west, you would set your compass to 12°.

2. Orient the map. Put the side edge of the compass baseplate in line with the north–south line on the map (usually the map's edge). Turn map and compass together until the north end of the magnetic needle is lined up inside the north-orienting arrow (put red in the shed).

3. Keeping the map oriented, place the edge of the compass base along the line from the trailhead to Moon Lake. Always make sure the DTA points toward your desired destination.

4. Holding the map and compass securely in place, turn the compass dial to line up the magnetic needle and the north-orienting arrow.

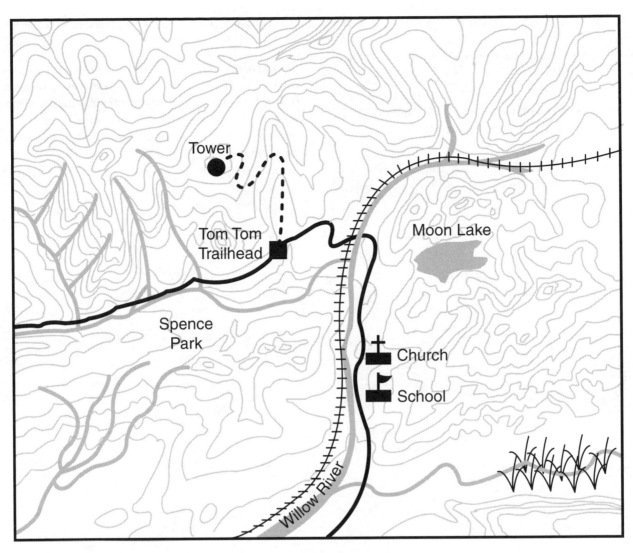

Contour interval 100 feet

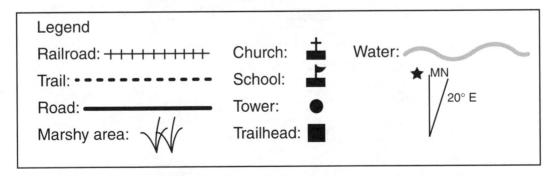

Figure 7.7 Sample topographic map for using a compass and map together.

From *Interdisciplinary Teaching Through Outdoor Education,* by Camille Bunting, 2006, Champaign, IL: Human Kinetics.

5. The degree reading (bearing) for the direction of travel will be lined up with the index line inside the compass dial and the DTA.

6. Pick up the compass, hold it level at waist height, and turn yourself until red is in the shed. You are now facing the direction you want to travel.

7. Sight an object in the distance that is in line with your DTA and walk to it. Repeat this process until you arrive at your destination.

Learning to use a map and compass is not only a useful skill, it can be fun and exciting. It has broad application in other subject areas such as math, geography, technology, and can be an excellent interdisciplinary activity. Many local orienteering clubs are happy to send one of their members to help students and teachers learn these skills.

LAND NAVIGATION UNIT PLAN

Unit Objectives

Students will:

- use a compass and follow bearings to get from point to point,
- analyze different maps to determine the location of various features and points,
- orient a map without a compass,
- use a map and compass together to get from one designated point to another, and
- exercise patience and caring with classmates while everyone is learning and practicing the skills.

Character Focus

Patience, caring, perseverance

Curriculum Areas

Physical Education, Science, Language Arts, Health, Math, Social Studies

Land Navigation Day Planner

Day	Topic	Concepts and skills	Teaching activities	Standards
1*	Using a compass	Cardinal directions; compass parts; orienting the compass; direction finding	Do cardinal direction story activity; do Silver Dollar Game in a triangle, square, and hexagon; do Circle Compass Game.	Language Arts 8; Math 2 and 5; Physical Education 1, 5, and 6
2*	Paces and pace factor	Counting paces to measure distance; using multiplication to figure pace factor; going around obstacles	Count paces per 100 feet (30 meters) three times and take average; do compass course with distances and bearings.	Math 2, 3, and 4; Physical Education 1 and 5
3*	Map and compass orienteering	Reinforcement of skills from previous 2 days; using a map	Do compass course with longer distances and multiple bearings; use map to locate markers around school.	Geography 1 and 4; Math 2 and 3; Physical Education 1 and 5
4*	Using a map	Different types of maps and their components; orienting a map	Students look at various maps and orient a map of their town and then a highway map that includes their town.	Geography 1 and 4; Language Arts 5 and 7; Physical Education 5
5	Map making	Making a rough map and making a map and compass course; using the compass to sight bearings	Students make rough maps of a large outdoor area on the school grounds; use the map to make a compass course for other students.	Geography 1 and 4; Language Arts 8; Physical Education 5 and 6
6	Map and compass orienteering	Reinforcement of knowledge and skills	Students race through a teacher-made map and compass course.	Physical Education 1, 5, and 6

* Has a corresponding lesson plan.

Lesson Objectives

Students will:

- use cardinal directions and a compass to orient themselves, and
- use a compass to follow degree readings (bearings).

Character Focus

Caring

Curriculum Standards

Language Arts 8; Math 2 and 5; Physical Education 1, 5, and 6

Materials

- One compass per student (ideal) but at least one for every pair of students
- Cardinal direction story (see Direction Story on page 119)

Circle Compass Game

- Lettered stakes or cones
- 50-foot (15-meter) tape measure or string
- Hammer

Preparation

Set up Circle Compass Game (see the Circle Compass Game on page 120 for diagram and details).

Lesson Sequence

1. Introduce the importance of being able to find your way and the useful tools of a compass and a map.
2. Teach students how use the compass, then a map, and then the two together.

Activity 1

1. Introduce the cardinal directions and read the Ninja Pet Blanket Story on page 119 with students facing the directions in the story.
2. About halfway through the story, move the markers for north, south, east, and west about two steps to the left or right and continue reading. See if the students pay attention to the markers and change their direction as the story continues.

Questions

- How many of you noticed that I changed the compass halfway through the story?
- How many of you adjusted to those new directions? It's important to pay attention to your compass.

Possible Character Affirmation

Caleb, it was caring of you to let others know about the change of directions.

Activity 2

1. Show a large diagram of a compass with all the parts labeled. △ ∟

2. Hand out the compasses and have students identify each part on their compass.

3. Explain how to use a compass to determine which direction is north. Have everyone face north, then west, then southeast, then 190°, until they can set a compass with a bearing they are given and face that direction.

Teaching Tip

Make sure everyone is holding the compass flat in one hand out in front of the stomach, with the DTA pointing straight out ahead. Some will have a tendency to hold the compass so the arrow points off to one side, which will make it difficult for them to walk in the intended direction.

Questions

Chantal, what object do you see that your compass is pointing to when it is set at 190°? Jackie, what object is your compass pointing to? Why aren't they both pointing to the same object?" (Chantal and Jackie should be in different places and pointing to two different places that are the same distance apart as the distance between Chantal and Jackie.)

Activity 3

1. Silver Dollar Game—Students spread out on the playground and mark their starting spot with their notebook. Have everyone set their compass to 0°. Have them spot a distant target and walk 10 paces. Then have them set their compass to 120° and walk 10 paces, and then 240° and 10 paces. (Students should be close to their starting spot.) △

2. Repeat Silver Dollar Game two more times, adding 90° after each set of 10 paces and then 60° and sets of 10 paces.

Questions

- What geometric shapes did we just walk? (A triangle with 120°, a square with 90°, and a hexagon with 60°.)
- What do the compass bearings represent in the geometric shapes? (Angles)
- If we wanted to walk in the shape of an octagon, how could we figure out what bearings to use? (Divide 360 by the number of sides of the shape.) ∟

Activity 4

Do the Circle Compass Game if time and resources are available. See the Circle Compass Game at the end of this chapter for instructions. This activity will provide students with additional practice at setting and sighting a line for travel.

Discussion and Review

- All directions are degree measurements from which cardinal direction? (North-0°)
- What are the major cardinal directions? (North, south, east, west)
- How can you go in a specific direction without looking down at the compass the whole time? (Before you start walking, spot a stationary object in line with the DTA and keep your eyes on it as you walk.)
- What number of degrees do you add each time if you want to walk in a triangle? Why? (A triangle has three sides, and 360° divided by 3 = 120°)
- Tomorrow, we'll learn how to go specific distances while using our compass.

Teaching Tips

Pair students who catch on quickly with students who need help. Sometimes it will be those who don't usually excel in physical activities helping those who do—a nice change for the new helpers!

Possible Character Affirmations

- If someone cared enough to help you out, it would be great if you would thank them for doing it. △ ☺
- Overall, this class has been caring, helpful, and patient with one another, and I would like to congratulate you all for that.

Direction Story

Have the class stand in an area around which you have placed signs indicating the cardinal directions. Ask everyone to face north while you give instructions for the activity.

Instructions

Tell students, "I am going to read a story that uses the directions we have just talked about. Each time you hear a directional word in the story, turn to face that direction. Be ready, because some of them might come pretty fast!"

Ninja Pet Blanket Story

Early one morning the Ninja King of the West brought many of his tribe to the South City to help the South Ninja tribe repair its eastern wall. As strange as it may seem, the Ninja King of the West had long golden hair. When the tribe members of the South saw the Ninja King of the West coming with his long golden hair and his many ninja tribesmen, they thought an attack was upon them. Because their eastern wall had crumbled and needed repair, the Ninja tribe members of the South decided to run outside of their crumbling Eastern wall and split into two groups. One group would hide outside of the southern wall and the other group would hide outside the northern wall.

Suddenly, the Ninja Prince of the Northwest arrived with his new bride, the Ninja Princess of the East. They had brought their most highly treasured pets: four southeast miniature donkeys, two potbellied northwest pigs, and one spotted east highland okappe. As soon as they saw the Ninja King of the West, they thought surely he would make a wonderful pet with his long golden hair. So the Ninja Prince of the Northwest and the Ninja Princess of the East plotted with the Prince and Princess of the South and they trapped the Ninja King of the West. But as soon as they got a closer look, they discovered he had bad breath and teeth that hung way below his northern and southern chins. So they cut off his long golden hair and made the east highland okappe, the northwest pigs, and the southeast donkeys beautiful blankets out of it. The rest of the hair, the hair of the north, east, and south was mixed with mud to make bricks to repair the South Ninja tribe's eastern wall.

From *Interdisciplinary Teaching Through Outdoor Education,* by Camille Bunting, 2006, Champaign, IL: Human Kinetics.

Circle Compass Game

This is a compass game which may be played in any open area. To play, the student must be able to find a bearing with a compass and face in the proper direction. The previous activities have helped the student master this skill. No pacing of distance is necessary. The course consists of eight labeled markers or cones placed in a large circle.

Equipment needed

Orienteering compasses; eight labeled markers or cones with one of the following letters—I, O, U, L, Z, E, A, P; one unlabeled center stake to measure from; and a measuring tape or string at least 50 feet (15 meters) long.

Preparing the course

The course consists of eight markers or cones in a large circle. The accuracy of the bearings used to place each marker is critical. Place the unlabeled stake in the center of the area to be used for the game. Attach the measuring tape or string to the center stake. Working from the exact center stake each time, set the compass bearing as indicated on the game clues (see pages 121 and 122) and place the properly labeled stake at the end of the 50 foot (15 meter) tape or string in the precise spot the bearing indicates. The radius of the course may be changed to suit either the available space or the number or skill of the players. Shortening the string to 25 feet (8 meters) also works well.

Playing the game

Each student receives an instruction card which tells her starting position as well as the bearings she is to follow in proper sequence. The student will stand at her starting mark, find her bearing on the compass, face the proper direction and look up to see which of the markers across the field is in her direct line of sight when the compass bearing is set. She will then put the compass at her side and walk directly to that marker. When she reaches it, she will record the letter located on the backside of the marker on her card. She then proceeds to the next bearing on the card and repeats the procedure until all bearings are completed. She will then take her card with the six-letter code (where the first letter represents the starting position) to be checked by the teacher for accuracy. If she is correct, she may try another one. If not, the teacher can direct her back to the spot where she got off track. Students may do this as a pair if it is too difficult for one to do alone. An important teaching hint is to point out that a very slight deviation at the start can translate to a couple of feet in the wrong direction and a wrong marker across the field. Also, keep any metal away from the compass as it will throw off the readings.

From *Interdisciplinary Teaching Through Outdoor Education,* by Camille Bunting, 2006, Champaign, IL: Human Kinetics.

Circle Compass Game Clues

#1 Start at A
305°, 29°, 100°, 162°, 221°

#8 Start at P
252°, 320°, 42°, 112°, 178°

#2 Start at E
358°, 68°, 140°, 198°, 252°

#9 Start at A
320°, 68°, 162°, 236°, 305°

#3 Start at I
42°, 112°, 178°, 236°, 305°

#10 Start at E
29°, 112°, 198°, 287°, 358°

#4 Start at O
100°, 162°, 221°, 287°, 358°

#11 Start at I
68°, 162°, 236°, 320°, 42°

#5 Start at U
140°, 198°, 252°, 320°, 42°

#12 Start at O
112°, 198°, 287°, 29°, 100°

#6 Start at L
178°, 236°, 305°, 29°, 100°

#13 Start at U
162°, 236°, 320°, 68°, 140°

#7 Start at Z
221°, 287°, 358°, 68°, 140°

#14 Start at L
198°, 287°, 29°, 112°, 178°

(continued)

From *Interdisciplinary Teaching Through Outdoor Education,* by Camille Bunting, 2006, Champaign, IL: Human Kinetics.

#15 Start at P
287°, 29°, 112°, 198°, 252°

#23 Start at P
302°, 83°, 206°, 351°, 139°

#16 Start at A
351°, 139°, 273°, 55°, 180°

#24 Start at A
351°, 112°, 178°, 273°, 125°

#17 Start at E
55°, 180°, 302°, 83°, 206°

#25 Start at E
93°, 319°, 112°, 263°, 42°

#18 Start at I
83°, 206°, 351°, 139°, 273°

#26 Start at I
122°, 335°, 139°, 273°, 70°

#19 Start at O
139°, 273°, 55°, 180°, 302°

#27 Start at O
139°, 236°, 26°, 263°, 122°

#20 Start at U
180°, 302°, 83°, 206°, 351°

#28 Start at U
140°, 206°, 56°, 286°, 42°

#21 Start at L
206°, 351°, 139°, 273°, 55°

#29 Start at L
263°, 83°, 206°, 56°, 273°

#22 Start at Z
273°, 55°, 180°, 302°, 83°

#30 Start at Z
319°, 112°, 263°, 122°, 287°

From *Interdisciplinary Teaching Through Outdoor Education,* by Camille Bunting, 2006, Champaign, IL: Human Kinetics.

Circle compass game answers

1. AEOUZP
2. EIULPA
3. IOLZAE
4. OUZPEI
5. ULPAIO
6. LZAEOU
7. ZPEIUL
8. PAIOLZ
9. AIUZAE
10 EOLPEI
11. IUZAIO
12. OLPEOU
13. UZAIUL
14. LPEOLZ
15. PEOLPA

16. AOZEUP
17. EUPILA
18. ILAOZE
19. OZEUPI
20. UPILAO
21. LAOZEU
22. ZEUPIL
23. PILAOZ
24. AOLZEA
25. EZOLIO
26. IPOZEL
27. OZALIP
28. ULAZIO
29. LILAZE
30. ZOLIPE

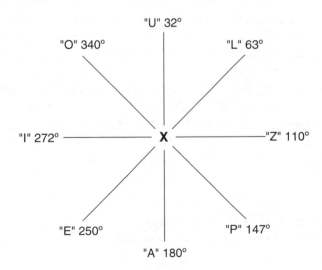

From *Interdisciplinary Teaching Through Outdoor Education,* by Camille Bunting, 2006, Champaign, IL: Human Kinetics.

USING PACES AND PACE FACTORS

Lesson Objectives

Students will:

- calculate their own average number of paces per 100 feet or 30 meters,
- use their pace factor and a compass to navigate a preset route (measured in feet or meters) and arrive at a specific destination, and
- demonstrate caring to their classmates and courage in gaining compass and pace-factor skills.

Character Focus

Caring, courage

Curriculum Standards

Math 2, 3, and 4; Physical Education 1 and 5

Materials

- One compass per student (ideal) or at least one for every pair
- Tape measure to measure off 100-foot (30-meter) distances
- Paper and pencils

Preparation

1. Measure a 100-foot (30-meter) distance for pacing.
2. Identify three or four starting points at least 20 feet (6 meters) apart.
3. From each starting point, select a compass bearing and follow that bearing a certain number of feet. Change the compass bearing and follow that bearing a different number of feet. Repeat this process one to three more times, varying the distance for each leg of the course.
4. At the end of each course, place an identifying stake. Make the ending stakes noticeably different from each other (i.e., different colors or numbers). See the sample pace-factor course on page 127. At the starting point, students should not know which ending point they are heading for.
5. Prepare several sets of directions for each course.

Lesson Sequence

Introduce the importance of knowing how far you have gone, and that knowing the length of your pace is one way to determine distance traveled.

Activity 1 △

Show students the 100-foot (30-meter) areas that have been measured off, and explain what a pace is. Demonstrate walking the distance and counting paces.

1. Have students walk the distance at least three times and average their number of paces together.
2. Put students in pairs and have them average their partner's paces, just as a check.

Activity 2 ◻ ◻

1. Ask students how many paces they would walk to go 50 feet (15 meters). They should be able to get the idea of halving the paces for 100 feet (30 meters).
2. Ask how many paces they would walk to go 32 feet (10 meters)? (This is hard to estimate very accurately.)
3. Introduce pace factor: Whatever the number of paces per 100 feet (30 meters), place a decimal point in front of it and multiply it by the distance you want to go. For example, if paces per 100 feet is 21 and distance to travel is 32 feet, $.21 \times 32 = 6.72$ paces, or approximately 6 3/4 paces. To go 165 feet (50 meters), $165 \times .21 = 34.65$ paces, or a little over 34 1/2 paces.
4. Have students line up on one of the 100-foot markers and have them figure their pace factor for going 20 feet (6 meters) (20 × paces/100 feet), and then 70 feet (21 meters). (Have these distances marked in some unobtrusive way.)
5. Ask students to get their partner to check their math and see if they can help each other.

Questions △ ◻

- How many of you allowed your partner to take part with you?
- How can working with a partner give you practice at caring and courage? (Caring—be patient and ask how they are doing; courage—it takes courage to ask someone for help.)

Activity 3 ◻

1. Show the students the different starting points for the pace-factor course.
2. Divide the pairs of students among the different starting points and give each pair a set of directions for that point. Remind them that it is not a race!
3. After each pair has completed one course, have them ask you if they ended up at the correct finish marker. If they did, give them another set of directions for a different course.

Teaching Tip

Make sure everyone is holding the compass flat in one hand out in front of the stomach, with the DTA pointing straight out ahead. Some will have a tendency to hold the compass so the arrow points off to one side, which will make it difficult to walk in the intended direction.

Questions ◻

- Delia, what can you tell us about how you and your partner demonstrated caring and courage?
- Why do you think we sometimes have a tendency to just follow another group instead of reading our own compass and figuring our own distances? (It's easier.)
- How does caring and courage relate to doing your own work?

Possible Character Affirmation ☺ ⊋

- I saw many of you caring about your partner and their understanding of how to use the compass and pace factor.
- When it is difficult to do something and you try anyway, it usually means that you are exercising courage. I'm proud of you courageous folks!

Discussion and Review

- If you are working with a partner and your directions tell you to go in a direction that you don't see anything to line up with your DTA, what can you do to be sure you keep going in the right direction? (Use your partner as a marker.)
- We are going to be using that technique tomorrow.

Teaching Tips

- Pair up the students yourself instead of saying, "Everyone get a partner." Choosing partners can be a terrible experience for some.
- Consider allowing students to bring calculators.

Possible Character Affirmations

- You were courageous, Nathan, because you kept working with the compass until you got it. ↺
- Martha, the help you gave to Kelsey was very caring, and I am proud of you.

Pace Factor Course

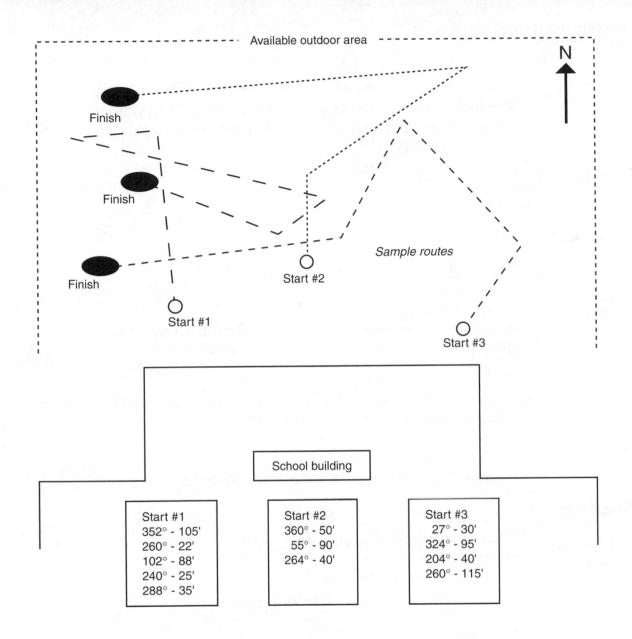

Available outdoor area

N

Finish

Finish

Finish

Sample routes

Start #1

Start #2

Start #3

School building

Start #1	Start #2	Start #3
352° - 105'	360° - 50'	27° - 30'
260° - 22'	55° - 90'	324° - 95'
102° - 88'	264° - 40'	204° - 40'
240° - 25'		260° - 115'
288° - 35'		

From *Interdisciplinary Teaching Through Outdoor Education,* by Camille Bunting, 2006, Champaign, IL: Human Kinetics.

MAP AND COMPASS ORIENTEERING

Lesson Objectives

Students will:

- navigate a preset route with a compass to arrive at a specific destination,
- demonstrate the ability to orient a map and use a map to find specific locations, and
- demonstrate trustworthiness as they search for designated points around the outside of the school building.

Character Focus

Trustworthiness

Curriculum Standards

Geography 1 and 4; Math 2 and 3; Physical Education 1 and 5

Materials

- Map of the school building and grounds with various points around the building marked in some manner (see example on page 130). The map can be hand drawn as long as key identifying features are included, such as the main entrance, doors, flag pole, and trees. Need one map per student pair.
- Markers with letters written on them, such as duct tape squares (write letters on the markers that will spell a word when they are all collected)
- Pencils
- One compass for each pair of students
- Directions for pace-factor course, one copy per pair of students

Preparation

1. Set up a pace-factor course with starting and ending points that are different from the previous day.
2. Prepare sets of directions for the course.
3. Draw and make copies of the school building and grounds map. The map indicates the location of each marker but does not show each marker's letter.
4. Place markers around the building and surroundings.

Lesson Sequence

Review pace factor, assign student pairs, and follow the activities in sequence.

Activity 1 └

1. Indicate the new starting points and have student pairs follow a new set of directions for the pace-factor course.
2. Ask if students have any questions.

Questions

- Who can tell me what a pace factor really is in math terminology? (Ratio)
- How would it be different if the directions were in meters rather than feet? (You would either have to measure pace factor in meters or do a conversion.)

Possible Character Affirmations

Sherri, thank you for being honest about not understanding and asking for another explanation. I'm sure there are others who also didn't understand and benefited from the additional discussion. That was being trustworthy, because you gave an honest answer when I asked whether anyone had a question.

Activity 2 └ ☺

1. Collect compasses from students and hand out school maps to each pair.
2. Have student pairs find all the markers and record the letter on each marker associated with the numbers indicated on the map. Tell them that the letters they collect from the markers will be used to spell something.
3. Have each pair of students write the word they think is correct on the back of their map.
4. When all students have returned, have them sit in one large circle with their maps in front of them so that the word they wrote is facing down.
5. Ask all pairs to turn their map over to reveal the word they wrote.

Questions

- When you got your map, what was the first thing you did before going to your starting marker? (Oriented the map and identified where we were on the map.)
- How did you figure out where you were on the map? (Identified the side of the building we were on.)
- What part did trustworthiness play in this last activity? (The teacher had to think the students were trustworthy to allow them to run around in all different directions around the school.)
- Have you ever experienced not getting to do something because someone doubted someone else's trustworthiness?
- What kind of things cause doubt about someone's trustworthiness? (A previous display of lack of trustworthiness, not keeping your word, not telling the truth.)

Possible Character Affirmations

- Jordan, I appreciate you not going over to the parking lot to talk with your friends in that other class while you had an assignment to do for this class. It lets me know that you are trustworthy.
- Raul, thank you for keeping your word that you would come back quickly.

School Map

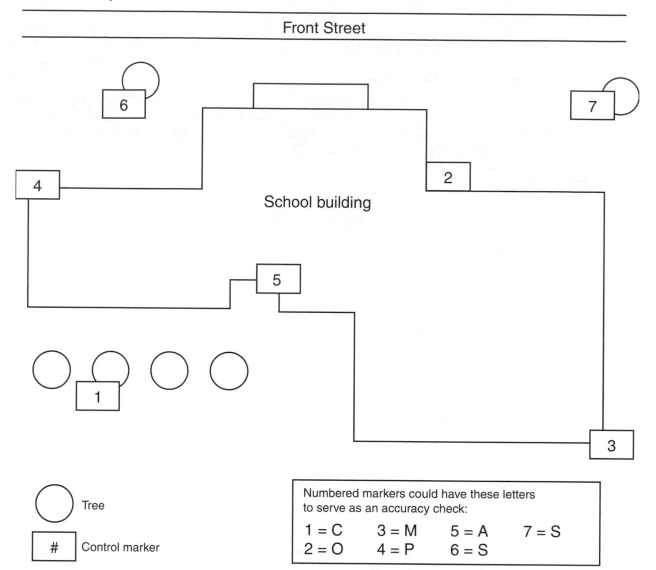

Front Street

6

7

4

2

School building

5

1

3

◯ Tree

☐ # Control marker

Numbered markers could have these letters
to serve as an accuracy check:

1 = C	3 = M	5 = A	7 = S
2 = O	4 = P	6 = S	

From *Interdisciplinary Teaching Through Outdoor Education,* by Camille Bunting, 2006, Champaign, IL: Human Kinetics.

USING A MAP

Lesson Objectives

Students will:

- orient a map to true north and magnetic north,
- identify different types of maps and the parts of those maps, and
- demonstrate diligence while learning the skills of using a compass with a map.

Character Focus

Diligence

Curriculum Standards

Geography 1 and 4; Language Arts 5 and 7; Physical Education 5

Materials

- One map of each type for each pair of students
  - Local area map
  - State highway map
  - Topographic map (can copy figure 7.7)
- One compass for each pair of students
- One protractor for each pair of students
- One 6- or 12-inch (15- or 30-centimeter) ruler for each pair

Preparation

Have maps ready to hand out to students and have other materials on hand.

Lesson Sequence

Introduce the concept of using a map to identify where you are and to identify a route for getting where you want to go. Follow the activities in sequence.

Activity 1 △

1. Put students in pairs.
2. Hand out local area maps and have students find where their school is located on the map. Then have them orient the map.
3. Students can go outside with compasses and determine the direction according to where the road lies in front of the school. This will help make the map-orienting process more accurate.
4. Have students point out different indicators on the map, such as the north indicator of the map legend.
5. Change to state highway maps and repeat the same process. Identify parts of the map, how they are marked, and orient the map.

Questions

- How can you tell if your area map and your highway map are oriented the same?(Find a road that is on both maps and see if they are running in the same direction.)

- How can we check to make sure we have oriented the maps correctly? (Check the direction of the actual road with a compass and then check the direction of that road on the map.)

Activity 2 ⌐

1. Have students go out with compasses and check the linear direction of a road next to the school. Then have students come back together as a single group with the maps.

2. Have students reorient the map to north with the compasses and then check the linear direction of the major road that they checked outside the school. If there is a difference between the two readings, it is probably due to the difference between true north and magnetic north.

Question

Why do you think there is a difference? (It could be because the teacher or student did the activity wrong, or because our compasses point to magnetic north and maps are drawn to true north.)

Activity 3 ⌐

1. Show a globe and large map of the world or North America and indicate where you are located and where magnetic north is located.

2. Draw a line with string from your location to true north and another string from where you are to magnetic north. The angle between the two lines is called the angle of declination.

3. Have students look again at the local area map and draw a long line across the map running from true north to south.

4. Line up the straight side of the protractor with the north–south line. If your area has an easterly angle of declination, the rounded side of the protractor should be on the east side of the line; if it has a westerly declination, it should be on the west side.

5. Count the number of degrees for your local declination from 0 on the protractor. Make a mark lined up with the number of degrees, and then draw a straight line from that mark to the north–south line. The angle should be the angle of declination for your area.

Questions

- What if you were using your compass with a map and didn't take into consideration the difference between magnetic north and true north? (You would miss your target.)

- In which situation would it make the most difference, if you were going 1/2 mile (1 kilometer) or 2 miles (3 kilometers), and why? (2 miles [3 kilometers], because on the angle of declination there is more difference between the two lines the farther away they are from where they meet.)

Activity 4 ⌐ ⌂

1. Hand out several topographic maps. If possible, have them all be the same. You can make copies of the sample map on page 113, but it would be good to have at least one or two real topographic maps as well.

2. Hand out the key sheet for topographic map symbols, or use an overhead transparency.

3. Point out and discuss several different parts and symbols on the map, and be sure to note the angle of declination at the bottom of the map.

Activity 5 ⌐ ⌂

1. Have students place their maps flat on the floor or ground and ask everyone to locate particular points on the map, such as Tom Tom Trailhead and then Moon Lake on the sample map. Say, "If you were at the trailhead and wanted to hike to Moon Lake to fish or swim,

how would you know what direction to go? That's what we're going to learn how to do now."

2. Guide students through orienting their maps to true north and then drawing a line from the trailhead to Moon Lake. Go through the process of finding the bearing from trailhead to lake.

3. Since the lake is small and the distance is not short, explain how to adjust the compass for the angle of declination.

4. Several different landmarks can be used to practice using the compass and map together.

Teaching Tips

- Make sure everyone has the DTA pointing in the direction they want to travel (Moon Lake, not the trailhead). The compass must be held securely on the line from trailhead to Moon Lake, and the map must not move.
- If your angle of declination is easterly, to adjust the compass turn the dial toward the east (right). If it is a westerly declination, turn the dial toward the west (left).

Questions

- What degree reading did you get?
- Who has a question about how to do this?
- How many of you have the same question?
- Who can answer that question?
- How about a different question?

Possible Character Affirmations ⊃

- This group is being diligent about learning this skill.
- Just because you don't catch on to something right away does not mean that it's too hard or that you won't get it. That's where diligence comes in. To practice something so that you get it right means that you are being diligent. I'm proud of you for being diligent.

Discussion and Review

- Who can tell me what the angle of declination is? (It's the difference between magnetic north and true north.)
- To which direction does the magnetic needle of the compass point? (Magnetic north)
- Why are magnetic north and geographic north different? (Magnetic north is not in the exact same spot as geographic north. Geographic north is where all of the longitude lines on the globe come together at the North Pole.)
- Tomorrow we are going to make a map and then use it with our compasses.

Teaching Tips

- If your class needs to go more slowly, divide the lesson into two.
- If some students are getting impatient, group them together and give them different problems more quickly. Then have those students help students who may be struggling.

Possible Character Affirmation ⊃

This was a hard task. Thanks to all of you who helped your teammates. Everyone was doing well by the end of class.

Casting and Angling   Chapter 8

One of America's favorite pastimes is fishing, and some statistics even show fishing to be America's number one sport (Sherman, 2004). Fishing provides opportunities to enjoy the great outdoors, spend time with friends and family, and occasionally add food to the table. Fishing comes in many varieties, such as reel or fly fishing; fishing on a lake or an ocean; or fishing from land, dock, or boat. This unit is designed to teach the basics of fishing, an activity that people can participate in throughout their entire lives.

Angling is the term used for the art of fishing with a hook, line, and rod. Fishing is one of the oldest and most popular outdoor activities. Archeological evidence shows that our ancestors fished using their hands and clubs. Throughout the years, methods and tools were invented to improve the fishing experience. Spears were made, dams were built to increase the number of fish, and fish traps were created. The first

hooks were made out of animal bones or shells thousands of years ago, and metal hooks became available in the 1600s. Vines, plant fiber, and human and horse hair were all used to enable early fishers to get their hook and bait closer to the fish. Attaching the line and hook to poles also extended the reach and provided extra leverage for landing a catch.

With the introduction of the reel, fishing became far more efficient. The first fishing reel was invented in 1810 by George W. Snyder in Kentucky. It greatly increased the distance that the bait could be cast, and it made it easier to control the catch and retrieve the line. The reel helped bring more of a sport aspect to fishing.

Fishing equipment is called *tackle*. Reel improvements enable anglers to enjoy fishing more and to be more successful. Because of improved fishing equipment and greater accessibility, more and more people have become avid fishers.

Reels and Rods

Four types of rods and reels can be used in both freshwater and saltwater.

• A spincast reel (figure 8.1, *a* and *b*) is ideal for beginners because it works smoothly and is easy to use without snarling the line. The spincast reel is mounted on top of the rod. Guides for the line are also on top of the rod. The reel has a thumb button for controlling the line when casting.

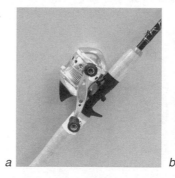

Figure 8.1   Spincast reel (*a*) and how to hold a spincast reel (*b*).

• A spinning reel (figure 8.2, *a* and *b*) is often called an open-face reel because the spool of line is not covered as it is in a spincast reel. Spinning rods have a straight handle rather than a pistol grip. They also have large line guides along the bottom of the rod. Spinning rods and reels allow you to cast longer distances because the line peels off the reel more quickly. A spinning reel is mounted on the bottom of a straight grip rod. Figure 8.2 shows the different positions of the spinning reel on a rod.

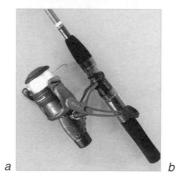

Figure 8.2   Spinning reel (*a*) and how to hold a spinning reel (*b*).

• A baitcast reel (figure 8.3, *a* and *b*) is generally used with some type of bait impaled on a hook, a sinker weight on the line, and a float or bobber attached to set the depth of your bait in the water. A baitcast reel is more difficult to learn to cast because the reel's line spool turns freely and the line can get snarled if it is not controlled with thumb pressure. Figure 8.3*b* shows a baitcast reel and the hand position for casting, how the thumb controls the spin of the line spool, and how the reel is positioned on the rod.

Figure 8.3   Baitcast reel (*a*) and how to hold a baitcast reel (*b*).

• A fly reel is different from the other types of reels. In fly-fishing, you cast the line that carries the fly, which is actually a lightweight lure made to look like some type of fly. Because it is so lightweight, the line is weighted to enable casting. With other fishing tackle the weight of the bait and sinker or lure pulls line from a reel. In fly-fishing, the reel is only used to store the line and is mounted on the bottom of a straight-grip rod. Fly casting is usually the most difficult casting technique to learn. However, with proper instruction anyone can learn the skill. Fly casting is beyond the scope of this book and will not be discussed. (No photo shown.)

The type of rod influences the way you cast. Casting is the skill of placing your bait or lure where you want it to go. Accuracy is much more important than distance. The best reel to start with is a spincast reel and a rod with a pistol grip. A practice plug is best to practice casting. It provides some weight, but does not have a hook.

Casting With a Spincast Reel

To cast with a spincast reel, grip the pistol grip with one hand. If you're right-handed, turn the rod sideways so the reel handle points straight up; if you're left-handed, point the reel handle straight down. Push the thumb button and hold it down.

Face the target area and turn your body at a slight angle. The arm holding the rod should be closest to the target. Aim the rod tip toward the target at about eye level. Swiftly and smoothly bend your casting arm at the elbow, raising your casting forearm until your hand reaches eye level. When the rod is almost straight up, it will be bent back by the weight of the practice plug. As the rod bends, move your forearm forward with a slight wrist movement. When the rod tip reaches eye level, release the thumb button and let the line travel freely.

If the practice plug lands close in front of you, you released the thumb button too late. If the plug went straight up, you released the button too soon. Casting with a spincast rod and reel is not too difficult, but it does take practice. A good beginning practice distance for a target is about 25 feet (8 meters).

Casting With a Spinning Reel

When casting with a spinning rod and reel, the reel is on the underside of the rod and as you grasp the rod's handle, the reel "stem" lies between your second and third fingers or between your third and fourth fingers, depending upon the size of your hand. Your thumb should be on top of the handle and your forefinger extended to touch the spool of line. With your other hand, rotate the reel spool until the line roller is directly beneath your extended forefinger. Pick up the line in front of the roller with your forefinger and open, or cock, the reel's bail with your other hand.

After this procedure, casting is similar to that for spincasting except that when the rod tip reaches eye level as you are casting, you release the line from your forefinger rather than releasing the thumb button. If the plug lands too close to you, you released the line too late. If the plug goes too high, you released the line too soon.

Casting With a Baitcast Reel

For casting with a baitcast reel, everything remains the same as with the spincast reel, except you do not have a button to control the line. Instead you use your thumb on the spool of line to control the spin, releasing pressure from the spool when you would have released the button on a spincast reel. When your bait is about to land, you must begin applying pressure again on the spool and stop the spin as the bait hits the water. If you do not stop the spin soon enough, the line will tangle on the spool, which is called backlash.

Angling Equipment

Entire books are written on the intricacies of fishing tackle. However, we will only scratch the surface and present the basics.

Line

Fishing line comes in a variety of sizes, or strengths, called pound test. For example, 10-pound (5-kilogram) test line is stronger than 4-pound (2.5-kilogram) test. You must match the pound-test line to the size of rod and reel, the bait, and the fish you want to catch. For example, small, ultralight spincasting and spinning reels can use up to 6-pound (3-kilogram) test line, while larger spinning reels can use stronger line. Baitcasting reels can use from 6- to 30-pound (3- to 14-kilogram) test line, but 8- to 16-pound (4- to 8-kilogram) test lines are the most common. Using heavier line than necessary may reduce the number of bites or strikes you get because heavy line is more visible in the water.

Hooks

Fish hooks come in a variety of sizes and styles. When you fish with natural or live bait, a package with an assortment of hooks ranging from size 6 through 10 is suitable. However, when you fish for catfish or bullheads, larger hooks are needed. Bend down the barbs on the hooks if you intend to release your catch. This will make your fishing more challenging and reduce fish mortality.

Knots

Several knots are used to connect fishing line to hooks or lures. The two knots presented here are commonly used because they weaken the line less than other knots and do not slip.

• The improved clinch knot (figure 8.4) is used to tie the line to the swivel, hook, or lure.

• The Palomar knot (figure 8.5) is used to tie the line to the hook or jig and is considered the strongest knot for this application.

Bait

As you learn more about fish behavior, you'll learn more about how to choose the best bait or lure for different situations. Always check the fishing regulations to make sure the bait you choose is legal for the body of water you are fishing.

Earthworms are a good bait for nearly all freshwater and saltwater fish, although sea worms are often used in saltwater fishing. You can find enough worms for fishing from a few shovels of dirt in your garden or from a shaded, damp area. You can also purchase worms in fishing-tackle stores and bait shops. If you have small worms, thread the hook through the side of the worm at several places along its body. For bait-stealing fish such as sunfish, thread the worm on the hook until the hook is completely covered.

Prepared baits for bottom-feeding fish like carp and catfish can be small pieces of cheese or canned corn. Commercially made baits are also available, but many anglers like to make their own bait for this type of fish, such as sweet doughballs or pieces of rotting, smelly bottom-feeding fish such as shad.

Lures

Lures come in many sizes, styles, colors, and patterns (figure 8.6). They are designed to mimic food that fish normally eat.

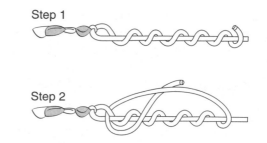

Figure 8.4 Improved clinch knot.

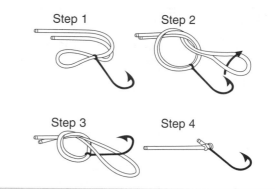

Figure 8.5 Palomar knot.

Figure 8.6 The types of lures include: jig (*a*), spoon (*b*), plastic worm (*c*), plug (*d*), spinner (*e*), popper (*f*), and fly (*g*).

• Jigs (8.6*a*) have weighted metal heads and a tail made of animal hair, soft plastic, feathers, or rubber.

• Spoons (8.6*b*) are metal lures designed to look like a swimming baitfish.

• Plastic baits (8.6*c*) come in the form of worms, minnows, and crayfish in all different sizes and colors. Some even have scents attractive to fish.

- Plugs (8.6*d*) have a body made of plastic or wood and are designed to be used on top of the water or to dive below the surface to certain depths.

- Spinners (8.6*e*) have one or more blades that spin or revolve around a straight wire shaft. Some spinners have tails made of soft plastic or animal hair.

- Poppers (8.6*f*) and flies (8.6*g*) are small lures used with spincast and fly-fishing tackle. These baits are good for fish that feed on the surface of the water.

Locating Fish

Not all fish live in the same kind of water. Some fish need salt in the water and others cannot live where there is much salt. Most ponds, reservoirs, and rivers across North America are freshwater. Some common freshwater fish are bluegill, carp, catfish, crappie, bass, perch, northern pike, trout, and walleye. Popular saltwater fish are bluefish, cod, flounder, striped bass, sea trout, rockfish, sea perch, and yellowtail. If you want to catch a specific type of fish, you have to know the type of water in which it lives.

Water Quality

Without an adequate supply of oxygen in the water, fish cannot survive, and some fish, such as trout, require more oxygen than bottom-feeding fish, such as carp. Several factors can affect the oxygen level of water. Living plants in a lake, stream, or river add oxygen to the water, and water moving over rocks in a way that makes the water bubble up also gets oxygen into the water. However, oxygen is reduced from the water by dead and decaying plants, as well as from various types of pollution such as chemicals and heating of the water from industrial use. Colder water can hold more oxygen than warm water, and clean water will support more species of fish and a larger population of fish than polluted water.

Locations

Fish tend to be near a food source. Aquatic plants, rocks, and logs provide food, protection, and a good location for catching an unsuspecting meal that is floating past. Different species of fish require or prefer certain habitats. They all must have adequate oxygen, appropriate temperature, adequate food, and hiding places (see figures 8.7 and 8.8).

Small fish often feed on insects that fall on the surface of the water, and larger fish often feed on the small fish. In deep water, the larger fish often are below the smaller fish, driving them up closer to the surface. Shallow water tends to have hiding places like brush and plants and thus attracts large and small fish. The early morning and evening low light is the time when larger fish come to shallow areas to feed. In moving water like streams and rivers, fish tend to be in areas where the current is not very strong. They are typically facing upstream and are either in deep areas where the current is slower or behind rocks or logs that create calm areas. A skilled angler is able to "read" the water and spot the slow, deep areas and the calm pools behind rocks where fish tend to rest.

Angling Ethics and Safety

As more and more people become involved in fishing, the need for courtesy and respect increases. Everyone's safety is related to how we behave when fishing, and fishing quality and regulations are affected as well. Following is a list of unofficial rules that reveal the ethics of fishing.

- If someone is fishing in a certain spot, do not go to that spot while the person is there.
- Remain quiet. Talk only in a low to normal voice. Don't laugh loudly or play music. Most people who fish do so to enjoy the natural surroundings as much as the catching of fish.
- If you are in a boat, keep your distance from other boats that are obviously trolling or anchored.

Cross Section of a Lake

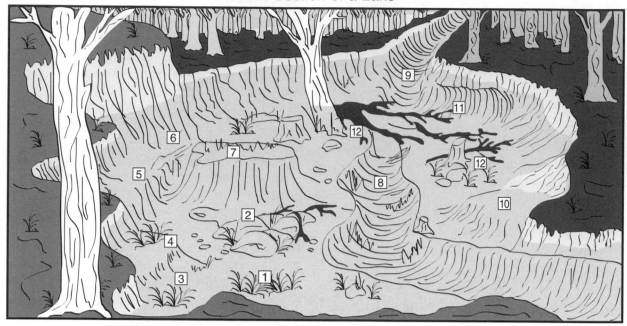

Like people, fish seek comfortable surroundings, and productivity of a particular area will vary with the seasonal water temperature. The general rule is fish shallow in spring, deep in midsummer, shallow in fall, and deep in winter.

1. **Brushy bank:** Good feeding area.
2. **Submerged rock pile:** Holding and feeding area. Rocks usually harbor small forage fish and crayfish.
3. **Weedy bay:** Good feeding area.
4. **Shallow submerged weedy bar:** Good feeding area. Weeds harbor minnows and small forage fish.
5. **Drop-off:** Game fish forage in shallows, hold on edge of drop-off, dart into deeper water at sign of danger.
6. **Cliffs:** Holding and feeding area. Game fish school on shelves. Minnows, small fish, crayfish-in-habit rocks and crevices.
7. **Submerged island:** Holding area. Possible feeding area, depending on cover and depth.
8. **Creek bed:** Edges with cover are good holding areas during midsummer and winter months.
9. **Creek mouth:** Food washed into lake creates good feeding area.
10. **Sloping point with drop-off:** Shallow point good feeding area. Drop-off into deep water good holding area.
11. **Overhanging bank:** Provides shade. Good holding area.
12. **Stump patches and brush patches:** Provide cover for minnows and small fish. Good feeding and holding areas.

Figure 8.7 Typical fish habitats found within a lake.

Adapted, by permission, from J. Grigg, *Cross section of a lake.* © The Estate of Jodie L. Grigg.

From *Interdisciplinary Teaching Through Outdoor Education,* by Camille Bunting, 2006, Champaign, IL: Human Kinetics.

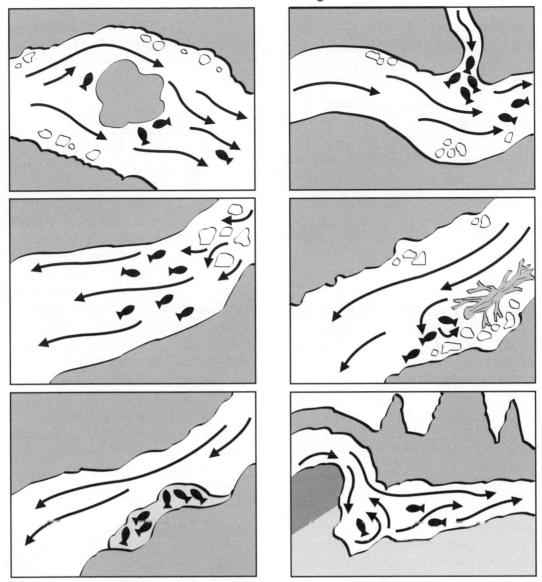

Figure 8.8 Typical fish locations within a stream.

Adapted, by permission, from D. Brown, 1980, Safari Club International Conservation Fund.

- Slow down and keep your boat's wake small when passing small crafts, anchored boats, or people fishing from the bank.
- Take your trash home with you and dispose of it properly. Leave no trace of your presence.
- Keep only the fish you will eat, and follow the local regulations on fish size and number limit.
- Always be ready to help someone in trouble.

Part of the ethics of fishing is abiding by state laws and regulations. Each state has fishing regulations and requires anglers to purchase a fishing license that helps provide funding for maintaining quality fishing opportunities. It is your responsibility to become aware of regulations for the area in which you plan to fish and to be a good citizen by following them. The Internet is an excellent source of information on fishing regulations.

Fishing is not an inherently dangerous activity; however, the environment can change quickly and unexpectedly. It is important to be aware of certain situations and health concerns that are common to this activity and to be prepared to respond appropriately. The following are common safety concerns while fishing.

- **Weather.** Make sure you have extra clothing and rain gear. If you see lightning, the best plan is to get off or away from the water. Do not keep your rod with you (it could become a lightning rod rather than a fishing rod). Be prepared for the unexpected.

- **Swimming.** Accidents happen that can have you in the water in the blink of an eye. Everyone who enjoys fishing should learn to swim and should also wear a PFD (personal floatation device) and fish with a buddy. The U.S. Coast Guard and most states require you to have an approved PFD when you are in a boat, but it is also a good idea to wear one while wade fishing. A nonswimmer should always wear a PFD when fishing.

- **Sun.** Wear appropriate clothing and apply sunscreen frequently to all exposed areas. Sunglasses are important for protecting your eyes from the sun. Polarized lenses are excellent for cutting glare from the sun on the water and will improve your vision into the water. You should also be sure to take plenty of drinking water. Soft drinks with caffeine do not help prevent dehydration as well as water does. Each person should consume at least one quart (one liter) of water every 4 to 6 hours. Of course, that requirement increases with hot temperatures and physical exertion.

- **Fish hooks.** Before casting, look around and be sure no one is too close and in danger of being hooked. Hooks and lures should be in a tackle box when not in use, not left on the ground or boat seats or floor. An embedded fishhook is a very painful injury. Another preventive measure is to avoid attempting to free a hook or lure by jerking it out of weeds or branches. The hook may suddenly come loose and come flying back toward you and your fishing partners. Instead of jerking the line, go to the lure. If a hook does become embedded past the barb (see figure 8.9), go to a doctor to have it removed.

- **Insects.** Insects like mosquitoes, chiggers, black flies, ticks, bees, and wasps are often found around good fishing areas. If at all possible, try to avoid areas with a high insect population. Insect repellent works well, but do not get it on your lures or bait because the fish may smell it and also

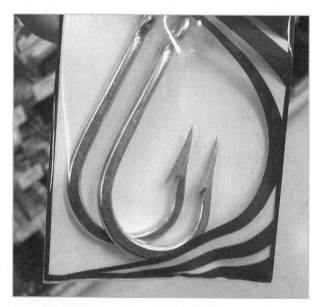

Figure 8.9 This hook uses a barb. If a hook becomes embedded in someone's skin past the barb, see a doctor to have it removed.

be repelled. Other tips for keeping insects less interested are to not use cologne or other scented products and not wear blue clothing. Blue seems to attract mosquitoes and some flies.

What if someone falls in the water? There is a recommended progression of actions for helping an angler or swimmer in trouble. It is called the reach-throw-row-go method.

1. Reach out with a long object if the person is close to you. A tree limb, a boat paddle, or a fish net are possibilities.

2. Throw a rope, PFD, float ring, or anything that floats to help the person stay afloat. Something with a rope attached is good because you can then pull the person to you.

3. Row a boat to the person in the water. The person should then be pulled into the boat over the stern. If you pull someone into a small boat over the side, you risk capsizing the boat.

4. Swim out to the person only as a last resort and only if you have appropriate training. Panicked swimmers may injure or drown their rescuer. If you don't have water life-saving training, go quickly to get help.

This progression illustrates the importance of being able to swim as well as the importance of being prepared to help someone in trouble by having the right equipment with you.

Fishing has become a widespread, enjoyable activity. It is encompasses a wide range of age groups, uses a variety of techniques, and can be accomplished in many types of settings. From the laid-back fishing trip to the competitive fishing arena, anyone can enjoy and participate in this pleasurable activity.

Unit Objectives

Students will:

- develop an understanding of casting and angling as a sport,
- become familiar with basic angling equipment,
- develop casting skills and skills for locating fish, and
- be able to identify safe fishing practices and understand the importance of water quality.

Character Focus

Caring, trustworthiness

Curriculum Areas

Language Arts, Science, Social Studies, Physical Education, Health

Assessment Activity

Have students cast a certain number of times at a target with concentric rings, similar to a large archery target, and record the score of their best three casts. Ask students to draw either a lake (underwater view) or a stream and indicate which places are most likely to have fish.

Casting and Angling Day Planner

Day	Topic	Concepts and skills	Teaching activities	Standards
1	Types of fishing and fishing equipment; how early humans caught fish and the evolution of techniques; knot tying for fishing	Definition of bait; presenting bait and using a hook; why catch fish; useful equipment and skills; how to tie the improved clinch knot	Show pictures of different types of fishing. Show types of equipment and how they are used. Discuss bait, bait presentation, and hooks. What do students experience in own lives where they are presented with bait to try to get them hooked?	Geography 6; History 2 and 8; Physical Education 6; Science 6 and 7
2*	Types of rods and reels; types of casting	Identification of rod and reel parts and how they work; how to cast	Review improved clinch knot. Display and demonstrate equipment and casting technique. Practice spincasting.	Physical Education 2, 5, and 6
3	Different reels and their casting techniques	Identification of rod and reel types; different casting techniques	Introduce differences between types of equipment. Demonstrate different casting techniques. Allow students to practice casting at targets.	Language Arts 8; Physical Education 2, 5, and 6
4	Types of bait; Palomar knot; hooking and landing a fish	Different fish and conditions require different bait and a new knot; skills for setting a hook and landing the catch	Display and discuss several different types of bait and demonstrate how they work. Let students handle the different baits. Demonstrate hooking and landing a fish and allow students to practice.	Science 1 and 6; Physical Education 1 and 5
5	Fishing safety	Safety equipment; knowledge for safe fishing; skills to prevent accidents; dealing with common accidents	Display safety equipment and safety guidelines. Demonstrate how to help someone in trouble in the water. Student groups develop skits illustrating a safety guideline.	History 2, 5, 7, and 8; Language Arts 8; Physical Education 2 and 5
6	Where to fish	Where fish live, what they eat, and how to locate them; using maps and knowing what you want to catch	Show lake maps and indicate locations where different types of fish prefer due to their diet. Show pictures of streams and where fish typically can be found.	Geography 1 and 2; Science 6
7*	Locating fish and casting with accuracy	Identifying spots to cast and casting for accuracy	Use various items to create a stream with fish hangouts for students to identify and cast toward.	Geography 1 and 2; Physical Education 1, 2, 5, and 6; Science 6
8*	Casting Golf	Casting for accuracy	Introduce Casting Golf. Student groups play for lowest number of casts.	Physical Education 1, 2, 5, and 6

* Has a corresponding lesson plan.

RODS, REELS, CASTING TECHNIQUES, AND CLINCH KNOTS

Lesson Objectives

Students will:

- be able to identify parts of a rod and different types of reels,
- cast with a spincast reel, and
- tie a clinch knot.

Character Focus

Perseverance, caring

Curriculum Standards

Physical Education 2, 5, and 6

Materials

- At least one rod and reel for every pair of students
- Two or three different types of rods to show
- Three different types of reels to show
- Several hula hoops for casting targets
- At least two casting plugs for each rod and reel
- Extra fishing line
- Ropes for knot-tying practice (8- to 10-foot or 2- to 3-meter lengths)
- Large poster or overhead display identifying parts of rod and reels

Preparation

- Set knot-tying ropes out for each student.
- Set practice targets (hula hoops) out in a selected practice area.
- Run a line between 20 and 30 feet (6 and 9 meters) away from the hula hoops to indicate the location for casting.

Lesson Sequence

1. Introduce the different types of rods and reels.
2. Pass them around for each student to see.
3. Prepare a large poster or an overhead display identifying the parts of the rods and reels. (See pages 148 and 149 for reproducibles.)

Activity 1 △ ⌂

1. Put students in pairs. Hand out knot-tying practice ropes.
2. Have students follow you in tying a clinch knot (see page 134), and then have them try it on their own as you walk around helping pairs.
3. Ask partners to help each other.
4. When both students in a pair are able to tie the knot, ask them to go around and help others.

Questions

Show a rod with a reel attached and ask, "What is missing? How do we get that on?" (Bait and hook are missing; they should be tied on with a clinch knot.)

Possible Character Affirmation

- That was great, Valentino, Richard, and Tawanda. You all stuck with it and kept working until you could tie that knot!
- Thank you, Paul and Maria, for caring enough to help teach the knot.

Activity 2

1. Give each pair of students a rod and reel and a casting plug.
2. The student who is the first to cast should tie the practice plug on the end of the line using a clinch knot.
3. Ask all students to get behind a designated casting line. Students with rods should spread out along the line.
4. Stand in front of the class and demonstrate casting. Talk about the main points of holding the rod and when to release the thumb button. Tell students that the objective is to cast their plug inside the hula hoop closest to them.
5. Each student gets six casts, and then the partner gets six casts.
6. Give individual help as students practice.
7. Casting practice continues until 5 minutes before the end of class.

Discussion and Review

- How many of you hit inside the target every time you cast?
- What happened with the accuracy of your casts the more you practiced? (Probably got more accurate. Perseverance pays off—you're probably not going to become really good at something without practice, and some things take a lot of practice.)
- What's the name of the reel we learned to cast with today? (Spincast)
- What's the name of the knot we tied today? (Clinch knot)

Teaching Tips

- It is best to teach this activity outside. Even high ceilings get hit with practice plugs when students are first learning to cast.
- Encourage students to give their partners tips for improving casting.
- If guest speakers come to show their equipment and pictures and talk about their love of the sport, students can become interested in putting their casting skills and knowledge to use.

Possible Character Affirmation

This group did well giving casting tips to your partners today.

References

Schmidt, B. (1995). *Sport fishing and aquatic resources handbook*. Dubuque, Iowa: Kendall/ Hunt.

Two-Piece Rod

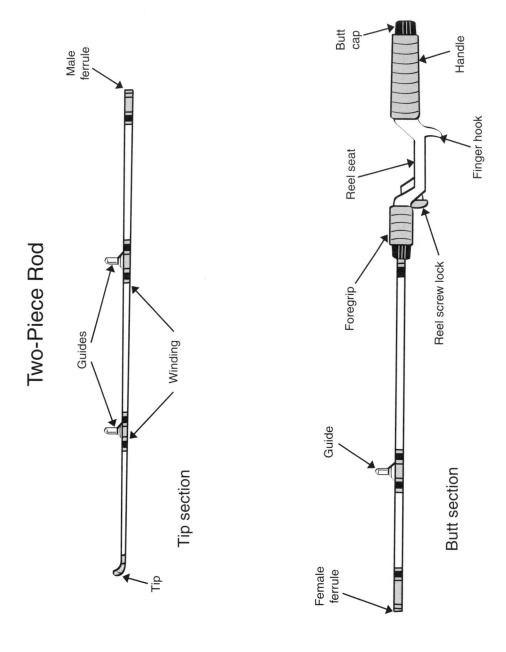

From *Interdisciplinary Teaching Through Outdoor Education,* by Camille Bunting, 2006, Champaign, IL: Human Kinetics.

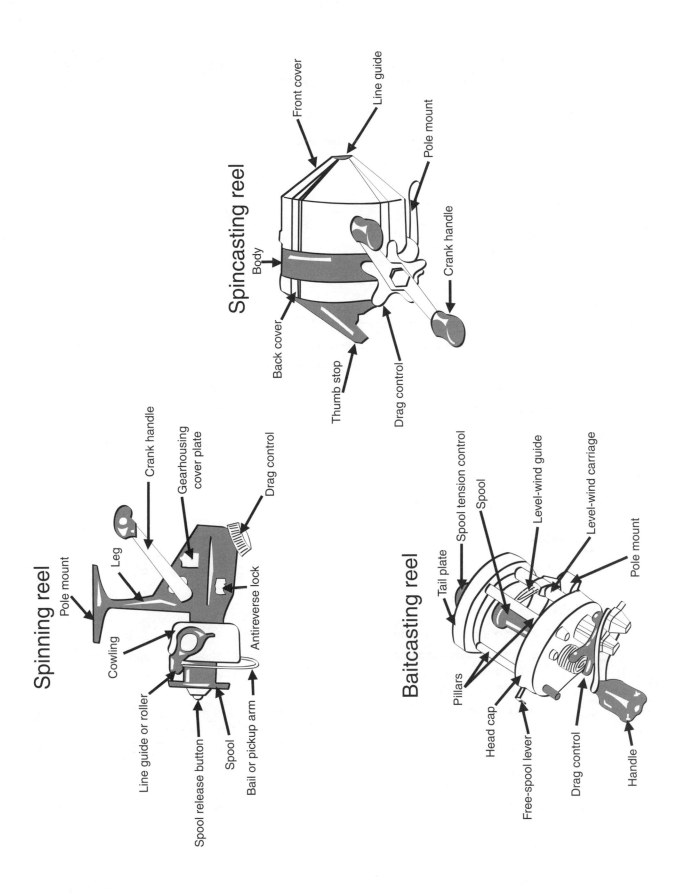

Spincasting reel

Front cover

Line guide

Pole mount

Body

Crank handle

Back cover

Thumb stop

Drag control

Spinning reel

Crank handle

Gearhousing cover plate

Drag control

Pole mount

Leg

Cowling

Antireverse lock

Line guide or roller

Spool release button

Spool

Bail or pickup arm

Baitcasting reel

Spool tension control

Spool

Level-wind guide

Level-wind carriage

Tail plate

Pole mount

Pillars

Head cap

Free-spool lever

Drag control

Handle

LOCATING FISH AND CASTING WITH ACCURACY

Lesson Objectives

Students will be able to identify places fish would typically be located and cast to those spots.

Character Focus

Fairness, self-control

Curriculum Standards

Geography 1 and 2; Physical Education 1, 2, 5, and 6; Science 6

Materials

- Long ropes for indicating the river bank
- Various materials to indicate large rocks, shallow areas, logs, and deep areas
- One rod and reel with casting plugs for every pair of students
- One copy of graphic river map per student (similar to the one on page 152)
- Casting targets (hula hoops)

Preparation

- Set up the river and its various characteristics so it is the same as the graphic map on paper.
- Make copies of graphic maps.

Lesson Sequence

The sequence of activities in this lesson will enable students to find probable fish locations and to practice accurate casting.

Activity 1 ⌐

1. Hand out river maps and have the students put their name on their map.
2. Give directions for students to place an X on the map on each place in the river where a fish would most likely be. Beside each X, they should select a (calm), b (deep), or c (shallow) as the reason fish would be there.
3. After approximately 5 minutes, walk down the river and ask the students to stop you by calling out "fish" when you get to a place close to where a fish would likely be.
4. Stop when a student says "fish" and have the student indicate exactly where the fish would be and why.
5. Place a casting target in each "fish location" that is correctly identified.

Activity 2 ⌂ ⌐

1. Students get with their fishing partner and each pair gets a rod and reel with casting plug.
2. Each student gets a chance to fish in the river. Students select a side of the river to fish from and they must stay at least 15 feet (5 meters) back from the edge of their bank (represented by a rope).

3. Students walk upstream along the bank and get two casts at each spot that has been indicated as a "fish spot."

4. Partners count the total number of casts and the number of fish spots the student hits.

5. The goal is to have a low number of casts and a high number of hits.

6. When a student leaves one spot another student can start at that spot.

7. You can allow students to spread out and fish from both banks of the river at the same time if they have gained control of their casts.

Discussion and Review

- Do fish face up- or downstream? (They face upstream, which is why we walked upstream so they would be less likely to see us.)
- Are fish most often found in swiftly moving water or slow and calm water?
- Why are they most often found in slow or calm water? (They are conserving energy and trying not to get washed downstream.)
- How are we sometimes like fish, wanting to be in the slow or calm water? (Sometimes we want the challenge of a faster pace, and sometimes we want to relax in calmer waters.)
- Why is it good sometimes to do things that seem really hard at first? (If we work at it and persevere we find out that we can do it and feel good about ourselves.)
- Would it have been fair to have taken more than two casts at each spot and not counted them? Why? (No, because it would have slowed everyone else down, and I would have cheated myself because I wouldn't know how well I really did.)

Teaching Tips

- Casting from both sides of the river is a good reason to keep students at least 15 feet (5 meters) behind their river bank.
- If students are too close to the bank and the river is not more than 10 to 15 feet (3 to 5 meters) wide, it is not challenging enough.
- The more students you have, the more river features you need to include.

Possible Character Affirmations ☺ ⋑

- This group is being very fair and not taking too much time from the others.
- Sonja, it was very good that you didn't get angry when Antonio's plug hit your arm. Thank you for that self-control.
- Congratulations on such good self-control in doing this activity.

Reference

Schmidt, B. (1995). *Sport fishing and aquatic resources handbook.* Dubuque, Iowa: Kendall/Hunt.

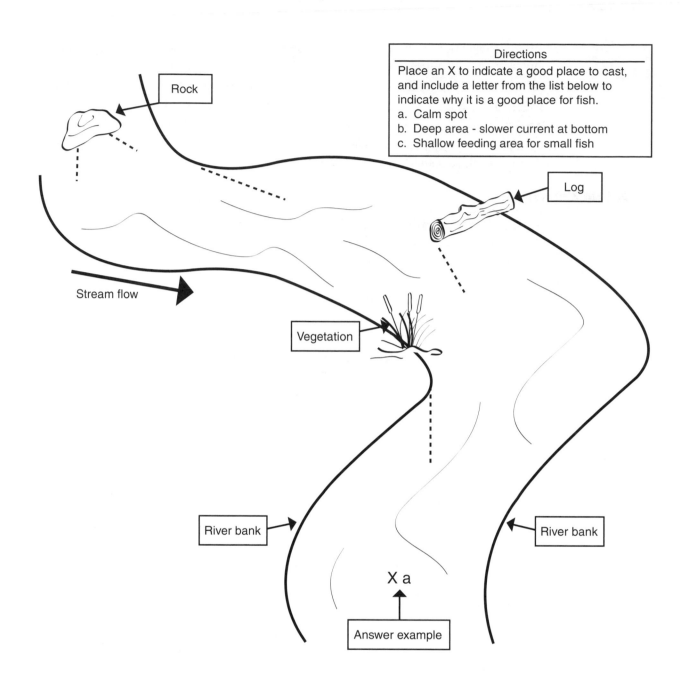

Rock

Log

Stream flow

Vegetation

River bank

River bank

X a

Answer example

From *Interdisciplinary Teaching Through Outdoor Education,* by Camille Bunting, 2006, Champaign, IL: Human Kinetics.

CASTING GOLF

Lesson Objectives

Students will be able to cast accurately from various distances.

Character Focus

Trustworthiness

Curriculum Standards

Physical Education 1, 2, 5, and 7

Materials

- Nine targets of various sizes (hula hoops, circles of rope, or other objects)
- Numbered traffic cones to indicate casting tees
- At least one rod and reel with casting plugs for every pair of students
- Casting Golf scorecards (see page 155)

Preparation

- Set up a nine-hole casting golf course. Make some holes farther from tee to target than others. The holes can range from 15 to 50 yards (14 to 46 meters), but will depend upon available space.
- Prepare scorecards. Indicate what a par score is for each hole.

Lesson Sequence ◠ ◣

1. Have pairs of students combine with another pair to create foursomes.
2. Use a shotgun start, meaning the foursomes all start at different tees. If class size allows it, skip one hole between foursomes.
3. Each group of four students shares two rods and reels. Students take turns casting from the "tee," handing off the rod and reel to another student and going to stand where their plug landed. Students then make their next cast from where their previous cast landed.
4. Students keep their own score on a scorecard.
5. Foursomes progress through the holes in consecutive order, completing as many holes as possible.

Discussion and Review ☺

- How did competition affect your casting form? Did it encourage you to be more careful or did you get careless?
- Why do you think we are sometimes tempted to cheat on things like our scores? (We want to do well and not be embarrassed.)
- How do you feel when you have worked hard to do well at something, compared to when you cheated to make it appear that you did well? (Cheating takes away the good feeling of accomplishment.)
- How did trustworthiness get tested today? (Casting from the tee and not in front; casting from exactly where your plug landed; counting your score correctly; recording your score correctly.)

153

Teaching Tips

- If possible, skip a hole between each foursome.
- You can join in and cast along with a group.
- Be a good role model for trustworthiness rather than strictly policing the group for following the rules.

Possible Character Affirmations ⤺

- This group is dong a great job of being honest.
- Jacob, thank you for not trying to enforce the rules for everyone and just making sure you were playing by them.

Casting Golf Scorecard

	Target #	1	2	3	4	5	6	7	8	9	
	Par										
Names											Total

From *Interdisciplinary Teaching Through Outdoor Education,* by Camille Bunting, 2006, Champaign, IL: Human Kinetics.

Casting Golf Scorecard

	Target #	1	2	3	4	5	6	7	8	9	
	Par										
Names											Total

From *Interdisciplinary Teaching Through Outdoor Education,* by Camille Bunting, 2006, Champaign, IL: Human Kinetics.

Archery

Archery has evolved from a skill for hunting food and materials for clothing to an Olympic sport. Stone arrowheads have been found in Africa that indicate bow and arrow use as early as 50,000 B.C. Archery has a fascinating history and connections to diverse curriculum areas such as math, physical education, physics, and history.

The first bows were made from tree branches and were probably fairly short so they could be used for hunting in wooded areas. In Egypt, a rock fresco, or drawing, of an archer has been dated to about 7,500 B.C. It is known as the Tassili rock fresco. It was the Egyptians who developed composite bows made from several different materials. These bows were much stronger than wooden bows and often required two people to get them strung. Warrior archers often rode and shot from chariots or horseback and used longbows with great success. During the 17th century, firearms became more accurate and reliable, and the bow's use as a war weapon gradually faded.

However, as the bow lost favor as a weapon, archery became a popular sport. Archery made its debut as an Olympic sport in 1900 in Paris. It was also included in the 1904, 1908, and 1920 Olympic Games. Due to a lack of organization and international rules, however, archery was dropped from the Olympics until the 1972 Munich Games. In 1931 the International Archery Federation was founded and began developing official rules for competition and promoting the sport of archery.

Archery is an excellent activity for actually experiencing principles of physics and the importance of perseverance, trustworthiness, and citizenship. It is often a very satisfying physical experience because improvement can be rapid and success comes as the student applies new concepts. Students will be proud of their progress as well as their growing understanding of physical principles. Safety concerns are the typical reason for not including archery in school programs, but safety can be managed with organization and structure.

This unit covers the basics of equipment, terminology, and shooting. Hitting the target consistently requires practice and a partner who can give feedback regarding form. Safety rules are also discussed.

Archery Equipment

As with any sport, equipment quality varies. This unit will only present basic equipment information and will not attempt to deal with the finer points of equipment design and comparisons. The two basic pieces of equipment are the bow and arrow.

Bows

There are three basic types of bows: recurve, compound, and longbow. The recurve bow (figure 9.1) is preferred by some because of its ability to shoot faster (velocity) and farther (distance) than a straight-ended bow of the same weight. The longbow is the most basic bow. Its shape has not changed since its invention between 9,000 and 6,000 B.C. Aiming is done by aiming the tip of the arrow while at a position of full draw. The archer must adjust the point of aim depending upon the target distance.

Compound bows have become the bow of choice for field archery and competitive target archery. They have a system of cams and pulleys at the ends of the bow limbs to increase arrow flight distance and speed. However, most school programs begin their archery activities with the more basic long or recurve bows. Compound bows are much more expensive and are not necessary for learning the fundamentals of the sport.

Stringing the bow is referred to as bracing the bow. It is the process of bending the bow so the ends of the bowstring can be securely placed in the string notches close to the ends of the upper and lower limbs. There are different methods for bracing a bow, but the recommended method for beginners is depicted in figure 9.2. Place the bowstring in one of the string notches and place that end of the bow in front of the left ankle. The bow should be turned so its back is against the left ankle. The right leg then moves between the bowstring and the bow face. When this position has been achieved, push the upper end of the bow away from the right leg and toward the front of the body. As the bow is bent, with the right hand slide the end of the bowstring up toward the end of the bow and into the string notch.

Bow Terminology

arrow plate—Part of the arrow rest lying flat against the side of the bow handle's sight

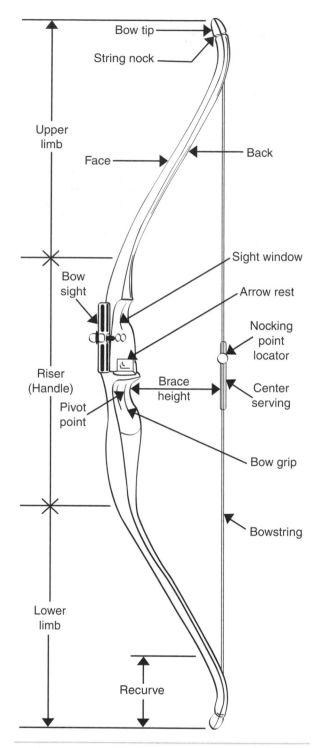

Figure 9.1   The recurve bow is often the bow of choice.

window and against which the arrow slides when being drawn or released.

arrow rest—Piece of plastic or metal that protrudes from the arrow plate to hold the arrow.

bow grip—Part of the bow handle that sits between the thumb and forefinger of the bow hand.

Figure 9.2 Bracing, or stringing, a bow.

bow sight—Mechanical device attached to the bow with which the archer can aim directly at the target.

bow tip—Very end of the bow.

string nock—Indention at each end of the bow that holds the string when the bow is braced.

brace—Process of stringing the bow.

center serving—Protective string wound onto bowstring at point where arrows are nocked.

nocking-point locator—Small metal bead located on bowstring to indicate proper nocking point.

Arrows

The arrow is the second main piece of archery equipment. Arrows can be made of a variety of materials, but wooden or plastic arrows are used for beginning target practice. Refer to figure 9.3 to become familiar with the parts of the arrow.

Arrow Terminology

nock—Plastic end of the arrow that is formed to fit onto the center serving of the bowstring.

pile—Point or tip of the arrow.

shaft—Body of the arrow.

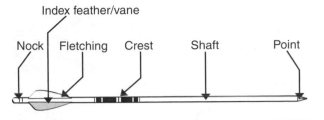

Figure 9.3 Parts of an arrow.

cresting—Decorative coloring on the arrow used for identification.

fletchings—Feathers attached to the arrow to help stabilize the arrow during flight.

index feather—Feather positioned at a right angle to the side of the bow when the arrow is nocked. Usually it is of a different color from the other two feathers on the arrow.

vanes—Plastic feathers used in place of fletchings.

Basics of Shooting

Now that you are familiar with the basic parts of the main equipment, it is time to learn the basics of actually shooting. The objective of target archery is to hit the center of the target. For this to happen, the archer must follow a number of steps. First, however, the archer must make a decision about which hand should hold the bow and which hand should draw the string. This decision is made by determining which eye is dominant. Just because a person is right-handed does not mean the right eye will be dominant or vice versa.

Eye Dominance

The dominant eye is the eye that does the aiming if both eyes remain open. A person who is right-eye dominant should hold the bow in the left hand and pull the bowstring with the right hand. The opposite applies for a left-eye dominant person. This allows the dominant eye to look down the arrow for aiming.

To determine which eye is dominant, hold your hands out at arm's length and form a triangle with the thumb and forefingers of your hands (figure 9.4a). Keeping both eyes open, look at an object in the distance through the hole formed by your hands. Now make the hole smaller by

a

b

Figure 9.4 Determining eye dominance includes holding the hands out at arm's length and forming a triangle *(a)*, making the triangle smaller *(b)*, and then moving the hands back to touch the face.

moving your hands closer together until the hole is only an inch or two in diameter (figure 9.4*b*). Keeping the spot in view, slowly move your hands toward your face until they touch your face. The hole formed by your hands should be over one eye. This eye is your dominant eye and will control your aiming. If you are right-handed but left-eye dominant, hold the bow with the right hand and draw the bowstring with the left hand. The other option is to close the dominant eye so you can aim with the nondominant eye.

Ten Steps to Shooting

These steps are the sequence that should be followed when shooting (figure 9.5, *a-i*). To progress as a precision archer, many other fine points must be learned. The information that follows is for beginners.

1. Stance—The archer stands in a comfortable, relaxed position with one foot on each side of the shooting line. The bow-hand side should be toward the target. Feet should be about shoulder-width apart with the weight evenly distributed between the feet and from the ball to heel of each foot. If there is a problem with bowstring clearance across the chest, use an open stance by moving the targetside foot back a few inches (see figure 9.5*a*).

2. Nocking the arrow—Hold the bow out toward the target and parallel to the firing line with the arrow rest pointing to the ceiling or sky. Place the nock of the arrow onto the bowstring under the nocking-point locator bead. If the string does not have a locator, make sure the arrow shaft is perpendicular to the bow handle. Make sure the index feather on the arrow is pointed toward the ceiling or sky and the nock is pushed firmly onto the bowstring. The arrow shaft should be placed onto the arrow rest. See figure 9.5*b*.

3. Bow-hand and string-hand placement—The bow grip is placed in the hand between the thumb and index finger. The thumb and fingers should stay relaxed with the fingers curled around until lightly touching the bow. This is not to grip the bow but to keep it from falling out of the hand when the string is released. The string hand uses

the index, second, and third fingers. Place the index finger above the arrow nock and the second and third fingers below the nock. The thumb tucks in toward the palm and does not touch the arrow. To set the fingers in position, pull slightly on the bowstring and maintain even pressure on all three fingers. See figure 9.5c.

4. Predraw—Push out with the bow arm to set the hand into the bow grip, and then raise the bow arm and draw arm together up to the position shown in figure 9.5d. Keep the shoulders level and in a natural position. The elbow of the draw arm should be raised to shoulder height.

5. Draw—From the predraw position, use the back muscles to pull the elbow of the drawing arm backward in one smooth motion until the drawing hand is against the jaw. The head and body should not move to meet the bowstring. See figure 9.5e.

6. Anchor—This is the location on the jaw where the bowstring hand comes back to and anchors on with each draw. The index finger is firmly against the jaw, the thumb is tucked under the jaw, and the bowstring touches the nose and chin. This position should be exactly the same with

Figure 9.5 The 10-step sequence for shooting a bow and arrow: stance (*a*), nocking the arrow (*b*), bow-hand and string-hand placement (*c*), predraw (*d*), draw (*e*), anchor (*f*), aiming (*g*), release (*h*), follow-through (*i*), and relax (not shown).

each draw. If there is any variation in the position, the amount of force transferred to the arrow will be different, which will affect its flight, which will in turn affect where it lands. See figure 9.5*f*.

7. Aiming—When the bowstring and hand are anchored, the sight pin is moved into the center of the target. Check to make sure that the string is vertical and parallel with the bow. If the hand is not anchored properly or the bow is not positioned correctly, let the bowstring down gently without releasing the arrow and start again. See figure 9.5*g* for proper aiming alignment.

8. Release—Most archers consider the release to be the most important step in the sequence. Two things must be done correctly to have a good release:

   • The fingers must allow the bowstring to slip off all three fingers at the same time.

   • When the release happens, the hand should move backward and come to rest under the ear. Figure 9.5*h* shows the correct position following the release.

9. Follow-through—The follow-through consists of maintaining your release position until the arrow hits the target. Nothing moves—the head, the draw hand, the shoulders, and especially the bow arm maintain the release position. Any movement before the arrow hits the target can affect where the arrow hits. See figure 9.5*i*.

10. Relax—Relax for a few seconds after each shot to allow the muscles to recover. If not allowed at least 15 to 20 seconds between shots to relax, the muscles may not perform consistently.

Safety

With any sport, safety is important. However, it is especially important to follow safety rules in archery since carelessness could result in someone getting shot. Getting shot is not the only safety consideration, though. Archers must take care to protect their bow arm from getting in the way of the string, to avoid blistering the fingers, and to avoid stepping across the shooting line before everyone is finished shooting. (See Archery Safety Rules, page 171.)

Bow-Arm Position

Bow-arm positioning is a safety issue for the archer. If the elbow of the bow arm hyperextends (see figure 9.6*a*), the inside of the elbow

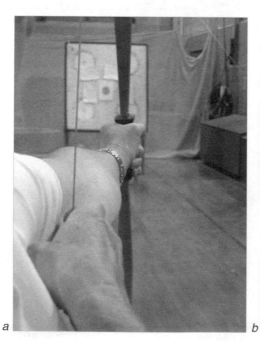

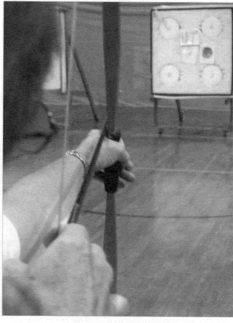

a *b*

Figure 9.6 Hyperextension when holding a bow should be avoided (*a*). The proper arm position involves rolling the elbow down and out of the way of the bowstring (*b*).

is in the path of the released bowstring. If the bowstring hits or slaps the forearm, a painful abrasion or blister can result. To prevent this, the elbow must not be hyperextended and must be consciously rolled down out of the way of the bowstring (see figure 9.6b).

Protective Equipment

Protective equipment can be worn to protect the forearm from injury and the fingers from blisters (figure 9.7). Although they are not absolute requirements, arm guards can be especially helpful. Finger tabs can prevent blisters, but for beginning archers they can also be cumbersome. Only when shooting many arrows is there a likelihood of getting finger blisters.

Shooting-Range Signals

Shooting-range signals are important for everyone to know so safety can be maintained. Three situations require signals. One signal indicates when it is safe for archers to begin shooting. The second signal indicates that shooting is over and it is safe to retrieve arrows from the target. The third signal communicates an emergency and everyone should stop shooting immediately and step back from the shooting line. These signals can be verbal signals if the group is small enough for everyone to easily hear. If hearing could be questionable, a whistle works well. For example, establish one whistle blast to begin shooting, two whistle blasts to indicate it is safe to retrieve arrows, and three blasts to indicate an emergency (see Archery-Range Signals, page 172).

Aiming

Most bows for beginners are not equipped with a sighting mechanism for aiming. Without a special mechanism for sighting, the tip of the arrow is used.

Sighting Mechanism

It is relatively simple to make a sighting aid by adding a strip of masking tape along the back of the bow handle. Stick a straight pin with a small bead head into the masking tape with the head extending out perpendicular to the bow. When shooting at distances of 70 to 30 feet (9 to 21 meters), the pin extends out somewhere in the area of the sight plate but well above where the fletchings will cross the bow. It will take several shots to locate the pin correctly.

Scoring

In an archery tournament, archers shoot what is called a *round*. A round consists of a certain number of arrows shot. That number is decided upon by tournament officials and can range widely. The round is divided into ends, which is the number of arrows each archer shoots before going to the target to retrieve the arrows. An end usually ranges from three to six arrows.

The target face has a color scheme for scoring, starting in the middle with a gold bull's-eye and then concentric rings in the order of red, blue, black, and white. Target faces can vary in the number of rings, but generally the bull's-eye is worth 10 points and each consecutive ring outward is worth 1 less point (see figure 9.8).

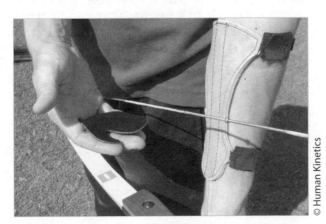

Figure 9.7 An arm guard and finger tabs are protective equipment for archery.

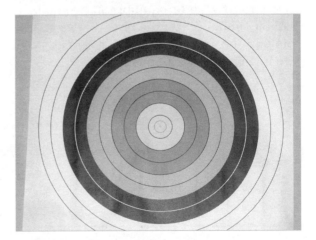

© Human Kinetics

Figure 9.8 A photo of the official National Archery Association (NAA) target face.

Groupings and Adjustments

When you hit the target, take several shots using the same point of aim before adjusting or changing your aim. The goal is to achieve a grouping of arrows in a relatively small area when using the same point of aim. When this is accomplished, you know that you are consistent in your aim, form, and release. You can then adjust the aim to get your arrows to hit closer to the bull's-eye. If your grouping is high, move your pin up. If your grouping is to the left of the bull's-eye, move the pin head farther out from the edge of the bow.

Science of Archery

As in many activities involving movement, archery is a process of converting energy from one form to another. In archery, energy is converted from the potential energy in the archer's arm and back to the potential energy in the bent limbs of the bow when the string is drawn back. When the string is released, the potential energy in the bow limbs is transferred back through the string and converted to kinetic energy in the arrow as it flies forward. In addition to the act of sighting down the arrow to aim or to align the sighting pin with the target, you should consider other factors when aiming. Some of these factors are force, trajectory, and weight (force × trajectory = distance).

Physics Terms Relevant for Archery

• **Potential energy.** Potential energy is the energy an object has stored due to its position relative to its zero or equilibrium position. For example, in figure 9.5*i* the bow is in its equilibrium position, and in figure 9.5*f* it is in its elastic potential-energy position (see page 161).

• **Kinetic energy.** Kinetic energy is the energy of motion. An object that has motion, whether it is vertical or horizontal motion, has kinetic energy. In archery, when the bowstring is released, the potential energy stored in the bow is transferred to the arrow through the string, producing kinetic energy.

• **Force.** Force is a push or pull upon an object resulting from the object's interaction with another object. For example, when the drawn bowstring is released, it exerts a push on the arrow. The weight that is required to bring the bowstring to a fully drawn position affects the amount of force that will be applied to the arrow. Bows vary by the pounds of pull required to draw the bowstring. For example, a bow for a young person might require 15 pounds (7 kilograms) of pull whereas a bow for an older, more muscular archer could be a 30-pound bow (14 kilograms). The greater the pounds of pull (force) required, the greater the force (push) that will be applied to the arrow and the greater the velocity of the arrow's flight.

• **Trajectory.** Trajectory is the angle at which the arrow flies. Trajectory angle is expressed in the number of degrees the arrow's flight is from level, or parallel, with the ground. See figure 9.9 for an illustration of the association between trajectory and distance.

Physical Training for Archers

All athletes must be in good physical condition to perform to their best ability. Three areas are of special importance to the physical conditioning of archers: flexibility, strength, and diet.

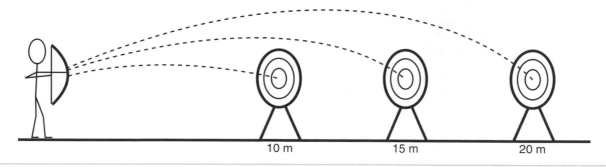

Figure 9.9   Trajectory and distance.

Flexibility

Flexibility is the range of motion possible in the joints and is influenced by bone structure, muscle bulk, and the length of tendons and ligaments. To increase range of movement in the joints that are important for archers, use the following stretching exercises.

- Posterior and anterior deltoid stretch

- Rhomboid stretch

- Rotator stretch

Strength

Strength in archery includes not only the muscle power required to draw a bow but also to maintain balance and remain steady as you aim. The muscle groups used in archery where strength is required are

- the upper back and shoulder muscles to draw the bow,
- the upper and lower shoulder muscles to control the draw arm,
- the arm muscles to extend the bow arm, and
- the finger muscles to hold the bowstring.

To strengthen these muscles, use exercises that imitate the movement of shooting a bow. When strengthening specific muscles be sure to include both the right and left sides to maintain a balance of muscle strength. The following exercises are examples of good strengthening exercises for archers.

- Strengthening the abdominals

- Strengthening the medial deltoid and trapezius with side flies

- Strengthening the trapezius, rhomboids, and deltoids with upright rows

ARCHERY UNIT PLAN

Unit Objectives

Students will:

- trace archery development from its beginnings to today,
- be able to string and shoot a bow with accuracy to consistently hit a target at 50 feet (15 meters), and
- apply principles of trajectory, velocity, and mass for adjusting their aim.

Character Focus

Citizenship, perseverance, trustworthiness

Curriculum Areas

Social Studies (History and Civics), Science, Physical Education

Assessment Activity

Record total score of each end shot during the last two days and drop all but the two highest end total scores. Have students label the parts of a bow and arrow and identify definitions of archery terms.

Archery Day Planner

Day	Topic	Concepts and skills	Teaching activities	Standards
1	What is archery?	Types of equipment; basic safety rules; archery terminology; eye dominance; archery's place in history	Show different types of equipment. Discuss how bows and arrows began and have evolved. Demonstrate eye dominance and how to find the dominant eye.	History 1 and 2; Science 7
2*	Steps of shooting a bow	Using equipment correctly; stringing the bow; ten steps of shooting	Review equipment parts and how to find the dominant eye. Demonstrate how to string the bow and the 10 steps. Student pairs practice stringing a bow and shooting from 30 feet (9 meters).	Civics 24; Physical Education 2 and 5; Science 9
3	Correct posture and sight alignment	Correct posture and string alignment; grouping arrows; sight adjustment	Demonstrate correct posture and shooting form. Explain sight alignment using arrow grouping. Students shoot from 30 feet (9 meters).	Civics 24; Physical Education 1, 2, and 5
4	Shooting for accuracy	Basic steps of tuning a bow; sight adjustments for greater distance	Introduce the tuning and sighting-in of a bow. Demonstrate the difference in sighting at a distance of 50 feet (15 meters) as compared to 30 feet (9 meters). Students practice shooting at 50 feet (15 meters).	Civics 24; Physical Education 1, 2, and 5
5*	Archery and physics	Relationship of velocity, trajectory, and weight and how they affect the flight of an arrow	Define archery terms and display in writing. Show the relationship between velocity and trajectory; demonstrate aiming and shooting from varying distances. Students shoot from 50 feet (15 meters).	Science 9 and 10, Physical Education 2 and 5
6	Archery as an Olympic sport	Types of archery competitions; how athletes train to compete in archery	Show pictures of competitions and charts of muscles involved. Hand out sample workouts of Olympic archers. Students try a few of the exercises to discover which muscles are worked and then shoot from 50 feet (15 meters).	Physical Education 2 and 5; History 1 and 2
7	Archery tournament	Tournament structure and competition	Run the class as an archery tournament. Each student shoots three ends of three arrows to complete one round.	Civics 24; Physical Education 2, 5, and 6

* Has a corresponding lesson plan.

STEPS OF SHOOTING A BOW

Lesson Objectives

Students will:

- correctly string a bow,
- follow the 10 steps of shooting,
- recognize the terms *potential energy* and *kinetic energy*,
- practice shooting from 30 feet (9 meters), and
- practice perseverance, trustworthiness, and good citizenship on the archery shooting range.

Character Focus

Perseverance, trustworthiness, citizenship

Curriculum Standards

Civics 24; Physical Education 2 and 5; Science 9

Materials

- One target for every pair of students
- One bow for every pair of students
- Six arrows for every pair of students
- One arrow quiver (can be a traffic cone with slightly enlarged opening at the top) to hold six arrows for each pair of archers
- 100-foot (30-meter) tape measure
- Shooting line parallel to the targets (if shooting indoors, it can be a line on the floor; if shooting outdoors, it can be a long rope or string)
- Poster with range safety rules
- Poster with shooting-range signals
- Posters with words and definitions for perseverance, trustworthiness, and citizenship (see Appendix C)
- Posters with words and definitions for potential energy and kinetic energy (see pages 173 and 174)
- Poster with the 10 steps of shooting a bow (see page 175)

Preparation

- Set up shooting range with all equipment and posters.
- Set up shooting line 30 feet (9 meters) from targets.
- If shooting indoors, hang sheets or canvas tarps a few feet behind targets to stop arrows that miss the targets. (Arrows should not be allowed to hit walls.)
- Be sure to set up targets so there is no danger to anything downrange.

Lesson Sequence △

1. Review equipment and parts.
2. Review how to find the dominant eye.
3. Introduce the safety rules of the shooting range and the shooting-range signals.
4. Introduce how the shooting range is set up (targets, quivers, shooting line).
5. Introduce how to brace (string) a bow.

Activity 1 △ ㄴ

1. Put students in pairs.
2. Have pairs stand along the shooting line, with one student in each pair standing on the line and the other student about 5 feet (152 centimeters) behind the line.
3. The student on the line practices bracing the bow two times, then the pair trades places and the other student braces the bow twice.

Activity 2 △ ㄴ

1. Demonstrate and explain the 10 steps of shooting a bow.
2. Demonstrate all steps twice.
3. Have student pairs take turns going through the 10 steps without an arrow and without actually releasing the bowstring. Correct form individually and in groups. There should be no dry firing (releasing the bowstring without an arrow)!

Questions ☺ ⤶

- Why do you think our character words for this unit are perseverance, trustworthiness, and citizenship? (It is going to take perseverance to be able to hit the bull's-eye. We have to be trustworthy and good citizens to make sure everyone stays safe, because if we're not, someone could get shot and hurt very badly.)
- Citizenship means that you will act in the best interest of the whole group. Is everyone willing to do that?
- Trustworthiness means that you each can be trusted to follow all of the rules. Is everyone willing to do that?
- Perseverance means that although you may not hit the target the first few times you shoot, you will continue to work to improve your skill. Is everyone willing to do that?

Possible Character Affirmations

- Granger, thank you for following the safety rules and being trustworthy.
- Joanne and Jonle, you are being excellent citizens when you help other students remember the steps for safe shooting.

Activity 3 △ ◠ ㄴ

1. Demonstrate and explain process of nocking the arrow, drawing, aiming, releasing, and following through.
2. Appoint two shooting-line monitors and two downrange monitors.
3. Remind students to follow shooting-range signals!
4. Partners take turns shooting four arrows each from 30 feet (9 meters).

Questions

- In shooting a bow, what do you think is potential energy? (The muscles have the potential to contract, draw the bowstring, and bend the bow; the bent bow has potential energy with the string drawn back.)
- How is potential energy transferred in shooting a bow? (The muscles actually contract, and that energy is transferred to the bow because it is now bent; that energy is transferred to the arrow, sending it flying.)

Activity 4

Repeat the shooting and retrieving process as time allows. Leave adequate time for questions.

Discussion and Review

How were our trustworthiness, citizenship, and perseverance today?

Teaching Tips

- Be vigilant about having the students follow all the safety rules.
- Triple-check the shooting range to make sure no one could possibly get behind the targets.
- When archers are retrieving their arrows, the partners should stay behind the shooting line and hold the bow.

Safety Tips

- Have four students serve as safety monitors. Two students take turns monitoring the shooting line, making sure no one steps in front of the line before the "retrieve arrows" signal. Two students take turns monitoring downrange, making sure all students are behind the shooting line before the "OK to shoot" signal.
- Shooting-line monitors also monitor that the shooting partners hold the bow and stay behind the shooting line when arrows are being retrieved.
- Downrange monitors also monitor how arrows are pulled from the targets. To pull an arrow, place one hand on the target with fingers on both sides of the arrow. With the other hand slowly pull the arrow out of the target. The tips are always held in the palm when returning to the shooting line.

Possible Character Affirmations ☺

- I am proud of this class for the way you followed the safety rules.
- Thank you for being trustworthy and good citizens today.
- This group has been very aware of the importance of following the safety rules, and I appreciate your trustworthiness.

Reference

http://library.thinkquest.org/27344/heavy.htm

Archery Safety Rules

1. Always straddle the shooting line when preparing to shoot.

2. Never draw, aim, or shoot your bow unless you have been given the signal to shoot.

3. Never cross the shooting line until you have been given the signal to do so.

4. Never dry fire your bow (release the bowstring without an arrow).

5. Draw your bow only while pointing the arrow at the target.

6. If an arrow falls in front of the shooting line, drag it back if you can reach it with your bow. If you cannot reach it, leave it there until the signal is given to retrieve the arrows.

7. Step back from the shooting line when you have finished shooting.

8. Make sure no one is standing behind you while you remove your arrows, and do not stand directly in front of the target when arrows are being removed.

9. Never leave anyone alone at a target. This reduces the possibility of the misperception that all is clear when it's not.

10. When returning to the shooting line with arrows, carry the tips in the palm of your hand to prevent accidents, and never run back to the line.

From *Interdisciplinary Teaching Through Outdoor Education,* by Camille Bunting, 2006, Champaign, IL: Human Kinetics.

ARCHERY-RANGE SIGNALS

One whistle—It's safe to shoot.

Two whistles—Shooting is over, retrieve arrows.

Three whistles—Stop!

From *Interdisciplinary Teaching Through Outdoor Education*, by Camille Bunting, 2006, Champaign, IL: Human Kinetics.

POTENTIAL ENERGY

The stored energy of an object when its position is altered from its usual position.

From *Interdisciplinary Teaching Through Outdoor Education*, by Camille Bunting, 2006, Champaign, IL: Human Kinetics.

KINETIC ENERGY

The energy of motion.

1. Take your stance
2. Notch the arrow
3. Position draw hand and bow hand
4. Position bow arm for pre-draw
5. Draw the bow
6. Anchor
7. Hold and aim
8. Release
9. Follow through
10. Relax

From *Interdisciplinary Teaching Through Outdoor Education,* by Camille Bunting, 2006, Champaign, IL: Human Kinetics.

PHYSICS AND ARCHERY

Lesson Objective

Students will use physics concepts to adjust their aim.

Character Focus

Trustworthiness, citizenship

Curriculum Standards

Physical Education 2 and 5; Science 9 and 10

Materials

- One outside target for each pair of archers
- One bow for each pair of archers
- Four arrows for each pair of archers
- 100-foot (30-meter) tape measure
- Moveable shooting line, such as a long rope
- One arrow quiver (traffic cone) for each pair of archers

Preparation

- Set up targets and 50-foot (15-meter) shooting line outside.
- Be sure to leave plenty of room behind the targets so arrows that miss will land in the grass without possibly hitting anything.

Lesson Sequence

1. Shoot to determine point of aim at a distance of 50 feet (15 meters).
2. Move shooting line back to explore trajectory.

Activity 1 (Setup for focus on physics concepts)

- Tell the class they will begin by shooting one end of four arrows each.
- Ask them to pay special attention to their point of aim.
- Remind students to follow shooting-range signals!
- Students shoot one end. Have students identify the point of aim to their partner and mark it on the target.

Activity 2

- Move the shooting line back to 70 feet (21 meters) and have students keep their same point of aim for at least their first arrow. Each student shoots one end of four arrows.
- After this end, have students mark their point of aim on the target.

Questions

- Where was your point of aim for this end compared to the first end you shot? (Higher)
- Why did your point of aim need to be higher? (Because we shot from farther back)

- We shot from 50 feet (15 meters) during the first end and from 70 feet (21 meters) during the second end. If we moved the shooting line up to 30 feet (9 meters), how would that affect your point of aim? (Point of aim would be lower.)

Activity 3

Show pictures of arcs with different trajectories. Then show pictures of arcs with the same trajectory but different velocities.

Questions

- When we moved our shooting line farther back from the targets, we had to move our point of aim higher than before. That raised the trajectory of our arrow. How could we keep the same point of aim when shooting from a greater distance and still hit the same point on the target? (Put more speed on the arrow—velocity.)
- How can we get more speed, or velocity, on the arrow? (Use a stronger bow, one that takes more strength, to draw back the bowstring.)
- Demonstrate how a greater velocity works by shooting one arrow with the bowstring drawn back only halfway and a second arrow from a full draw. Make sure the trajectories of both are the same.
- What would you have to do to be able to draw a more powerful bow? (Have stronger back and arm muscles)
- Do you know which muscles would have to be stronger, their names, and what exercises to do?

Possible Character Affirmation ☺

Jesse and Wu Lee, I really appreciated your trustworthiness with the equipment while I was doing the demonstration.

Activity 4

Three or four students shoot at one time to see which one can shoot an arrow the farthest. (Limit to three or four for safety.)

1. Remind students of how trajectory and draw affect the distance of the arrow.
2. When the arrows land, mark the farthest arrow by putting a piece of paper with the student's name on the arrow and leaving it in the ground. Retrieve all other arrows.
3. The next group of students shoot, mark the farthest arrow, and retrieve all other arrows.
4. Repeat this procedure until all students have had a chance to shoot.

Possible Character Affirmation ☺ ᕙ

Both of you have been very good to stay behind the shooting line. Thank you for being good examples for your classmates.

Discussion and Review ⌂ ⌐

- If you were going to have a contest between archers (both using 20-pound [9-kilogram] bows) to see who could shoot an arrow the farthest, would you want to sponsor the archer who was the strongest or the one who knew the exact trajectory to get the most distance from their shot? (If both archers were shooting bows that require equal pounds of pull, then the more knowledgable archer would have the advantage. However, if the stronger archer were shooting with a bow requiring more pounds of pull than the more knowledgable archer, the stronger archer would have the advantage.)

- Let's say that two archers are competing in target archery. One archer has a 35-pound (16-kilogram) bow and the other a 20-pound (9-kilogram) bow. The targets are placed at 75 feet (23 meters). Which archer will have the highest point of aim and why? (The archer with the 20-pound bow.)
- Tomorrow we are going to talk about how to become an archer who can use a 35-pound bow.

Teaching Tips

- Be vigilant about having the students follow all the safety rules.
- Triple-check the shooting range to make sure no one could possibly get behind the targets.
- When archers are retrieving their arrows, partners should stay behind the shooting line and hold their partner's bow.

Safety Tips

- Have four students serve as safety monitors. Two students take turns monitoring the shooting line, making sure no one steps in front of the line before the "retrieve arrows" signal. Two students take turns monitoring downrange, making sure all students are behind the shooting line before the "OK to shoot" signal.
- Shooting-line monitors also monitor that the shooting partners hold the bow and stay behind the shooting line when arrows are being retrieved.
- Downrange monitors also monitor how arrows are pulled from the targets and that tips are held in the palm when returning to the shooting line.

Possible Character Affirmation ☺

This group has been trustworthy with the equipment and with following the safety rules, and I'm proud of you.

Reference

http://library.thinkquest.org/27344/heavy.htm

Rock Climbing

Chapter 10

© Human Kinetics

Rock climbing is probably as old as the rocks. However, the difference between ancient rock climbing and modern rock climbing is the difference between necessity and recreation. Long ago, people climbed to get from one place to another if they couldn't find another way around. Today, people climb for fun. Rock climbing is one component of a broader sport called mountaineering. Mountaineering is the sport of climbing to the top of mountain peaks 14,000 feet (4,267 meters) and higher and often requires multiple activity skills. Some of the activities involved in mountaineering are backpacking, camping, and hiking, as well as climbing snow, ice, and rock. Today, most of these activities can be done individually and rock climbing has become very popular—so popular, in fact, that there are now indoor climbing gyms all over the United States and many schools even have artificial climbing walls. These facilities are excellent venues for learning some of the skills of rock climbing, and they are great places to train and practice. However, climbing in the outdoors makes for an even greater experience due to the added benefit of the natural environment.

AUTHOR'S NOTE

This chapter makes no attempt to teach the skills of climbing or rappelling. These skills should be learned from an experienced instructor. Background information is provided that can be shared with students, but the teacher is encouraged to acquire safety knowledge and skills before conducting any climbing or rappelling activities.

Climbing Basics

Before we can begin discussing technical aspects of climbing, we need to present some common terms and their definitions. Only the main terms are included, but many others can be accessed on some of the Web sites or books listed in the references and resources at the end of the book.

Climbing Terms

belay—Safety system used in climbing.

artificial anchors—Various pieces of hardware placed in cracks of rock with rope run through them. Also called protection, the anchors provide an anchor point for the belay rope so the climber is protected from falling to the ground.

natural anchor—A large boulder, large rock outcropping, or strong tree that can be used as an anchor for a belay or rappel rope.

climbing techniques—Ways for climbers to place their hands and feet to maneuver up a climb. Techniques differ according to the type of climb and skill of the climber. Some techniques take more finesse and flexibility, while others take more strength.

top rope—A top-rope climb is climbing with the belay rope anchored at the top of the climbing route. For this type of climb, the belayer can be either at the top or bottom of the climb. If climbers fall, they only fall a distance equal to the amount of slack in the belay rope plus the stretch in the rope.

lead climbing—Climbers use protection (artificial anchor) by placing it, pulling the belay rope up from behind, clipping it into the protection, and progressing on up the climb. If climbers fall, they will fall the distance they have climbed above the last anchor and that same distance below the anchor.

pitch—Segment of a climb. Lead climbing allows climbers to climb long vertical distances. However, the climbs must be completed in segments or pitches no longer than the length of the rope.

route—A way to the top, or the path of a particular climb. Some climbs are negotiated according to any way a climber decides to go. When the climb is completed, that climber completed a particular route. The same area of rock might be climbed via a different route by another climber. For example, El Capitan in Yosemite National Park has many specific routes, each with its own name.

As people climb, they choose their route to the top. To allow climbers to communicate the difficulty of various routes, grading systems have been developed. There are a number of different grading systems, but the one most often used in the United States is the Yosemite Decimal System (YDS). This system categorizes terrain according to the techniques and equipment required to ascend the terrain. It uses two terms: class (difficulty of each move) and grade (overall length of time to climb).

- Class 1—A hiking scramble on a rocky incline with no use of hands or equipment.

- Class 2—Scrambling up a rocky incline with use of hands, but most will not need a rope.

- Class 3—Simple climbing with moderate exposure and frequent use of hands. A rope should be available for inexperienced climbers.

- Class 4—Climbing with exposure presenting some increased degree of risk. All beginning climbers should have a belay.

- Class 5—Climbing that involves the use of rope and natural or artificial anchors to protect against a serious fall. In this chapter, all rock climbing is class 5 or 6.

- Class 6—This is direct aid climbing, meaning that ropes and supports are climbed rather than the actual rock.

  - 5.0-5.4—Physically fit climbers can climb at this level with little or no rock-climbing skills, using only natural ability.

  - 5.4-5.7—Requires strength and use of rock-climbing techniques, such as hand jamming.

  - 5.7-5.9—Rock-climbing shoes, good skills, and some strength are usually needed at this level.

  - 5.10-5.14—Requires excellent skills and strength, training for climbing techniques, and time commitment to maintain skills and strength. To get even more precise, 5.10-5.14 climbs can also be broken down into four subcategories (a, b, c, d) to indicate multiple moves at that classification level.

Grade refers to the amount of time required to complete a climb. For top-rope climbing, the type of climbing done in school programs, grade is not an issue. All climbs set up with a top-rope anchor are grade I climbs. However, for lead climbing, grade is a significant consideration.

- Grade I—Single-pitch climbs.
- Grade II—Several pitches.
- Grade III—Many pitches, takes most of a day.
- Grade IV—Many pitches, takes a full day, better keep moving if you don't want to spend the night on the climb.
- Grade V—Most climbing parties will spend two to three days.
- Grade VI—Most climbing parties will spend more than three days to complete the climb.

Most school-based climbing involves grade I top-roped single-pitch climbs, primarily because they can accommodate greater numbers of participants in a given amount of time. In addition, there are limited locations for multipitch climbing and multipitch climbing requires someone to lead climb, which has a much higher level of risk because of the possible fall distances.

Components of Climbing

As with all activities, climbing has certain vital components. We will cover only the components most important for climbing in a school-based program.

Climbing Equipment

Climbing equipment is quite specialized and is often a matter of personal preference. However, there are a few pieces of equipment that are fairly standard in school climbing programs (see figure 10.1, *a-i*).

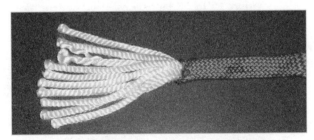

Figure 10.1 *a* Kernmantel rope.

Figure 10.1 *b* Seat harness.

© Human Kinetics

- **rope**—A kernmantel rope is generally the top choice of climbers because of its ease of handling and its core-and-sheath construction that offers some protection to the inner core of the rope. It is made from nylon, is generally 10 to 11 millimeters in diameter, and can either have a lot of shock absorbency or stretch (dynamic) or very little stretch (static). It is good to use a static rope for rappelling to provide the rappeler with a better sense of stability. It is also safe to use a dynamic rope; it just feels less secure at the beginning of the rappel because the rope has more stretch (see figure 10.1*a*).

- **seat harness**—This piece of equipment is worn by the climber and, when attached to the rope, offers support in the event of a fall. It should have leg loops that are securely fitted around the top of each leg and an integrated belt that can be secured against unexpected lengthening (see figure 10.1*b*).

- **chest harness**—This equipment is used with beginners, especially those who are extremely fearful of rappelling. It provides extra security for maintaining an upright position (see figure 10.1c).

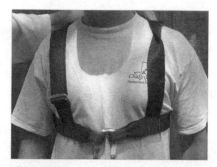

Figure 10.1c Chest harness.

- **carabiner**—Climbing carabiners are used in a number of ways. They allow a rope to be secured to an anchor, they attach a belayer to the belay device and an anchor, and they attach the descending friction device to the rappeller's harness. Carabiners come in a variety of shapes and are either locking or nonlocking styles. The most common shapes and styles are shown in figure 10.1d.

Figure 10.1d Carabiners.

- **belay device**—This device attaches to the climber's harness. The rope is threaded through it for belaying (figure 10.1e). Its primary purpose is to create friction quickly in the event of a fall so the belayer can stop the rope, which stops the fall. It permits a belayer to feed out rope or take in slack while maintaining a sharp bend in the rope so the rope's movement can be stopped at any time.

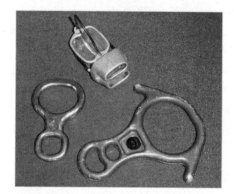

Figure 10.1e Belay devices.

- **helmet**—In a natural rock-climbing area, protective headgear (figure 10.1f) should always be worn by a climber and anyone in the climbing area. Its main purpose is to protect against falling rock and debris, but also it protects the climber from head injury during a fall. The helmet should be specifically produced for climbing and should fit snugly and squarely on the head to protect the forehead and the temples.

Figure 10.1f Helmets.

- **technical hardware (chocks, nuts, hexes, cam)**—Many types of hardware are used in climbing. However, a top-rope climbing program generally does not need this type of equipment. The hardware shown in figure 10.1g is for setting anchors for rope when natural anchors are not available.

Figure 10.1g Chocks, cam, hex.

- **climbing shoes**—Beginning climbers just need a pair of tennis shoes. As the climber improves and the climbs increase in difficulty, climbing shoes are a big advantage (figure 10.1*h*). These shoes fit tightly and have a rubber sole that is especially "sticky" on rock to improve the climbers' grip.

Figure 10.1*h*   Climbing shoes.

- **webbing**—One-inch (3-centimeter) tubular nylon webbing is used in rock climbing to set anchors for belay ropes and belayers. The webbing is generally tied in to a circle, called a sling (figure 10.1*i*), by using a water knot. The sling can then be used as an anchor.

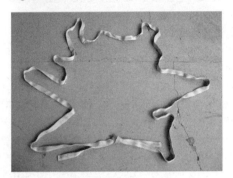

Figure 10.1*i*   Webbing.

Climbing Skills

Climbing skills extend beyond the act of climbing. They involve everything from setting up the climbing anchors to climbing, belaying, and then taking down the rope and anchor equipment. The safety system for climbing is a belay system. The term "belay" means to keep a climber safe by holding onto and taking up any slack in the rope that the climber is using. The person that handles the rope is called the "belayer" and the rope is referred to as the "belay rope."

Knot Tying

There are two main knots for safe climbing, a water knot and a figure 8 follow-through knot. A water knot (figure 3.3, page 39) is used to tie two ends of webbing (flat material) together to form a sling for setting anchors. An overhand knot is tied loosely in one end of the webbing, and then the other end is used to trace the knot in the opposite end backward so the ends of the webbing are pointing in opposite directions from the knot. When the knot is pulled tight, at least 3 inches (8 centimeters) of webbing should extend from the knot on each side. The knot tightens

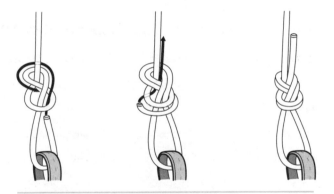

Figure 10.2   A figure 8 follow-through knot.

Reprinted, by permission, from J. Stiel and T.B. Ramsey, 2004, *Climbing walls* (Champaign, IL: Human Kinetics), 95.

down on itself. To untie the knot, push toward the center of the knot from each side.

A figure 8 follow-through knot (figure 10.2) is used to tie the end of the climbing rope to the climber's harness. A loose figure 8 is tied 3 to 4 feet (91 to 122 centimeters) from the end of the belay rope. The loose end is threaded through the leg-loop attachment point and the waist-belt attachment point and then traces the figure 8 knot backward until the end extends out from the knot, pointing away from the climber.

Communication Signals Between Belayer and Climber

Belaying has become the universal term for the safety system of protecting a climber from a serious fall. In belaying, the rope is secured through a belay (friction) device, and as the climber goes up, the belayer takes up the slack in the rope by pulling it through the belay device (see figure 10.3). In the event of a fall, the climber will not fall very far, and the friction of the rope going through the belay device will make it possible for the person belaying to hold the weight of the climber on the rope.

It is imperative that the climber and belayer communicate well with each other. If the climber begins before the belayer is ready to begin taking up the slack in the rope, a serious injury could result. If the belayer thinks the climber has reached the top of the climb and unclips from the belay, the climber could be injured. For this reason, systems have been created to aid the communication process. There are some variations for the calls and responses in table 10.1, but

© Human Kinetics

Figure 10.3   The belayer has the vital role of helping to keep the climber safe.

Table 10.1   Rock-Climbing Calls and Responses

Person speaking	What is said	What it means
Climber	"On belay?"	I'm tied in and ready to go. Are you ready?
Belayer	"Belay on."	I'm ready to belay.
Climber	"Climbing."	I'm starting to climb.
Belayer	"Climb."	I'm taking up the slack in the rope.
Climber	"Up rope."	The rope is too loose.
Belayer	"Thank you."	I heard you and did it.
Climber	"That's me."	The slack is out and I feel the pull of the rope. The rope is not stuck in a crack.
Belayer	"Thank you."	I heard you.
Climber	"Tension."	Put the brake on the rope, I might slip.
Belayer	"Thank you."	I heard you and you've got it.
Climber	"Slack."	I need a little slack. (Each call for slack means the belayer should feed out 1 foot [30 centimeters] of slack toward the climber).
Belayer	"Thank you."	I heard you, and you've got it.
Climber	"Off belay."	I have finished the climb and am in a secure place.
Belayer	"Belay off."	I am no longer belaying you.

Not all climber's signals are always necessary. However, if they are used, the belayer responds with "thank you" as a way of letting the climber know that the belayer heard her and is responding.

these are the commands taught by the National Outdoor Leadership School. The thank-you responses that are shown allow climbers to know the belayer has heard them and has responded.

These signals were developed in mountaineering situations, where communication between climber and belayer often occurs without eye contact and in windy conditions. However, it is good practice to use the signals even when such conditions do not exist, such as in an indoor situation.

Climbing Holds and Moves

There are many different types of handholds, footholds, and ways to move the body to climb certain routes. Figure 10.4 illustrates a few such holds and moves. Rock climbing is more like a combination of gymnastics and ballet than like climbing a ladder.

- **bouldering**—Climbing on large boulders that offer several opportunities to practice climbing holds and moves while remaining fairly close to the ground (see figure 10.4*a*). The safety system for bouldering is spotting and using a crash pad under the climbing area. A good rule of thumb is not to allow the climber's feet to get more than 4 to 5 feet (122 to 152 centimeters) off the ground.

Figure 10.4 *a*   Bouldering.

- **chimney**—A parallel-sided constriction wider than the body (see figure 10.4*b*).

Figure 10.4 *b*   Chimney.

- **edge**—A small, horizontal hold, or to stand on an edge with the corner of a shoe maximizing the pressure applied to a small area of rubber (see figure 10.4*c*).

Figure 10.4 *c*   Edge.

- **hand jam**—Using your hand to gain purchase in a crack by twisting the hand, squeezing or spreading the palm, pulling the thumb down, making a fist, stacking both hands, and so on (see figure 10.4*d*).

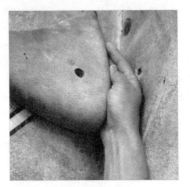

Figure 10.4 *d*   Hand jam.

- **jamming**—Wedging a body part into a crack in order to hold yourself on the wall (see figure 10.4*e*).

Figure 10.4 *e*   Jamming.

- **layback**—Pulling with arms to the side and pushing with the feet in the opposite direction (see figure 10.4*f*).

Figure 10.4 *f*   Layback.

- **mantel**—Climbing technique involving the transfer of upward force from a pulling action to a pushing action, much like a child would climb the kitchen counter to reach the cabinets above (see figure 10.4*g*).

Figure 10.4 *g*   Mantel.

- **rappel**—Self-belaying down a length of a rope to descend (see figure 10.4*h*). This is a method for coming down after getting to the top of a climb if there is no way to walk down. The principle of rappelling is to belay yourself down a rope that is secured at the top. To accomplish this without the rope burning your hands, hardware known as a descender or belay device is used to allow for control over the rate of descent. The more bends the rope makes around the belay device and the tighter the rope is held, the slower the descent will be. The pieces of hardware shown in figure 10.1*e* are typical friction devices used for rappelling.

Figure 10.4 *h*   Rappel.

- **smear**—Placing a large surface area of shoe rubber on a hold to create maximum friction (see figure 10.4*i*).

Figure 10.4 *i* Smear.

- **stem**—Movement requiring opposing outward pressure, used in climbing chimneys (see figure 10.4*j*).

Figure 10.4 *j* Stem.

- **undercling**—Hold that requires fingers to face upward rather than downward (see figure 10.4*k*).

Figure 10.4 *k* Undercling.

Climbing is a great adventure and a wonderful physical-development activity. It is a highly recommended activity that both teachers and students will enjoy. All it takes is some safety training, knot-tying and belaying instruction, and quality equipment.

Climbing in School

The majority of school programs will not be able to take students to a natural rock-climbing area to experience rock climbing. However, it can still be introduced and some of the basic skills taught. Many schools even have artificial climbing walls such as the ones in figure 10.5. But even without a climbing wall, certain skills and concepts can be taught.

For example, belaying can be taught with ropes thrown over the crossbar of a football goal post, the top of a horizontal ladder, or the supports of a basketball goal. Students can belay for each other to climb ladders or trees. Of course, the top of ladders should always be secured to something unmovable. Another possibility is to hang static ropes from a gym or playground pavilion's rafters and have students climb the ropes using prusik slings while being belayed by a team. A prusik is a knot that will slide on another rope when there is no tension on the knot. When tension is put on the not, it tightens around the rope it is tied to and does not slip. These options have all been successfully implemented and have worked quite well in situations without climbing walls. However, before attempting any of these activities, the teacher should be well trained in climbing safety.

Interdisciplinary Connections With Climbing

As with other outdoor activities, climbing offers connections to a variety of curriculum areas. You can choose to emphasize the personal development aspects of climbing, such as confronting fear, being perseverant, or being responsible for another person's safety. Another option is to focus on academic subjects and how they relate to the experience of climbing.

Figure 10.5 Climbing facilities at various schools.

Following are a few examples of curricular connections:

Science

- Friction—The more bends and points of contact with a descender or belay device, the more friction is provided.
- Heat—Friction produces heat. The faster the rope runs through a carabiner or descender, the more heat is produced.
- Why descenders get scored (worn down) right where the rope goes through them (the heat from friction destroys the metal).
- Implications of wear for the brakes on your bicycle or car (the heat from friction wears down and destroys the brake pads).
- What effect does heat have on nylon, such as nylon climbing ropes? (Heat melts nylon.)
- What is the principle of opposing forces, and how might that be used in climbing? (Chimney move, layback move)

Geology or Earth Science

- What are the characteristics of granite, limestone, and sandstone?
- How would these types of rock differ for climbing?
- Compare the types of rock at well-known climbing areas across the United States, such as Yosemite, Red Rocks, Joshua Tree, and Huaco Tanks.

Language Arts

- Describe how the arm and the hand that is gripping the rock feel when you are moving the other hand and arm.
- Describe how your stomach or heart feels when you get to the top of a climb.
- What is the difference between the sensations you feel while belaying as compared to climbing?
- Talk someone else through the beginning part of a rappel.

Climbing and rappelling are excellent educational activities. Leading them does require some training and experience, but that should not prevent you from exploring the options. Many companies build artificial climbing areas that range from not too expensive to quite elaborate. Do a little investigation and give it some thought. This exciting and challenging activity could enhance many curriculum areas.

Character Connections With Climbing

Just as there are curricular connections with climbing and rappelling, there are also opportunities to observe and exhibit positive character qualities. Following are some possible affirmations.

- That was very responsible of you to check her harness and figure 8 follow-through knot to make sure they were secure.
- Nathan, you are being a trustworthy belayer for Adela. You are paying attention and keeping the slack out of the rope, which means you are being trustworthy.
- It is good to be caring and help your classmates get tied into their harness correctly.
- You are being a good citizen by helping put up the harnesses and helmets for the next class.
- Lyndscy, that was courageous of you to hold onto the belay rope securely while Reed caught his breath. Even though your hand got tired, you did your job.
- Class, all of you demonstrated excellent perseverance by continuing to work at that climb until you got it.

To successfully accomplish the activities of climbing and rappelling, people must confront situations that require focused attention, patience, and courage. They must recognize the importance of acting responsibly and follow through with those actions. Failure to act with focused attention, patience, responsibility, and courage can result in tragic consequences. Therefore, these activities provide excellent opportunities to reinforce positive behaviors that really matter.

Canoeing and Kayaking Chapter **11**

anoeing and kayaking are nature-oriented activities. They take place in the great outdoors and can take you to places that are difficult to access by any other means. You have a floating craft to navigate and you are its motor. What could be more fun on this blue planet with all of its water to explore?

Canoeing and kayaking are activities that most schools will not be able to do during a class period. However, boats can be introduced, a few basic skills taught, equipment explained, and wilderness travel options explored. These activities can be fun and educational even without actually getting on the water. If you can work out a way to get on the water, it will be even better. Just remember, it is not only about doing the activity, but also about learning from it.

There are many types of boats we could consider, but this chapter will present three boats, all of which require paddles for propulsion and steering: the open canoe, the white-water kayak, and the sea kayak. Each has a different experience to offer. For the skills discussion, the focus is on the open tandem canoe.

Types of Boats

The canoe, white-water kayak, and sea kayak have many features in common as well as features unique to their particular function. Hull shape and size, decking, and outfitting are some of the characteristics that distinguish the types of boats.

AUTHOR'S NOTE

As with climbing, canoeing and kayaking require specialized safety skills. Teachers should not attempt to take students on the water in boats without an expert or without adequate training themselves. A trained lifeguard should be present if the teacher does not have lifeguard training.

• Canoes can be made for solo paddling or for tandem paddling and typically have an open hull (see figure 11.1). In general, solo canoes are shorter than tandem canoes and their seat is positioned close to the center of the boat. Tandem canoes have two seats—a seat or kneeling position for the bow paddler close front of the boat, and a similar place for the stern paddler close to the back of the boat.

• White-water kayaks have evolved into short little boats, with hull and bottom shape determining the type of paddling it is designed for (see figure 11.2*a*). A flat bottom will help the boat spin on the water, while a more rounded bottom will facilitate downriver paddling. Flat-bottomed kayaks are considered to be play boats and often are taken to a set of rapids for practicing various maneuvers. Downriver kayaks are put on the river at one point and paddled downstream to a different point on the river, usually a distance of several miles.

• Sea kayaks (figure 11.2*b*) are designed for open water, such as lakes or the ocean, rather than rivers. The kayaks may be either a sit-on-top or decked design. If the boat is used for short periods of play during a day, a sit-on-top is a great. If the purpose is touring, where you will pack camping gear in the boat and be out for more than a day

at a time, a decked boat with a cockpit that can be covered is preferable.

The one thing these three types of boats have in common is that they each have specific hull designs (see figure 11.3). Flat bottoms allow for easy turning, V bottoms allow for good tracking or maintaining a direction of travel, and arch- or U-shaped bottoms have less initial stability but good secondary stability (as you are leaning into a turn).

Another component of hull shape is the boat bottom's shape from bow to stern. The straighter the underwater keel line (from a side view), the less maneuverability and the greater tracking ability are available. If the keel line curves upward at the ends of the boat, it is said to have rocker, like the curve of the rocker of a rocking chair. Greater rocker means greater maneuverability and less tracking ability (see figure 11.4).

Since sea kayaks are typically used for traveling distances, they need to be able to track well, so there is less need for rocker and more need for a V- or arch-shaped hull. A white-water kayak that is intended to make sharp turns and spins needs a flat bottom with significant rocker. A tandem canoe can have any combination of the hull designs previously discussed. A canoe can be designed especially for white-water maneuverability, for traveling downriver, or for cruising on lakes. The primary way a boat is used will indicate the most appropriate hull design.

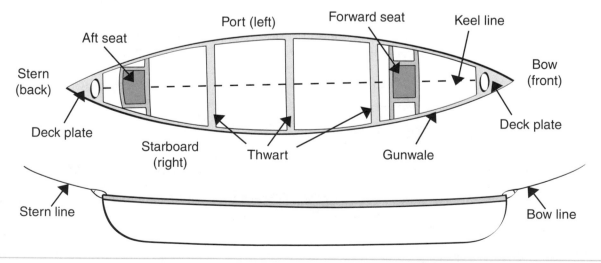

Figure 11.1 Canoe nomenclature.

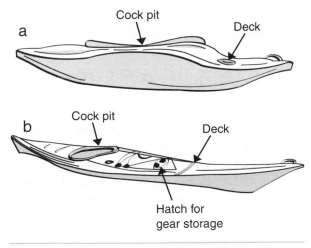

Figure 11.2 White-water kayak (*a*) and sea kayak (*b*) nomenclature.

Equipment

Another thing canoeing, white-water kayaking, and sea kayaking have in common is that they each require the use of a paddle. Each should be paddled only when wearing a personal floatation device (PFD), also known as a life jacket. Other equipment is also a part of these sports.

- Paddle—The paddle is the equipment inserted into the water for maneuvering the boat (see figure 11.5).
- PFD—Personal floatation device, or life jacket. PFDs should be U.S. Coast Guard–approved for the size of the wearer. PFDs provide buoyancy, body protection, and warmth.

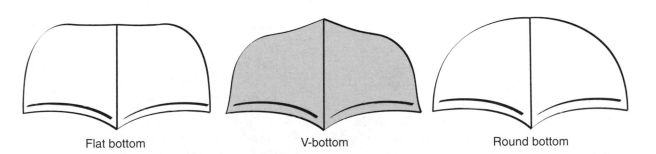

Flat bottom · V-bottom · Round bottom

Figure 11.3 Hull shape makes a difference when selecting a boat for a specific water activity.

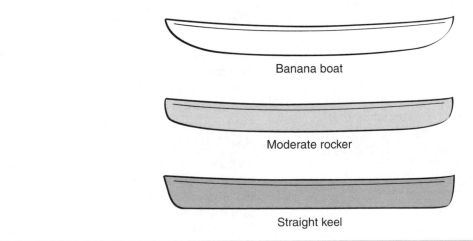

Banana boat

Moderate rocker

Straight keel

Figure 11.4 The curve of a hull rocker determines the maneuverability and tracking ability of the boat.

- Helmet—Head protection to be worn when paddling in rocky areas or in the surf with an increased probability of capsizing. Helmets should be well padded, high quality, and properly fitted.

- Appropriate clothing—Air and water temperature will determine appropriate clothing. Even if the air is warm, when the water temperature plus the air temperature is less than 100 degrees Fahrenheit (38 degrees Celsius), insulating clothes should be worn and a wet suit is recommended. There are nylon-coated splash jackets and pants that can be worn over fleece, wet suits made from neoprene, and even dry suits, all of which provide increasingly warm protection for these water activities. Here are some clothing suggestions:
  - Synthetic shirt and shorts
  - Protective footwear, such as sturdy river sandals or old tennis shoes
  - Extra clothes for warmth in unexpected conditions (synthetic)
  - Sun-protective hat and sunscreen
  - PFD—Always wear one when boating!

- Water bottle—Use one with a short leash and carabiner to clip to the boat. The leash should be short enough that it cannot wrap around your arm or ankle. It should be clipped to the boat so it will not get away and become litter if you capsize.

- Dry bag—Waterproof bag that can carry extra clothes and food. It should also be tied to the boat.

- Whistle—Should be on a very short leash for emergency signaling.

- First aid kit and duct tape—These supplies should be kept in a dry bag and should be easy to access. The duct tape can serve multiple functions, from blister prevention to splinting assistance.

Paddling Skills

Three types of boats have been introduced in this chapter, and each requires unique skills. However, there are also several fundamentals that all three boats have in common. The following presentation of skills is not intended as a substitute for paddling instruction but as an introduction to a few skills for each type of paddle sport.

Five Fundamentals

The basic skills are referred to by the American Canoe Association (ACA) as the five fundamentals. Most of the fundamentals relate to posture while paddling. The idea is to have your larger muscle groups do most of the work and protect your shoulder joints. This text adds a sixth fundamental that is especially important as you are being introduced to a particular boat.

1. Posture. Keep your back relatively straight and in line with your hips and head. This will help keep your weight at the midline of the boat, improve your balance, and facilitate efficient paddle strokes.

2. Keep body weight over the boat. This assists with balance and enables you to lean or edge the boat while maintaining balance. You lean or edge the boat, not your body.

3. The boat moves, not the paddle. Think of paddle strokes as planting your paddle in the water so you can move the boat, not moving the paddle through the water. This mindset will also help engage the larger muscle groups. Visualize planting your paddle in peanut butter and pulling your boat forward.

4. The body turns with the paddle blade. Some people refer to this as "paddling as if you were in a box." Keep your paddle, and therefore your hands, in front of your body. If you have the paddle in the water beside your hip, turn your shoulders to face the paddle (see figure 11.6). This will

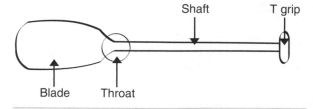

Figure 11.5   Paddle nomenclature.

protect your shoulders from undue stress and vulnerable positions and will allow the larger muscles in your back, chest, and abdomen to do most of the work.

5. Vision. Look beyond the front of the boat to select your route and stay on your chosen course. Work to expand your vision beyond the front of the boat just as you work to perfect your skills with the paddle.

Figure 11.6 Box paddling.

6. When getting in and out of your boat, maintain three points of contact with your hands and feet to improve your weight distribution and balance.

Canoe Skills

A canoe can either be paddled by two people (tandem paddling) or by one person (solo). There are even special solo canoes that are shorter and outfitted for only one person. In this chapter, we will only address tandem paddling.

The following list of skills is specific to canoeing.

• Getting into a canoe can be tricky if you don't remember the rule about three points of contact. For best results, bring the canoe parallel with the shore or dock. The bow paddler holds the boat steady as the stern paddler steps into the center of the boat while holding both gunwales (the top of each side of the canoe). Still holding the gunwales, the stern paddler walks the midline to the stern seat, all the while staying low and centered. At the seat the paddler turns, kneels in a wide-kneed position, rests her rear end on the front edge of the seat, and puts her paddle in the water to stabilize the boat. The bow paddler then repeats the procedure to access her bow-paddling position (see figure 11.7).

Figure 11.7 The proper method for getting into a canoe.

- A canoe paddle has only one blade. It is gripped with one hand on top of the grip (not around the shaft). The other hand is loosely placed around the shaft about an arm's length down from the other hand. The bottom hand should not be at the throat of the blade where it joins the shaft (see figure 11.8).

- Tandem canoeists paddle on opposite sides of the boat and in rhythm with each other. The stern paddler is responsible for steering the boat, but when obstacles are being negotiated the bow paddler helps with the steering.

- The forward stroke is the most important stroke for paddlers, and in canoeing it should be done with the hands stacked one above the other so the top hand is out past the gunwale. Stacked hands allow the paddle shaft to be vertical, and the direction of pull will be parallel to the side of the canoe. For best results, twist at the waist and turn your shoulders away from the paddle as you put it in the water out in front of your knee. As

you pull the boat up to the paddle, untwist at the waist until the paddle is by your hip (see figure 11.9, *a* and *b*).

There are more canoe strokes to learn, but they are best learned from an experienced instructor rather than a book. The second boat we will consider is the white-water kayak. Unlike the canoe, which can be paddled as a tandem or solo boat, white-water kayaks are for solo paddlers.

White-Water Kayak Skills

Kayaks are paddled with a double-bladed paddle (a blade on each end of a shaft) and in a seated position with your legs stretched out in front of you. Because you are almost sitting on the bottom

Figure 11.9 When the paddle first enters the water, it is called the "catch." The upper body should be rotated *(a)*. Using the abdominal and back muscles, the upper body "un-rotates" as the paddle comes back in a straight line and causes the boat to move forward *(b)*.

Figure 11.8 The proper way to grip a canoe paddle.

of the boat, you are much closer to the water than in a canoe. This position limits your ability to see down the river, but the lower center of gravity adds maneuverability and compensates for the shorter field of vision. A tandem canoe is to a sedan as a white-water kayak is to a sports car.

The following is a list of beginning kayak skills.

- Getting into a white-water kayak can be tricky (see figure 11.10, *a-c*). A kayak tips more easily than a canoe, so it is a good idea to get in for the first time while it is on land. You can get the feel for the foot pegs, the seat, and the back support. If you need to adjust anything to fit properly, now is the time to do so. When getting in the boat when it's in the water, pull the boat parallel to the shore and brace the paddle across the cockpit with the blade at the shore actually resting on land to provide extra stability. The cockpit size will determine if you can put one leg in at a time or if you will have to sit on the back of the cockpit opening and slide both legs in simultaneously.

- The next step is snapping the spray skirt into place (see figure 11.11). It is best to position the back of the spray skirt first and then pull forward on the skirt's loop to snap over the cockpit in front. The sides can then be secured in place. Kayakers often will need help from another person to get their spray skirt on the cockpit.

Figure 11.10 Getting into a kayak involves careful balance (*a*), getting your legs and foot in a comfortable position (*b*), and adjusting the position of your hips and back support (*c*).

- To position your hands correctly on the paddle shaft, hold it above and centered over your head. Then adjust the placement of your hands so that your elbows are at right angles. Your grip should be relaxed, with the main grip being between your thumb and index fingers, like the OK sign (see figure 11.12).
- As with the forward stroke in a canoe, your body should twist as you reach forward

to put the blade in the water and then untwist, using the muscles of your back, abdomen, and shoulder to complete the stroke. Again, your body turns to face the paddle blade that is in the water (see figure 11.13).

Just as your grip on the paddle should be relaxed, your hips should be relaxed and allowed to rock from side to side. Loose hips save ships, and stiff hips sink ships (or, more accurately, stiff

Figure 11.11 Stretching the spray skirt.

Figure 11.12 Hand placement on the kayak paddle shaft.

Figure 11.13 Forward stroke in a kayak.

hips flip ships). This principle applies to canoes and all types of kayaks.

Sea Kayak Skills

There are no specific paddling skills for sea kayaks that are different from white-water kayaks. However, in white-water kayaking it is important to have the ability to read the water so you can determine the best route through a set of rapids. In sea kayaking the ability to see obstructions is needed less often, but knowledge of tides and ocean currents is very important. This type of knowledge is best learned by taking a course from an experienced instructor. Check out the Internet for classes in sea kayaking. A good source of information is the American Canoe Association (www.acanet.org).

Interdisciplinary Connections With Canoeing and Kayaking

Numerous curriculum areas can be connected with canoeing and kayaking. Whether you want to focus on canoeing as a method of travel for early hunters, the science of buoyancy, or the language of water, students can be inspired by the act of paddling a boat. Following are examples of possible curricular connections.

Social Studies

- Characteristics of places (geography)—The diverse locations for traveling by canoe or kayak and how they differ
- Boats in different cultures—Different types of paddling that did and still do take place in different cultures
- Pros and cons of damming rivers—How canoeing and kayaking are affected by changes that occur in the meaning, use, and importance of resources
- Territorial expansion westward in the United States—The role canoes and kayaks played

Science

- Motion and forces and the transfer of energy—How the transfer of energy causes a boat to move through the water
- Recognizing natural hazards—Being aware of boating safety and precautions
- Personal health—How to dress appropriately for paddling in differing weather and water conditions

Language Arts

- Read literature about early explorers who traveled by canoe.

- Write a story about what it might be like to travel in a canoe or kayak for a week down a particular river from one town to another. What supplies would you need, what weather would you expect, and what problems might you encounter?

- Write a description of what it feels like to be in a boat floating on the water with your eyes closed.

Character Connections With Canoeing and Kayaking

Tandem canoeing involves challenging interpersonal communication. Following are examples of possible character connections to capitalize on when canoeing or kayaking.

- Trustworthiness—When your partner is talking to you, you are listening. You make sure that you understood correctly.

- Caring and kindness—When you do not understand why your partner cannot do a particular stroke correctly, you encourage him nicely to get someone different to show him how to do the stroke (i.e., "Let's get Ms. Larson to watch us and give us some help.").

- Patience—When you or your partner are having difficulty with a new skill, you do not get mad and quit, you ask for help and remember that it takes time to learn a new skill. Take a deep breath and think of the two things that are the most important to you in your life. Then return your focus to the task at hand, remembering to be kind and patient to yourself and your partner.

- Respect—You show respect in how you treat your paddling partners. Kindness and patience are signs of respect.

- Courage—To paddle a canoe or kayak, you need loose hips. It takes courage to let the hull of the boat rock from side to side while you keep your head and shoulders in the middle of the boat. It also takes courage to get both hands on the paddle out over the water (stacked hands) to do a forward stroke. Both of these things may initially seem like they will cause you to capsize. However, with courage they will actually make you a better paddler.

The two paddlers sharing the canoe have to communicate so they can maneuver the boat where they want to go. If they fail to work together to accomplish their goal, it can be a frustrating experience. Therefore, the character qualities of patience, kindness, and respect are critical. (Note that people learn and understand a new skill at different rates and usually want their partner to perform at their same rate.)

Being on the water is a wonderful experience. It is made even better by being able to navigate a boat. Canoeing and kayaking are two of the most inexpensive and accessible boating activities. Having the knowledge and skills for safely paddling one or both of these types of boats offers the potential for a lifetime of enjoyable physical activity and recreation.

Part **III**

Outdoor Education Programming for Schools

Starting a School-Based Outdoor Education Program

Chapter **12**

© Jim Whitmer

You can do it! Start small. Begin with just one class and one activity. You can even recruit students' help by making it an experiment for all of you. Starting a program means different things to different people, depending on the situation and personal interests. Some different approaches include the following:

- Adjusting your teaching methods and incorporating activities such as the ones presented in this book
- Involving other teachers at your school and moving toward a program that incorporates more curriculum diversity
- Planning for a districtwide outdoor education center

Regardless of which approach most closely fits your dream, a main ingredient is your passion.

The first two chapters of this book covered the outdoor education teaching method and the reasons for using it. Chapters 3 through 11 introduced 11 different outdoor activities and supplied basic information for using them as the focus activities of interdisciplinary lessons. However, you must consider additional information if you would like to initiate a program beyond using the outdoor education methodology in your own classes. This chapter will present steps for starting a school-based outdoor education program that extends beyond your own classroom.

Clarify Your Vision

It's a good idea to brainstorm what you would like to see happen. For example, are you thinking about starting a school-based program that takes a two- to three-week period of the school year to focus on the environment? This might involve several teachers structuring lessons in their field to relate to the environment, with some coordinated overlap with other curriculum areas. Are you thinking about teaching outdoor pursuit skills such as backpacking or canoeing in physical education and collaborating with a science teacher who would cover the ecology principles of those different environments? Do you want to take students on field trips to experience different environments and use skills they have learned in class? Or do you want to start an outdoor education center that could facilitate many types of programs? All are worthy ideas, and there is no single correct way to begin a program. Even so, a few suggestions from other people can be helpful if your vision goes beyond your own classroom.

Next, you should put your vision in writing. Become familiar with your school district's mandated curriculum standard and scope and sequence requirements. Get help, if necessary, for developing a clear and rational written explanation of your vision with measurable objectives and an evaluation plan. You will then have a document to give to people with whom you speak about your ideas.

Get Support

If you are the only person invested in getting a program underway, there is less chance for success. Recruit others to help in brainstorming, planning, and further recruiting. Important partners for your program include

- community members and organizations,
- special outdoor interest groups,
- parents,
- school district administrators, and
- other teachers in your school.

Consider yourself lucky if you already have people from one or two of these groups who are interested in working with you to get a program started. Let's consider how these groups can be influential and how you can approach them with your ideas.

• Community members and organizations such as service clubs and businesses can be help-

Community organizations like the YMCA can help you educate your class and provide you with ideas for integrating outdoor education into your curriculum.

ful in acquiring start-up funds for purchasing equipment and supplies. They will also represent other entities that need to be stakeholders, such as parents and school administrators. Experts on various topics can typically be found in each community, and if groups are aware of your program, you will have help in locating speakers.

• Special outdoor interest groups or clubs such as angling, orienteering, canoeing, and hunting clubs are excellent sources of information. They also may have equipment they would allow you to use on a limited basis. Members of these organizations are usually eager to assist beginners who may be interested in their organization's interest, and they could also be another source of funds.

• Parents are critical to the success of any program. Of course, parents are often in one or two of the previously mentioned groups, and they are the most likely to be interested. On the other hand, it will also be helpful to acquire support from parents who are not currently involved in outdoor activities. They will likely be hesitant about something new if it is unfamiliar.

• Your school principal and district administrators are equally important for developing a successful program. Typically, the first questions from this group will be, "How much will it cost?" and, "What's the liability of those activities?" You will be prepared to answer those questions if you and your support group have done your homework. That homework should consist of a brief written description of your vision, a sequenced plan for implementation over a three to five year period, and a cost estimate for each year. The best position for you and your dream is to have already acquired fund commitments from one or two groups that will cover the costs of the first year. The program does not have to be costly if you start small and allow it to grow over several years. An excellent way to end your proposal is with a plan for evaluating the success of the program. The evaluation must be structured to evaluate how well your objectives were met, so keep that in mind when writing the program objectives. It is not possible to measure an objective such as, "Students will benefit from learning activities typically unique to a school setting." On the other hand, the following objectives can be measured: "Students will be able to explain and demonstrate science and math concepts present in archery, cooking, and orienteering"; "Student absences and behavior referrals will decrease during the outdoor education program"; and "Students will exhibit positive character qualities following the outdoor education program." The objectives will depend upon the type of program you propose; just make sure to include measurable objectives.

• Having at least two teachers working together on a program is a big advantage. The old saying, "Two heads are better than one," is definitely true in this case. Ideas will tend to be more creative and problems will seem less daunting. Equally important is the opportunity for an effective interdisciplinary program. Teachers can often feel isolated, but with enjoyable collaborative programs, that sense of isolation will be diminished.

Training and Certification

Do not become an outdoor educator only by trial and error. Outdoor educators cannot afford to let their students always serve as guinea pigs. Some trial and error is to be commended, but not when safety is an issue. How students are organized, taught, and supervised can be critical for safety in some outdoor activities. For example, don't take a class on a canoe trip down a river without adequate prior teaching and supervision as well as readily available skilled help. Even if the river is not white water, things can happen that can lead to serious accidents. This is not to say that such a trip cannot be done safely, but you need to learn what that means before you take the trip. Do not just assume you can figure it out when you get there.

Training

Some activities require more training than others simply because of the possible consequences if an accident happens or because the activities are much less familiar. Following is a list of training possibilities:

- Many local canoe clubs teaching ACA canoe classes.
- Local Sierra Clubs often offer rock-climbing and rappelling workshops.
- Some state park and wildlife departments offer various workshops for outdoor skills.

In addition, the Association for Experiential Education (AEE) offers a program accreditation, as well as a publication that details accepted peer practices in outdoor pursuits. AEE also holds an annual international conference and annual regional conferences. These often provide excellent opportunities for training and sharing ideas with peers. Other organizations that conduct helpful workshops and conferences are the American Alliance for Health, Physical Education, Recreation, and Dance (AAHPERD), the Wilderness Education Association (WEA), and the National Outdoor Leadership School (NOLS).

Certification

Several specific activity certifications can be acquired. Certifications are not always necessary, but documented training is a significant component of risk management. Following is a list of activities for which you can receive certification:

- Challenge-course facilitation, provided by a variety of organizations
- Top-rope climbing site management, provided by American Mountain Guides Association (AMGA)
- Canoeing or kayaking—flatwater, moving water, white water—provided by the ACA
- First aid and CPR, provided by the American Red Cross and American Heart Association
- Wilderness leadership, provided by the WEA

To use the units and lessons presented in this book, no special certifications are needed. Nevertheless, as you gain experience in these activities, you or other teachers may be interested in specialized training that will help you plan and

© Human Kinetics

Specialized training such as training offered at a local climbing organization can help you use the lessons presented in this book.

deliver lessons that go beyond the basics presented in this book.

Assess and Minimize Risks

Any new program has associated risks. However, a program involving diverse physical activities in an outdoor setting involves a few risks that are different from other teaching programs. Too often outdoor programs are nixed because of risk aversion. Don't let risk be an insurmountable obstacle, because with information and planning, you can reduce and manage risk. Most of the risks that are unique to outdoor education activities can be minimized with proper planning and organization. For example, there is risk involved with allowing students to cook over open fires or on gas stoves. Nonetheless, that risk can be reduced in the following ways:

- Teach a few students (team leaders) in a small group ahead of time how to safely use the stoves or fire. These students can then serve as "teaching assistants," which allows for smaller instructional groups.

- Use stoves that have been tested for operating safety.

- Use butane-canister stoves rather than white-gas stoves. Butane-canister stoves are less prone to malfunctions and do not have to be primed (pumped or heated with a separate flame).

- Give clear directions, both verbal and written, as well as instruction in what to do if an accident happens.

- Conduct the activity in a location with adequate ventilation and minimal wind.

Similar steps can be taken to reduce risk with any activity. The following chapter further discusses risk management for field trips, but risk management is also important for school-site classes. Appropriate levels of risk can actually serve as a motivator for learning. They just need to be managed by reducing the risks through planning, organization, instruction, and supervision.

Summary

Exercise your courage. Develop your vision, write it down, specify measurable objectives, recruit partners, adjust and tune the plan, and seek approval for implementation. Notice that "your vision" changed to "the plan" in the previous sentence. Sometimes we hesitate to get others involved because we know what we want to do and do not want anyone to change it. However, when others are invited to join in the planning process, the vision becomes more refined as well as more possible. Remember, your passion is the key!

Field Trips

Chapter 13

© M Holmes

Outdoor education programs do not require field trips. Nonetheless, field trips are an excellent way to allow students to observe and put to use the skills and concepts they have been learning. Unfortunately, field trips present many problems for schools, including travel expenses, time away from "school," and heightened exposure to liability lawsuits. The information found in this chapter will not solve these problems, but hopefully it will provide some ideas for addressing the issues and increasing the chances that field trips remain a safe, well-planned, and educational option. The information is for field trips in general and is not specifically for backcountry expeditions.

There are many possibilities for field trips, so this chapter is only going to address two general areas for consideration:

- Risk-management planning
- Educational planning

Risk management is listed first because it will be one of the administrators' first questions. There is no way to eliminate risk from a field trip, just as there is no way to eliminate risk when driving a car unless you opt not to go. Unfortunately, that option is often chosen when it comes to field trips. Although you cannot eliminate the risk involved, you can minimize it. If you show a thoughtful plan for risk management coupled with an educational plan that clearly shows the value of the field trip experience, the elimination option will probably not be chosen.

Risk Management

Risk management is "the systematic analysis of one's operations for potential risk exposures and then setting forth a plan to reduce the severity and frequency of such exposures. It is the diagnostic process with preventive actions which forestall problems. Risk management plans have three primary parts:

- the analysis of risks,
- the policies and procedures for reducing risks, and
- the implementation of the plan" (van der Smissen, 1997).

Risk Analysis

Risk analysis consists of considering the activity, location, participant competence, leader competence, environmental conditions, supervision capabilities, foreseeable scenarios for harm, potential consequences, and likelihood of potential consequences. The purpose of the analysis process is to weigh the consequences of harm against the likelihood of their occurrence. The greater the consequences, the more measures should be taken to reduce the likelihood of harm occurring. The analysis process will also assist in identifying what can be done to reduce the severity and frequency of injury or suffering.

Developing policies and procedures for reducing risks is the natural step following risk analysis. Attempting to reduce the number and severity of accidents is the heart of a risk-management plan. Most of the time this is a matter of education and training, which includes developing an awareness of possible situations and appropriate procedures to follow to prevent accident occurrences. An example might be a class going on a hike in a remote area. Two possible risks are

- a student could become separated and lost from the group, and
- a student could have a severe allergic reaction to a bee sting.

Both of these risks are foreseeable and the resulting harm can be reduced. In the first instance, each student could be instructed to have a hiking partner and each pair a buddy pair. The instructions would also specify the responsibility to stay in sight of the pair behind and to pass a message up the trail to an adult if a problem arises. Adults are dispersed throughout the group and are at the front and end of the hiking group, so all students have easy access to an adult.

Many people are allergic to bee stings. For this reason, teachers should know if a student

has such an allergy. With that information, the teacher can make sure the student carries the appropriate medication. However, there is always the possibility of a bee stinging someone who did not know they were allergic and thus brought no medicine. If the hike is in a remote area, the first aid kit accompanying the group should be equipped with appropriate medications, and before the trip parents should have had the opportunity to agree to emergency treatment.

A procedure or policy that can significantly contribute to risk reduction is informing participants and parents of as many potential dangers as possible along with offering instructions on how they can minimize their risk of harm from these

Even something as insignificant as a bumblebee can pose a great hazard to some people and you should prepare for it as part of your risk analysis.

dangers. The scenarios presented here illustrate the necessity of providing information and instruction. Written information that requires a signature is also important for documentation purposes, but it does not negate the need for verbal information regarding risks and how they can be reduced. A school district attorney should be on the writing team for health forms and risk-acknowledgment forms.

Implementing the Plan

Implementing the plan is the next step. Do not create policies and procedures that you do not follow. Make sure that more than one adult knows the policies and procedures for field trips in the event that the field trip teacher becomes ill or injured. The most important part of implementing the risk-management plan is vigilant supervision. A teacher has a duty to provide as safe an environment as the activity will allow, without an unreasonable exposure to risk. Breaching that duty by a lack of supervision or instruction or doing something in a substandard manner is the basis of negligence. Following through is important. Be sure to find out about any specific rules or guidelines of your particular school district and follow them.

Most teachers are extremely conscientious and do an excellent job of supervision and organization. So let's move on to the educational plan for field trips.

Educational Field Trips

A field trip should fit into a unit or lesson plan in one or more of the following ways:

- Provide a real-world observation experience related to a subject being studied
- Provide an opportunity to put concepts and skills to use in context
- Provide an experience that will excite and motivate students for an upcoming unit

Whatever reason a field trip is planned, its presentation to the class should receive careful consideration, the organization of activities or experiences on the trip should be thoughtfully structured, and what will happen in class following the field trip should be planned so the maximum benefits can be achieved. The following outline is modified from Camp Silos Web site and serves as a detailed checklist for field trip planning (www.campsilos.org).

Pretrip Planning

There are many things to consider when planning a field trip. Everyone involved should have a clear understanding of where, how, and why the group is going.

Trip Selection

- Identify the rationale, objectives, and plan of evaluation for the field trip.
- Select the site to be visited. Contact the educational coordinator for the site and arrange the date and time. Obtain the pretrip information package if one is available. Record addresses, directions, contact persons, phone numbers, e-mail addresses, and so on.
- Visit the site to familiarize yourself with the major features of the field trip. Take digital photographs to share with students before the trip.

Logistics Planning

- Apply for administrative approval from the departmental chairperson, curriculum administrator, or building principal.
- File a requisition for transportation reservation.
- Make arrangements for meal or sack lunch if needed.
- Develop the schedule for the day.
- Arrange for special equipment such as supplies, film, video camera, or digital camera.
- Arrange for chaperones (usually parents).
- Prepare name tags for students and chaperones.
- Compose a parent permission letter that includes the following:
  - Date and location of the field trip and transportation arrangements
  - Educational purpose of the field trip
  - Provision for special needs
  - Cost

- Clothing for the trip
- Lunch arrangements
- Money needed
- Trip schedule
- Whether a child will need prescribed medication administered
- Emergency contact information
- Parent signature

- Send a letter to parents or include in the class newsletter a request for help as chaperones. Communicate assigned responsibilities, review field trip objectives, and list activities and schedule.

- Provide alternative arrangements for pupils who will not be going on the trip.

- Inform the cafeteria staff if students will be away during the lunch hour.

- Submit a list of students who will be attending the field trip to other teachers if their schedules will be affected.

Don't forget to line up adequate transportation for your field trip.

© Human Kinetics

- Collect the money for the trip and deposit it in your school's account. If required, send the advance fee to the field trip site.

- Create a list of all student names and home phone numbers for use in an emergency.

Preparing Students for the Trip

- Discuss the purpose of the field trip and how it relates to the current unit of study.

- Introduce visual observation skills. Let students describe in detail ordinary objects such as a paper clip, paintbrush, clothespin, or comb.

- Introduce vocabulary words that will be used by lecturers or guides during the tour.

- Show photographs or posters of the field trip site or of things that are related to exhibits that will be viewed.

- Assign students "specialist" roles in one aspect of the topic that they will be studying during the field trip. Group students in different subject areas to research topics related to the field trip (e.g., history, art, religion, science, the environment).

- Explore the Web site of the location you will be visiting.

- As a class, brainstorm standards of conduct for the trip and discuss spending money, lunch plans, and appropriate clothing, including gear for rainy weather.

- Discuss how to ask good questions and brainstorm a list of open-ended observation questions to gather information for during the visit. Record questions on chart paper or in student field trip journals.

- Check with the school nurse about prescription medications that must be administered.

- Review the field trip schedule and make sure timelines are realistic.

Final Planning

- Check all permission slips the day before the field trip.

- Leave the original permission slips and trip plan with the school office and take a copy of each slip on the trip.

Conducting the Trip

On the day of the trip, do the following:

- Pass out name tags.
- Divide the class into small groups and assign chaperones to groups.
- Assign each student a partner and each pair a buddy pair.
- Place a class list and student emergency forms in a folder.
- Secure a cell phone if possible.
- Take along an emergency first aid kit.
- Take inventory of food, equipment, and other supplies pertinent to the field trip.

Activity Ideas

Plan activities that allow students to work alone, in pairs, or in small groups. Activities should include experiences that encourage the use of different senses and motivate the students to make observations and wonder about things. Some types of activities might include the following:

- A mystery to solve with various clues found throughout the day
- Papers with partial drawings of objects for students to complete based on their observations
- Peepholes in construction paper (cut different-sized holes in construction paper and have students view part of something through the peepholes; ask them to describe what they see, what they notice now that they missed before, and how their perspective changes with each new view)
- Field notebooks for recording answers to prepared questions based on clues

Ask follow-up questions as students make observations.

- How are these two objects different from one another?
- What clues does this _____ provide about _____ ?
- In what ways do these two objects relate to one another?

- If you could change one thing about _____, what would it be?
- Pretend you are an archaeologist in the future who is observing this object. What would you be able to conclude about the culture of the past?
- If you were drawing the situation that we are in right at this moment, what caption would you give it? Write a sentence or paragraph caption in your field book.
- Pretend you are a character in or component of this environment. Tell us as much as you can about your life.

Provide time for students to observe; ask questions; and record key words, ideas, and phrases as journal entries in their field book.

- Schedule a particular segment of the field trip for a scavenger hunt where students look for particular objects and record them in their field book or on an observation sheet.
- Provide time for students to work in their field book writing questions and describing things they have seen or heard or ideas they have had.

Post-Trip Activities

Just as quality preplanning is essential to the success of a field trip, planning appropriate follow-up activities will facilitate student learning and multiply the value of hands-on experiences outside the classroom. The following activities provide a general guide when planning post-trip classroom experiences.

- Provide time for students to share general observations and reactions to field trip experiences in small groups before a large group discussion takes place.
- Share assignments students completed while on the field trip.
- Create a classroom bulletin board displaying materials developed or collected while on the field trip.
- Develop a classroom museum that replicates and extends displays students observed on the field trip. For example,

if the field trip involved an art museum, develop a classroom art museum containing student artwork.

- Link field trip activities to multiple curriculum areas. For example, students can develop vocabulary lists based on field trip observations; record field trip observations in a classroom journal; or complete math problems related to actual field trip budget planning

- Share and evaluate student assignments from the field book.

- Have the class compose and send thank-you letters to the site host, chaperones, school administrators, and other persons who supported the field trip.

- Create a short news report about what happened on the field trip. Publicize the trip via your local newspaper, the school bulletin board, a trip presentation for parent's night, or the class Web page.

Evaluating the Trip

Complete your own teacher journal regarding the field trip. This will provide a reference for future field trips.

- What was of unique educational value in this field trip?

- Did the students meet the objectives and expectations?

- Was there adequate time?

- Was there adequate adult supervision?

- What might be done differently to make this an even better experience in the future?

- What special points should be emphasized next time?

- What special problems should be addressed in the future?

- What would improve a visit to this site in the future?

Share the evaluation with the students, volunteers, hosts from the site, and school administrators.

Although field trips are not necessary for outdoor education programs, they are excellent extensions of in-school learning experiences. One of the biggest headaches in field trip planning is the paperwork associated with it. This process is much easier if there is a protocol to follow in making the requests and getting permission. Appendix B contains planning tips that you can adapt to fit your trip. Use the forms to develop your own protocol, and share them with other teachers to facilitate the field trip process.

Adapted, by permission, from Silos and Smokestacks National Heritage Area (2002, October 1) CampSilos History Center Excursion. Retrieved 4/21/05 from the World Wide Web: http://campsilos.org/excursions.hc.

Summary

Outdoor education field trips serve two main purposes. One purpose is the application of learned knowledge and skills in an appropriate context to further develop understanding and the ability to apply the skills. The other main purpose is to enable meaningful connections among a variety of subjects. It is exciting for students to discover that they can apply their learning in real situations. They can make decisions based on previous learning that will result in immediate consequences. For example, if they have learned how to select a campsite and cook with a small single-burner stove, on a camping trip their comfort depends upon the application of what they learned. It is quite a boost to student's self-efficacy when they experience successes they can attribute to their own learning. And nothing is a better motivator for a teacher than seeing students excited about what they have learned. In essence, field trips are good for both students and teachers, providing both with opportunities for discovery.

Appendix A

National Standards

The standards listed in this appendix are applicable to ages 5 through 18, or kindergarten through 12th grade.

National Standards for Civics

What Is Government and What Should It Do?

1. Understands ideas about civic life, politics, and government.
2. Understands the essential characteristics of limited and unlimited government.
3. Understands the sources, purposes, and functions of law, and the importance of the rule of law for the protection of individual rights and the common good.
4. Understands the concept of a constitution, the various purposes that constitutions serve, and the conditions that contribute to the establishment and maintenance of constitutional government.
5. Understands the major characteristics of systems of shared powers and of parliamentary systems.
6. Understands the advantages and disadvantages of federal, confederal, and unitary systems of government.
7. Understands alternative forms of representation and how they serve the purposes of constitutional government.

What Are the Basic Values and Principals of American Democracy?

8. Understands the central ideas of American constitutional government and how this form of government has shaped the character of American society.
9. Understands the importance of Americans sharing and supporting certain values, beliefs, and principles of American constitutional democracy.
10. Understands the roles of voluntarism and organized groups in American social and political life.
11. Understands the role of diversity in American life and the importance of shared values, political beliefs, and civic beliefs in an increasingly diverse American society.
12. Understands the relationships among liberalism, republicanism, and American constitutional democracy.
13. Understands the character of American political and social conflict and factors that tend to prevent or lower its intensity.
14. Understands issues concerning the disparities between ideals and reality in American political and social life.

How Does the Government Established by the Constitution Embody the Purposes, Values, and Principles of American Democracy?

15. Understands how the United States Constitution grants and distributes power and responsibilities to national and state government and how it seeks to prevent the abuse of power.
16. Understands the major responsibilities of the national government for domestic and foreign policy, and understands how government is financed through taxation.
17. Understands issues concerning the relationship between state and local governments and the national government and issues pertaining to representation at all three levels of government.

18. Understands the role and importance of law in the American constitutional system and issues regarding the judicial protection of individual rights.

19. Understands what is meant by "the public agenda," how it is set, and how it is influenced by public opinion and the media.

20. Understands the roles of political parties, campaigns, elections, and associations and groups in American politics.

21. Understands the formation and implementation of public policy.

What Is the Relationship of the United States to Other Nations and to World Affairs?

22. Understands how the world is organized politically into nation-states, how nation-states interact with one another, and issues surrounding U.S. foreign policy.

23. Understands the effect of significant political and nonpolitical developments on the United States and other nations.

What Are the Roles of the Citizen in American Democracy?

24. Understands the meaning of citizenship in the United States, and knows the requirements for citizenship and naturalization.

25. Understands issues regarding personal, political, and economic rights.

26. Understands issues regarding the proper scope and limits of rights and the relationships among personal, political, and economic rights.

27. Understands how certain character traits enhance citizens' ability to fulfill personal and civic responsibilities.

28. Understands how participation in civic and political life can help citizens attain individual and public goals.

29. Understands the importance of political leadership, public service, and a knowledgeable citizenry in American constitutional democracy.

National Standards for Economics

1. Understands that scarcity of productive resources requires choices that generate opportunity costs.

2. Understands characteristics of different economic systems, economic institutions, and economic incentives.

3. Understands the concept of prices and the interaction of supply and demand in a market economy.

4. Understands basic features of market structures and exchanges.

5. Understands unemployment, income, and income distribution in a market economy.

6. Understands the roles government plays in the United States economy.

7. Understands savings, investment, and interest rates.

8. Understands basic concepts of United States fiscal policy and monetary policy.

9. Understands how gross domestic product and inflation and deflation provide indications of the state of the economy.

10. Understands basic concepts about international economics.

National Standards for Geography

The World in Spatial Terms

1. Understands the characteristics and uses of maps, globes, and other geographic tools and technologies.

2. Knows the location of places, geographic features, and patterns of the environment.

3. Understands the characteristics and uses of spatial organization of the earth's surface.

Places and Regions

4. Understands the physical and human characteristics of place.

5. Understands the concept of regions.

6. Understands that culture and experience influence people's perceptions of places and regions.

Physical Systems

7. Knows the physical processes that shape patterns on the earth's surface.

8. Understands the characteristics of ecosystems on the earth's surface.

Human Systems

9. Understands the nature, distribution, and migration of human populations on the earth's surface.

10. Understands the nature and complexity of the earth's cultural mosaics.

11. Understands the patterns and networks of economic interdependence on the earth's surface.

12. Understands the patterns of human settlement and their causes.

13. Understands the forces of cooperation and conflicts that shape the divisions of the earth's surface.

Environment and Society

14. Understands how human actions modify the physical environment.

15. Understands how physical systems affect human systems.

16. Understands the changes that occur in the meaning, use, distribution, and importance of resources.

Uses of Geography

17. Understands how geography is used to interpret the past.

18. Understands global development and environmental issues.

National Standards for Health

1. Knows the availability and effective use of health services, products, and information.

2. Knows environmental and external factors that affect individual and community health.

3. Understands the relationship of family health to individual health.

4. Knows how to maintain mental and emotional health.

5. Knows essential concepts and practices concerning injury prevention and safety.

6. Understands essential concepts about nutrition and diet.

7. Knows how to maintain and promote personal health.

8. Knows essential concepts about the prevention and control of disease.

9. Understands aspects of substance use and abuse.

10. Understands the fundamental concepts of growth and development.

National Standards for History

1. Understands and knows how to analyze chronological relationships and patterns.

2. Understands the historical perspective.

National Standards for Language Arts

Writing

1. Uses the general skills and strategies of the writing process.

2. Uses the stylistic and rhetorical aspects of writing.

3. Uses grammatical and mechanical conventions in written compositions.

4. Gathers and uses information for research purposes.

Reading

5. Uses the general skills and strategies of the reading process.

6. Uses reading skills and strategies to understand and interpret a variety of literary texts.

7. Uses reading skills and strategies to understand and interpret a variety of informational texts.

Listening and Speaking

8. Uses listening and speaking strategies for different purposes.

Viewing

9. Uses viewing skills and strategies to understand and interpret visual media.

Media

10. Understands the characteristics and components of the media.

National Standards for Math

1. Uses a variety of strategies in the problem-solving process.

2. Understands and applies basic and advanced properties of the concepts of numbers.

3. Uses basic and advanced procedures while performing the processes of computation.

4. Understands and applies basic and advanced properties of the concepts of measurement.

5. Understands and applies basic and advanced properties of the concepts of geometry.

6. Understands and applies basic and advanced concepts of statistics and data analysis.

7. Understands and applies basic and advanced concepts of probability.

8. Understands and applies basic and advanced properties of functions and algebra.

9. Understands the general nature and uses of mathematics.

National Standards for Physical Education

Physical activity is critical to the development and maintenance of good health. The goal of physical education is to develop physically fit individuals who have the knowledge, skills, and confidence to enjoy a lifetime of healthful physical activity.

1. Demonstrates competency in motor skills and movement patterns needed to perform a variety of physical activities.

2. Demonstrates understanding of movement concepts, principles, strategies, and tactics as they apply to the learning and performance of physical activities.

3. Participates regularly in physical activity.

4. Achieves and maintains a health-enhancing level of physical fitness.

5. Exhibits responsible personal and social behavior that respects self and others in physical activity settings.

6. Values physical activity for health, enjoyment, challenge, self-expression, and/or social interaction.

National Standards for Science

Earth and Space Sciences

1. Understands atmospheric processes and the water cycle.

2. Understands the earth's composition and structure.

3. Understands the composition and structure of the universe and the earth's place in it.

Life Sciences

4. Understands the principles of heredity and related concepts.

5. Understands the structure and function of cells and organisms.

6. Understands relationships among organisms and their physical environment.

7. Understands biological evolution and the diversity of life.

Physical Sciences

8. Understands the structure and properties of matter.

9. Understands the sources and properties of energy.

10. Understands forces and motion.

Nature of Science

11. Understands the nature of scientific knowledge.

12. Understands the nature of scientific inquiry.

13. Understands the scientific enterprise.

Appendix B

Leave No Trace Principles

Plan Ahead and Prepare

Adequate trip planning and preparation helps backcountry travelers accomplish trip goals safely and enjoyably, while simultaneously minimizing damage to the land.

Pretrip Planning

Poor planning often results in miserable campers and damage to natural and cultural resources. Rangers often tell stories of campers they have encountered who, because of poor planning and unexpected conditions, degrade backcountry resources and put themselves at risk.

Why Is Trip Planning Important?

You may want to create additional answers for this list:

- It helps ensure the safety of groups and individuals.
- It prepares you to leave no trace and minimizes resource damage.
- It contributes to accomplishing trip goals safely and enjoyably.
- It increases self-confidence and opportunities for learning more about nature.

Seven Elements to Consider When Planning a Trip

1. Identify and record the goals (expectations) of your trip.
2. Identify the skill and ability of trip participants.
3. Select destinations that match your goals, skills, and abilities.
4. Gain knowledge of the area you plan to visit from land managers, maps, and literature.
5. Choose equipment and clothing for comfort, safety, and Leave No Trace qualities.
6. Plan trip activities to match your goals, skills, and abilities.
7. Evaluate your trip upon return, noting changes you will make next time.

Other Elements to Consider

- Weather
- Terrain
- Regulations and restrictions
- Private land boundaries
- Average hiking speed of group and anticipated food consumption (Leftovers create waste, which leaves a trace!)
- Group size (Does it meet regulations, trip purpose, and Leave No Trace criteria?)
- All Leave No Trace principles

Meal Planning

Meals are another element to trip planning that can have a profound effect on the impacts a group has on a backcountry area.

Benefits of Good Meal Planning

- Reduced trash
- Reduced pack weight, resulting in faster hiking times and less fatigue
- Reduced dependence upon campfires for cooking

One-Pot Meals and Food Repackaging

- Planning for one-pot meals and lightweight snacks requires a minimum of packing and preparation time, lightens loads, and decreases garbage. One-pot meals require minimal cooking utensils and eliminate the need for a campfire. Two backpack stoves can be used to cook all meals for large groups if you have two large pots (one large pot can be balanced on two stoves when quick heating is desired). Remember, a stove leaves no trace.

- Most food should be removed from its commercial packing and placed in sealable bags before packing your backpacks. Sealable bags secure food and reduce bulk and garbage. Empty bags can be placed inside each other and packed out for reuse at home. This method can reduce the amount of garbage your group must pack out at the end of the trip and eliminate the undesirable need to stash or bury unwanted trash.

What Are Some Examples of Results of Poor Trip Planning?

- A group that is inexperienced or unfamiliar with the geography of an area may put people at risk by traveling through areas susceptible to flash floods or along ridgetops vulnerable to lightning activity. Groups traveling in arid lands often fail to carry adequate water or a way of purifying water from natural sources. Checking with local land managers and studying maps and weather conditions can contribute to a low-risk existence.

- A poorly prepared group may plan to cook meals over a campfire only to discover upon arrival at their destination that a fire ban is in effect or that firewood is in scarce supply. Such groups often build a fire anyway, breaking the law or affecting the land simply because they have not planned for alternatives. Fire bans and scarce wood supplies are signs that an area is experiencing the cumulative effects of heavy recreation use.

- A group that has failed to develop good travel plans may be unable to travel as fast as expected. The terrain may be too steep or the trails too rugged. These groups often resort to setting up camp late at night, sometimes in an unsafe location. Poor campsite selection usually leads to unnec-

essary resource damage. In addition, the group may never even reach their planned destination.

Travel and Camp on Durable Surfaces

Travel on Durable Surfaces

The goal of backcountry travel is to move through the backcountry while avoiding damage to the land. Understanding how travel affects the environment is necessary to accomplish this goal.

Travel damage occurs when surface vegetation or communities of organisms are trampled beyond recovery. The resulting barren area leads to soil erosion and the development of undesirable trails. Backcountry travel may involve travel over trails and off-trail areas.

Travel on Trails

Concentrate activities when traveling in heavily used areas. Land-management agencies construct trails in backcountry areas to provide identifiable routes that concentrate foot and stock traffic. Constructed trails in themselves are an effect on the land; however, they are a necessary response to the fact that people travel in backcountry. Concentrating travel on trails reduces the likelihood that multiple routes will develop and scar the landscape. It is better to have one well-designed route than many poorly chosen paths.

Trail use is recommended whenever possible. Encourage travelers to stay within the width of the trail and not shortcut trail switchbacks (trail zigzags that climb hillsides). Travelers should provide space for other hikers if taking breaks along the trail. The principles of off-trail travel should be practiced if the decision is made to move off-trail for breaks. (Hikers in the same group should periodically stop to rest and talk. Avoid shouting to communicate while hiking. Loud noises usually are not welcome in natural areas.)

Travel Off-Trail

Spread use and impact in pristine areas (except in some desert areas). All travel that does not utilize a designed trail such as travel to remote areas, searches for bathroom privacy, and explorations near and around campsites is defined as off trail. Two primary factors influence how off-trail travel affects the land: durability of surfaces and vegetation, and frequency of travel (or group size).

Durability refers to the ability of surfaces or vegetation to withstand wear or remain in a stable condition. Frequency of use and large group size increase the likelihood that a large area will be trampled or that a small area will be trampled multiple times.

Surface Durability

The concept of durability is an important one for all backcountry travelers to understand. The following natural surfaces respond differently to backcountry travel.

- Rock, sand, and gravel. These surfaces are highly durable and can tolerate repeated trampling and scuffing. (However, lichens that grow on rocks are vulnerable to repeated scuffing).

- Ice and snow. The effect of travel across these surfaces is temporary, making them good choices for travel assuming safety precautions are followed and the snow layer is of sufficient depth to prevent vegetation damage.

- Vegetation. The resistance of vegetation to trampling varies. Careful decisions must be made when traveling across vegetation. Select areas of durable vegetation or sparse vegetation that is easily avoided. Dry grasses tend to be resistant to trampling. Wet meadows and other fragile vegetation quickly show the effects of trampling. Trampling ensures new travelers take the same route and leads to undesirable trail derailment. As a general rule, travelers who must venture off trail should spread out to avoid creating paths that encourage others to follow. Avoid vegetation whenever possible, especially on steep slopes where the effects of off-trail travel are magnified.

- Cryptobiotic crust. Cryptobiotic crust, found in desert environments, is extremely vulnerable to foot traffic. Cryptobiotic crust consists of tiny communities of organisms that appear as a blackish and irregular raised crust upon the sand. This crust retains moisture in desert climates and provides a protective layer preventing erosion. One footstep can destroy crypic crust. It is important to use developed trails in these areas. Travel across crypic crust should only be used when absolutely necessary. Walk on rocks or other durable surfaces if you must travel off trail. In broad areas of crypic crust, where damage is unavoidable, it is best to follow in one another's footsteps so the smallest area of crust is affected—exactly the opposite rule from travel through vegetation. (Cryptobiotic crust is also extremely vulnerable to mountain-bicycle travel.)

- Desert puddles and mud holes. Water is a preciously scarce resource for all living things in the desert. Don't walk through desert puddles or mud holes or disturb surface water in any way. Potholes are also home to tiny desert animals.

Camp on Durable Surfaces

Selecting an appropriate campsite is perhaps the most important aspect of low-effect backcountry use. It requires the greatest use of judgment and information and often involves making trade-offs between minimizing ecological and social effects. A decision about where to camp should be based on information about the level and type of use in the area, the fragility of vegetation and soil, the likelihood of wildlife disturbance, an assessment of previous effects, and your party's potential to cause or avoid affecting the area.

Choosing a Campsite in High-Use Areas

Avoid camping close to water and trails and select a site that is not visible to others. Even in popular areas the sense of solitude can be enhanced by screening campsites and choosing an out-of-the-way site. Camping away from the water's edge also allows access routes for wildlife. Be sure to obey regulations related to campsite selection. Allow enough time and energy at the end of the day to select an appropriate site. Fatigue, bad weather, and late departure times are not acceptable excuses for choosing poor or fragile campsites.

Generally, it is best to camp on sites that are already so affected that further careful use will cause no noticeable effect. In popular areas, these sites are obvious because they have already lost their vegetation cover. Also, it is often possible to find a site that naturally lacks vegetation, such as exposed bedrock or sandy areas.

At high-impact sites, tents, traffic routes, and kitchen areas should be concentrated on already-affected areas. The objective is to confine camping effects to places that already show use and avoid enlarging the area of disturbance. When leaving camp, make sure that it is clean, attractive, and appealing to other campers who follow.

Camping in Undisturbed Remote Areas

Pristine areas are usually remote, see few visitors, and have no obvious traveler effects. Visit these special places only if you are committed to, and highly skilled in, Leave No Trace techniques.

In pristine sites it is best to spread out tents, avoid repetitive traffic routes, and move camp every night. The objective is to minimize the number of times any part of the site is trampled. In setting up camp, disperse tents and the kitchen on durable sites. Wear soft shoes around camp. Minimize activity around the kitchen and places where packs are stashed. The durable surfaces of large rock slabs make good kitchen sites. Watch where you walk to avoid crushing vegetation, and take alternate paths to water. Minimize the number of trips to water by carrying water containers. Check regulations, but camping 200 feet (61 meters or 70 adult steps) from water is a good rule of thumb.

When breaking camp, take time to naturalize the site. Covering scuffed areas with native materials (such as pine needles), brushing out footprints, and raking matted grassy areas with a stick will help the site recover and make it less obvious as a campsite. This extra effort will help hide any indication where you camped and make it less likely that other backcountry travelers will camp in the same spot. The less often a pristine campsite is used the better chance it has of remaining pristine.

Camping in Arid Lands

The most appropriate campsites in arid lands are on durable surfaces such as rock and gravel or on sites that have been so highly affected that further use will cause no additional disturbance. Previously affected sites are obvious because they have already lost their vegetation cover or the rocky soils have been visibly disturbed. If choosing this type of site, make sure your spot is large enough to accommodate your entire group.

A pristine campsite with no evidence of previous use is appropriate in arid lands provided it is on a nonvegetated, highly resistant surface. Expanses of rock, gravel, or sand are all excellent choices. It should never be necessary to camp on cryptobiotic soil, islands of vegetation, or within the precious green ribbons of desert creeks or streams. Beware when camping on sandy river bottoms and areas susceptible to flash floods.

Cooking Areas, Tents, and Backpacks

These should be located on rock, sand, or gravel. Consciously choose durable routes of travel between parts of your camp so that connecting trails do not develop. Vary your routes since the objective is to minimize the amount of trampling and compaction on any specific part of the campsite. Limit your stay to no more than two nights.

Never scrape away or clean sites of organic litter like leaves, and always minimize the removal of rocks and gravel. The organic litter will help to cushion trampling forces, limit the compactability of soils, release plant nutrients, and reduce the erosive forces of rainfall. Disturbing the lichen-coated and varnished rocks known as desert pavement can leave a visible effect for hundreds of years. Once overturned, these rocks are difficult to replace and the lichens and varnish will not grow back within our lifetime.

Camping in River Corridors

River corridors are narrow strips of land and water with little room to disperse human activities. Campsites are often designated. It is generally best to camp on established sites located on beaches, sandbars, or nonvegetated sites below the high-water line.

Properly Dispose of What You Can't Pack Out: Minimize Human Effects

Human Waste

Proper disposal of human waste is important to avoid pollution of water sources, avoid the negative implications of someone else finding it, minimize the possibility of spreading disease, and maximize the rate of decomposition.

In most locations, burying human feces in the correct manner is the most effective method for meeting these criteria. Solid human waste must be packed out from some places, such as narrow river canyons. Land-management agencies can advise you of specific rules for the area you plan to visit.

Contrary to popular opinion, research indicates that burial of feces actually slows decomposition (at least in the Rocky Mountains). Pathogens have been discovered to survive for a year or more when buried. However, in light of the other problems associated with feces, it is still generally best to bury it. The slow decomposition rate causes the need to choose the correct location, far from water, campsites, and other frequently used places.

Catholes

Catholes are the most widely accepted method of waste disposal. Locate catholes at least 200 feet (61 meters or about 70 adult steps) from water, trails, and camp. Select an inconspicuous site where other people will be unlikely to walk or camp. With a small garden trowel, dig a hole 6 to 8 inches (15 to 20 centimeters) deep and 4 to 6 inches (10 to 15 centimeters) in diameter. The cathole should be covered and disguised with natural materials when finished. If camping in the area for more than one night, or if camping with a large group, cathole sites should be widely dispersed.

The advantages of catholes are as follows:

- They are easy to dig in most areas.
- They are easy to disguise after use.
- They are private.
- They disperse the waste rather than concentrate it, which enhances decomposition.
- It is usually easy to select an out-of-the-way location where you can be certain no one is going to casually encounter the cathole.

Selecting a Cathole Site

1. Select a cathole site far from water sources; 200 feet (61 meters or 70 adult paces) is the recommended range.

2. Select an inconspicuous site untraveled by people. Examples of cathole sites include in thick undergrowth, near downed timber, or on gentle hillsides.

3. If camping with a group or if camping in the same place for more than one night, disperse the catholes over a wide area; don't go to the same place twice.

4. Try to find a site with deep organic soil. This organic material contains organisms that will help decompose the feces. (Organic soil is usually dark and rich in color.) The desert does not have as much organic soil as a forested area. (See principle 2 under Digging a Cathole.)

5. If possible, locate your cathole where it will receive maximum sunlight. The heat from the sun will aid decomposition.

6. Choose an elevated site where water would not normally be during runoff or rainstorms. The idea here is to keep the feces out of water. Over time, the decomposing feces will percolate into the soil before reaching water sources.

Digging a Cathole

1. A small garden trowel is the perfect tool for digging a cathole.

2. Dig the hole 6 to 8 inches (15 to 20 centimeters) deep (about the length of the trowel blade) and 4 to 6 inches (10 to 15 centimeters) in diameter. In a hot desert, human waste does not biodegrade easily because there is little organic soil to help break it down. In the desert, the cathole should be only 4 to 6 (10 to 15 centimeters) inches deep. This will allow the heat and sun to hasten the decay process.

3. When finished, the cathole should be filled with the original dirt and disguised with native materials.

Catholes in Arid Lands

A cathole is the most widely accepted means of waste disposal in arid lands. Locate catholes at least 200 feet (61 meters or 70 adult steps) from water, trails, and camp. Avoid areas where water visibly flows, such as sandy washes, even if they are dry at the moment. Select a site that will maximize exposure to the sun in order to aid decomposition. Because the sun's heat will penetrate desert soils several inches, it can eventually kill pathogens if the feces are buried properly. South-facing slopes and ridgetops will have more exposure to sun and heat than other areas.

Latrines

Though catholes are recommended for most situations, there are times when latrines may be more applicable, such as when camping with young children or if staying in one camp for longer than a few nights. Use similar criteria for selecting a latrine location as those used to locate a cathole. Since this higher concentration of feces will decompose very slowly, location is especially important. A good way to speed decomposition and diminish odors is to toss in a handful of soil after each use. Ask your land manager about latrine-building techniques.

Toilet Paper

Use toilet paper sparingly and use only plain, white, nonperfumed brands. Toilet paper must be disposed of properly! It should either be thoroughly buried in a cathole or placed in plastic bags and packed out. Natural toilet paper has been used by many campers for years. When done correctly, this method is as sanitary as regular toilet paper, but without the negative effects. Popular types of natural toilet paper include stones, vegetation, and snow. Obviously, some experimentation is necessary to make this practice work for you, but it is worth a try! Burning toilet paper in a cathole is not generally recommended.

Toilet Paper in Arid Lands

Placing toilet paper in plastic bags and packing it out as trash is the best way to leave no trace in a desert environment. Toilet paper should not be burned. This practice can result in wild fires.

Tampons

Proper disposal of tampons requires that they be placed in plastic bags and packed out. Do not bury them because they do not decompose readily and animals may dig them up. It will take a very hot, intense fire to burn them completely.

Urine

Urine has little direct effect on vegetation or soil. In some instances urine may draw wildlife, which are attracted to the salts. Animals can defoliate plants and dig up soil. Urinating on rocks, pine needles, and gravel is less likely to attract wildlife. Diluting urine with water from a water bottle can help minimize negative effects.

Special Considerations for River Canyons

River canyons often present unique Leave No Trace problems. The most common practice is to urinate directly in the river and pack out feces in sealed boxes for later disposal. Check with your land manager for details about specific areas.

Leave What You Find

Allow others a sense of discovery by leaving rocks, plants, archaeology artifacts, and other objects of interest as you find them.

The activities for this Leave No Trace principle deal with cultural artifacts; however, leaving what you find involves many aspects of outdoor use. The following information addresses a variety of ways to respect natural settings.

Minimize Site Alterations

Leave areas as you found them. Do not dig trenches for tents or construct lean-tos, tables, chairs, or other rudimentary improvements. If you clear an area of surface rocks, twigs, or pine-cones, replace these items before leaving. On highly affected sites, it is appropriate to clean up the site and dismantle inappropriate user-built facilities, such as multiple fire rings and constructed seats or tables. Consider the idea that good campsites are found and not made.

In many locations, properly located and legally constructed facilities, such as a single fire ring, should be left. Dismantling them will cause additional effects because they will be rebuilt with new rocks and thus affect a new area. Learn to evaluate all situations you find.

Avoid Damaging Live Trees and Plants

Avoid hammering nails into trees for hanging things, hacking at them with hatchets and saws, or tying tent guy lines to trunks, thus girdling the tree. Carving initials into trees is unacceptable. The cutting of boughs for use as sleeping pads creates minimal benefit and maximum negative effects. Sleeping pads are available at stores catering to campers.

Picking a few flowers does not seem like it would have any great effect and, if only a few flowers were picked, it wouldn't. But, if every visitor thought "I'll just take a few," much more significant effects might result. Take a picture or sketch the flower instead of picking it. Experienced campers may enjoy an occasional edible plant, but they are careful not to deplete the surviving vegetation or disturb plants that are rare or are slow to reproduce.

Leave Natural Objects and Cultural Artifacts

Natural objects of beauty or interest such as antlers, petrified wood, or colored rocks add to the mood of the backcountry and should be left so others can experience a sense of discovery. In national parks and some other areas it is illegal to remove natural objects.

The same ethic is applicable to cultural artifacts found on public land. Cultural artifacts are protected by the Archaeological Resources Protection Act. It is illegal to remove or disturb archeological sites, historic sites, or artifacts such

as pot shards, arrowheads, structures, and even antique bottles found on public lands.

Minimize Use and Effects From Fire

Fires Versus Stoves

The use of campfires, once a necessity for cooking and warmth, is steeped in history and tradition. Some people would not think of camping without a campfire. Campfire building is also an important skill for every camper. Yet the natural appearance of many areas has been degraded by the overuse of fires and an increasing demand for firewood. The development of lightweight, efficient camp stoves has encouraged a shift away from the traditional fire. Stoves have become essential equipment for minimum-effects camping. They are fast, flexible, and eliminate firewood availability as a concern in campsite selection. Stoves operate in almost any weather condition, and they leave no trace.

Should You Build a Fire?

- The most important consideration to be made when deciding to use a fire is the potential damage to the backcountry.
- What is the fire danger for the time of year and the location you have selected? Are there administrative restrictions from the agency that administers the area?
- Is there sufficient wood so its removal will not be noticeable?
- Does the harshness of alpine and desert growing conditions for trees and shrubs mean that the regeneration of wood sources cannot keep pace with the demand for firewood?
- Do group members possess the skill to build a campfire that will leave no trace?

Lessening Effects When Campfires Are Used

Camp in areas where wood is abundant if building a fire. Choose not to have a fire in areas where there is little wood at higher elevations, in heavily used areas, or in desert settings. A true

Leave No Trace fire shows no evidence of having been constructed.

Existing Fire Rings

The best place to build a fire is within an existing fire ring in a well-placed campsite. Keep the fire small and burning only for the time you are using it. Allow wood to burn completely to ash. Put out fires with water, not dirt. Dirt may not completely extinguish the fire. Avoid building fires next to rock outcrops where the black scars will remain for many years.

Mound Fires

Construction of a mound fire can be accomplished by using simple tools: a garden trowel, a large stuff sack and a ground cloth or plastic garbage bag.

To build this type of fire, collect some mineral soil, sand, or gravel from an already disturbed source. The root hole of a toppled tree is one such source. Lay a ground cloth on the site and then spread the soil into a circular, flat-topped mound at least 3 to 5 inches (8 to 13 centimeters) thick. The thickness of the mound is critical to insulate the ground below from the heat of the fire. The ground cloth or garbage bag is important only in that it makes cleaning up the fire much easier. The circumference of the mound should be larger than the size of the fire to allow for the spreading of coals. The advantage of the mound fire is that it can be built on flat exposed rock or on an organic surface such as litter, duff, or grass.

Fire Pans

Use of a fire pan is a good alternative for fire building. Metal oil drain pans and some backyard barbecue grills make effective and inexpensive fire pans. The pan should have sides at least 3 inches (8 centimeters) high. It should be elevated on rocks or lined with mineral soil so the heat does not scorch the ground.

Firewood and Cleanup

Standing trees, dead or alive, are home to birds and insects, so leave them intact. Fallen trees also provide bird and animal shelter, increase water holding capacity of the soil, and recycle nutrients back into the environment through decomposition. Stripping branches from standing or fallen trees also detracts from an area's natural appearance.

- Avoid using hatchets, saws, or breaking branches off standing or downed trees. Dead and downed wood burns easily, is easy to collect, and leaves less of an effect.
- Use small pieces of wood no larger than the diameter of an adult wrist that can be broken with your hands.
- Gather wood over a wide area away from camp. Use dry driftwood on rivers and seashores.
- Burn all wood to white ash, grind small coals to ash between your gloved hands, thoroughly soak with water, and scatter the remains over a large area away from camp. Ashes may have to be packed out in river corridors.
- Replace soil where you found it when cleaning up a mound or pan fire.
- Scatter unused wood to keep the area as natural looking as possible.
- Pack out any campfire litter. Plastic items and foil-lined wrappers should never be burned in a campfire.

Safety

- Provide adequate supervision for young people when using stoves or fires.
- Follow all product and safety labels for stoves.
- Use approved containers for fuel.
- Never leave a fire unattended.
- Keep wood and other fuel sources away from fire.
- Thoroughly extinguish all fires.

Respect Wildlife

Learn about wildlife through quiet observation. Do not disturb wildlife or plants just for a better look. Observe wildlife from a distance so they are not scared or forced to flee. Large groups often cause more damage to the environment and can disturb wildlife, so keep your group small. If you have a larger group, divide into smaller groups if possible to minimize your effects.

Quick movements and loud noises are stressful to animals. Travel quietly and do not pursue, feed, or force animals to flee. (One exception is in bear country where it is good to make a little noise so as not to startle the bears.) In hot or cold weather, disturbance can affect an animal's ability to withstand the rigorous environment. Do not touch, get close to, feed, or pick up wild animals. It is stressful to the animal, and it is possible that the animal may have rabies or other diseases. Sick or wounded animals can bite, peck, or scratch and send you to the hospital. Young animals removed or touched by well-meaning people may cause the animal's parents to abandon them. If you find sick animals or animals in trouble, notify a game warden.

Considerate campers observe wildlife from afar, give animals a wide berth, store food securely, and keep garbage and food scraps away from animals. Remember that you are a visitor to their home.

Allow animals free access to water sources by giving them the buffer space they need to feel secure. Ideally, camps should be located 200 feet (61 meters or 70 adult paces) or more from existing water sources. This will minimize disturbance to wildlife and ensure that animals have access to their precious drinking water. By avoiding water holes at night, you will be less likely to frighten animals because desert dwellers are usually most active after dark. With limited water in arid lands, desert travelers must strive to reduce their negative effects on the animals struggling for survival.

Washing and human-waste disposal must be done carefully so the environment is not polluted and animals and aquatic life are not injured. Swimming in lakes or streams is okay in most instances, but in desert areas leave scarce water holes undisturbed and unpolluted so animals may drink from them.

Be Considerate of Other Visitors

One of the most important components of outdoor ethics is to maintain courtesy toward other visitors. It helps everyone enjoy the outdoor experience. Many people come to the outdoors to listen to nature. Excessive noise, unleashed pets, and damaged surroundings take away from everyone's experience. So, keep the noise level down while traveling and if you bring a radio, tapes, or CDs, use headphones so you will not disturb others. Also keep in mind that the feeling of solitude, especially in open areas, is enhanced when group size is small, contacts are infrequent, and behavior is unobtrusive. To maximize your feeling of privacy, avoid trips on holidays and busy weekends or take a trip during the off-season.

Groups leading or riding livestock have the right of way on trails. Hikers and bicyclists should move off the trail to the downhill side. Talk quietly to the riders as they pass, since horses are spooked easily. Take rest breaks on durable surfaces well off the designated trail. Keep in mind that visitors to seldom-used places require an extra commitment to travel quietly and lightly on the land.

When selecting a campsite, choose a site where rocks or trees will screen it from others' view. Keep noise down in camp so not to disturb other campers or those passing by on the trail. Goofing off or pranks are undesirable social behavior and may lead to serious or fatal injuries. Also, events need to fit the setting—save game playing for the city park. Bright clothing and equipment such as tents that can be seen for long distances are discouraged. Especially in open natural areas, colors such as fluorescent yellow are disturbing and contribute to a crowded feeling; choose earth-toned colors (i.e., browns and greens) to lessen visual effects.

Stay in control when mountain biking. Before passing others, politely announce your presence and proceed with caution.

Keep pets under control at all times. Bowser is not in the wildlife category. Dogs running free can be unwelcome, frightening people or leaving behind unwanted "presents." Please pick up dog feces from camps and trails. Some areas prohibit dogs or require them to be on a leash at all times.

Leave gates as you find them, and leave the land undisturbed for others to enjoy. Remember, our open spaces and wildlands are protected for all generations. It is up to us to keep them healthy, beautiful, and open to the public for recreation, reflection, and revitalization! Enjoy and learn from historical and archeological sites but respect these sites and treasures. Some of these are sacred to Native Americans or are important cultural reminders of our heritage.

Reprinted, by permission, from Leave No Trace: Center for Outdoor Ethics, 2005. Available: http://www.leavenotrace.org. Assessed 5/2/2005.

Appendix C

Character Qualities

CARING

Being kind and compassionate; expressing gratitude and forgiveness; helping those in need.

CITIZENSHIP

Doing your share to make your school and community better by cooperating, protecting the environment, and being involved.

From *Interdisciplinary Teaching Through Outdoor Education*, by Camille Bunting, 2006, Champaign, IL: Human Kinetics.

COURAGE

The steadfastness to commit yourself to what is good and right and actively pursue it, even if it is not convenient or popular.

From *Interdisciplinary Teaching Through Outdoor Education*, by Camille Bunting, 2006, Champaign, IL: Human Kinetics.

PATIENCE

Being able to wait or slow your pace without becoming irritable.

PERSEVERANCE

Continuing steady action or effort toward an undertaking in spite of counterinfluences, opposition, or discouragement.

From *Interdisciplinary Teaching Through Outdoor Education*, by Camille Bunting, 2006, Champaign, IL: Human Kinetics.

RESPECT

Being considerate of the feelings of others; dealing peacefully with anger, insults, and disagreements; considering others worthy of high regard even though there are differences.

From *Interdisciplinary Teaching Through Outdoor Education*, by Camille Bunting, 2006, Champaign, IL: Human Kinetics.

RESPONSIBILITY

Thinking before you act by considering the consequences; being accountable for your choices; using self-control and doing what you are supposed to do.

From *Interdisciplinary Teaching Through Outdoor Education*, by Camille Bunting, 2006, Champaign, IL: Human Kinetics.

TRUSTWORTHINESS

Being honest and reliable; doing what you say you will do; being worthy of someone's confidence.

From *Interdisciplinary Teaching Through Outdoor Education*, by Camille Bunting, 2006, Champaign, IL.: Human Kinetics.

References and Resources

References

American Canoe Association. (1996). *Introduction to paddling: Canoeing basics for lakes and rivers.* Birmingham, AL: Menasha Ridge.

Bandura, A. (1986). *Social foundations of thought and action: A social cognitive theory.* Englewood Cliffs, NJ: Prentice-Hall.

Cain, J. and Jolliff, B. (1998). *Teamwork and teamplay.* Dubuque, IA: Kendall/Hunt.

Caine, G. and Caine, R.N. (2001). *The brain, education, and the competitive edge.* Lanham, MD: Scarecrow Education.

Center for the Advancement of Ethics and Character. (1996). *Character education manifesto.* www.bu.edu/education/caec/documents/CharacterEdManifesto.html.

Cox, S. and Fulsaas, K. (Eds.) (2003). *Mountaineering: The freedom of the hills.* Seattle: The Mountaineers Books.

Csikszentmihalyi, M. (1975). *Beyond boredom and anxiety.* San Francisco: Jossey-Bass.

Csikszentmihalyi, M. and Larson, R. (1984). *Being adolescent: Conflict and growth in the teenage years.* New York: Basic Books.

Duffy, E. (1957). The psychological significance of the concept of arousal or activation. *Psychological Review, 64,* 265-275.

Guillion, L. (1987). *Canoeing and kayaking: Instruction manual.* Birmingham: Menasha Ridge.

Hammerman, D.R., Hammerman, W.M., and Hammerman, E.L. (1964). *Teaching in the outdoors.* Minneapolis: Burgess.

Maslow, A.H. (1970). *Motivation and personality.* New York: Harper & Row.

McDonald, H. (1997, Fall). Look Ma, no smoke: Solar cooker to relieve suffering. *Brigham Young Magazine,* http://webs.byu.edu/bergeson/physics1/atomic/solar.htm.

McNeill, C., Cory-Wright, J., and Renfrew, T. (1998). *Teaching orienteering* (2nd ed.). Champaign, IL: Human Kinetics.

Mid-Continent Research for Education and Learning (MCREL), 2005, *Standards and benchmarks.* Aurora, CO: MCREL, www.mcrel.org.

Miller, R.J., Brickman, P., and Bolen, D. (1975). Attribution versus persuasion as a means for modifying behavior. *Journal of Personality and Social Psychology, 32*(3), 430-441.

Raleigh, D. (1998). *Knots and ropes for climbers.* Mechanicsburg, PA: Stackpole Books.

Ray, S. (1992). *The canoe handbook.* Harrisburg, PA: Stackpole Books.

Rillo, T.J. (1980). Contributions of Llyod B. Sharp. In Hammerman, W. M. (Ed.), *Fifty years of resident outdoor education (1930-1980): Its impact on American education.* Martinsville, IN: American Camping Association.

Rohnke, K. (1977). *Silver Bullets.* Hamilton, MA: Project Adventure.

Rohnke, K. and Butler, S. (1995). *QuickSilver.* Dubuque, IA: Kendall/Hunt.

Schmidt, B. (1995). *Sport fishing and aquatic resources handbook.* Dubuque, IA: Kendall/Hunt.

Sherman, B. (2004). The history of fishing. *Oldmaster85,* www.oldmaster85.com/history_of_fishing.htm.

Simmons, G.A. and Cannon, E.C. (1991). *It is outdoors: A guide to experiential activities.* Reston, VA: AAHPERD.

Smith, T. and Cain, J. (2002). *The book on raccoon circles.* Tulsa: Learning Unlimited.

Thomas, F. (1999). *Target archery for beginners* (3rd ed.). Edina, MN: Burgess.

Van der Smissen, B. (1990). *Legal liability and risk management for public and private entities.* Cincinnati, OH: Anderson.

Weiner, B. (1972). Attribution theory, achievement motivation, and the educational process. *Review of Educational Research, 42*(2), 203-215.

White, R. (1959). Motivation reconsidered: The concept of competence. *Psychological Review, 66,* 297-333.

www.acanet.org—Several articles on everything from the basics to advanced paddling. The American Canoe Association.

http://www.aee.org/customer/pages.php?pageid=47—Defines experiential education for educators.

http://gorp.away.com/gorp/activity/main.htm—Wonderful information on outdoor activities and where to go for those activities.

http://library.thinkquest.org/27344/heavy.htm—Excellent site for learning about archery and how to teach it.

www.ancientarchery.com—Information on the history of archery.

www.angelfire.com/80s/shobhapardeshi/ParvatiCooker.html—Directions for constructing a solar-funnel cooker.

http://www.campsilos.org/excursions/hc/three/t1.htm—Field trip checklist.

www.charactercounts.org—Discussion of character qualities; offers many resources for teachers.

www.solarcookers.org/basics/why.html—Information on solar cooking and its benefits.

www.lnt.org—Leave No Trace Web site with detailed explanations, teaching resources, and publications.

Resources

http://camping.about.com/cs/advicetips/a/campingbasics.htm—Articles on everything from how to find a camping spot to leaving the area the same as you found it.

http://camping.about.com/cs/beinggoodcampers/index.htm—Links to articles about how to avoid poisonous plants and dangerous animals and how to camp with the least effect on the environment.

http://camping.about.com/od/campinggearchecklists—Checklists of what to take when camping.

http://get.to/climbbetter—Tips and techniques for beginners through advanced climbers.

http://paddling.about.com—Links to several articles explaining all aspects of canoeing and paddling.

www.backpacking.net/ethics.html—Several articles on how to select a campsite, how to minimize effects on the environment, and how to protect your belongings from wild animals.

www.backpacking.net/winter.html—Site with tips and equipment lists for winter hiking and backpacking.

www.businessballs.com/teambuilding.htm—Informative site, though activities tend to be indoor-oriented.

www.camping-usa.com/checklist.html—Checklist for all camping from frontcountry to backcountry.

www.canoeinstructor.net—Descriptions of a variety of canoes and kayaks and paddling skills.

www.character.org—Describes the principles of character and character education.

www.characterfirst.com—Defines character and lists 45 character qualities that are organized with resources by grade level.

www.davidlnelson.md/ElCapitan/DefinitionClimbGrade.htm—Personal report on climbing big walls, but also good general information on rock climbing.

www.ens.gu.edu.au/ciree/LSE/DOWNLOAD/MOD_8.DOC—Good ideas for teaching about the outdoors to students of all ages.

www.fishingonly.com/teaching_novices.html—Lessons on how to teach casting and angling as well as tons of tips for freshwater and saltwater fishing.

www.fix.net/~ggoven/p29.html—Description of how to go about teaching archery to children and the equipment needed, basic descriptions such as how to string and shoot the bow, and good games to play.

www.funteambuilding.com—Although there are no game descriptions, this site is worthwhile for its Top 10 Tips About Team Building.

www.globalserve.net/~codyak/CampCooking/KARENBURNS.HTM—Includes several tips and methods for outdoor cooking while camping.

www.hikingwithmike.com—Includes a list of FAQs as well as tips on survival and gear for backpacking and hiking.

www.learn-orienteering.org/old—Detailed information on how to use a compass and illustrations to make the lesson easier.

www.letsflyfish.com/fly_casting.htm—Basic instructions on how to get started as well as several articles in the archives on proper equipment.

www.lovetheoutdoors.com/camping/Outdoor_Cooking.htm—Includes a checklist for cooking while camping, safety tips, and suggested cooking methods and recipe ideas.

www.ncsu.edu/kenan/fellows/2001/cmoser/scavenger.html—Ideas on outdoor activities for young children.

www.online-orienteering.net—Gives an overview of what orienteering is and how to set up a competitive orienteering course as well as how to read a compass and use a map.

www.passemontagne.com—Pertinent information for climbing programs in schools.

www.peakware.com/encyclopedia—Wide variety of climbing information, from rating systems to equipment.

www.seakayak.ws/kayak/kayak.nsf—Glossary of kayak and nautical terms.

www.teambuildingusa.com/team-building-exercise.asp—Provides links to useful team-building activities.

www.toxophily.com/beginners/beginners.htm—Lots of information for beginners about getting started in archery and many useful and informative articles.

www.urbanext.uiuc.edu/SchoolsOnline/charactered.html—Information on character education and teaching kids to care; offers training for teachers

www.us.orienteering.org/OYoung—Site for designing a course for children to learn orienteering.

www.wilderdom.com/games/InitiativeGames.html—Free descriptions of team-building and problem-solving exercises plus links to recommended Web sites that also have free descriptions.

www.wilderdom.com/Indigenous.html—Gives an overview of theories and principles to apply to outdoor education in order to relate to all age groups.

www.yale.edu/archery/about.html—Detailed summary of archery equipment as well as a glossary of terms for easier understanding.

About the Author

Camille J. Bunting, PhD, is an associate professor in the department of health and kinesiology and director of the Outdoor Education Institute at Texas A&M University. She has been an active professional in the field of experiential education for nearly 30 years. She helped start an undergraduate major and minor emphasis in outdoor education at Texas A&M, and she is certified by the Wilderness Education Association as an outdoor leadership instructor. Bunting has conducted numerous teacher trainings and conference programs on the topics in this book and was instrumental in starting and expanding the Texas Outdoor Education Association. She is a past president of the Council on Outdoor Education for the American Alliance for Health, Physical Education, Recreation and Dance.

In addition to administering the programs of the Outdoor Education Institute, teaching graduate and undergraduate classes, and facilitating adventure education experiences, Bunting maintains a research agenda focusing on the physiological and psychological responses to outdoor adventure activities. Bunting is also the president of a consulting business, Success Dimensions, Inc. In her leisure time she enjoys doing many of the activities in this book, including canoeing, kayaking, and backpacking.